AGRICULTURE ISSUES AND POLICIES

GLOBAL AGRICULTURE PROJECTIONS TO 2020 AND U.S. TRADE TRENDS

AGRICULTURE ISSUES AND POLICIES

Additional books in this series can be found on Nova's website
under the Series tab.

Additional e-books in this series can be found on Nova's website
under the e-books tab.

TRADE ISSUES, POLICIES AND LAWS

Additional books in this series can be found on Nova's website
under the Series tab.

Additional e-books in this series can be found on Nova's website
under the e-books tab.

AGRICULTURE ISSUES AND POLICIES

GLOBAL AGRICULTURE

PROJECTIONS TO 2020 AND U.S. TRADE TRENDS

CHRISTOPHER R. FISHER
AND
WADE P. ELLIS
EDITORS

Nova Science Publishers, Inc.
New York

Library of Congress Cataloging-in-Publication Data

ISBN: 978-1-61942-859-1

Published by Nova Science Publishers, Inc. † New York

CONTENTS

PREFACE

This book provides projections for the agricultural sector through 2020. Projections cover agricultural commodities, agricultural trade, and aggregate indicators of the sector, such as farm income and food prices. The projections are based on specific assumptions about macroeconomic conditions, policy, weather and international developments, with no domestic or external shocks to global agricultural markets. Provisions of current law are assumed to remain in effect through the projection period. The projections are one representative scenario for the agricultural sector for the next decade.

Chapter 1- This report provides projections for the agricultural sector through 2020. Projections cover agricultural commodities, agricultural trade, and aggregate indicators of the sector, such as farm income and food prices. The projections are based on specific assumptions about macroeconomic conditions, policy, weather, and international develop-ments, with no domestic or external shocks to global agricultural markets. Provisions of current law are assumed to remain in effect through the projection period. The projections are one representative scenario for the agricultural sector for the next decade. The projections in this report were prepared during October through December 2010, reflecting a composite of model results and judgment-based analyses.

Prospects for the agricultural sector in the near term reflect market adjustments to the supplyand-demand conditions underlying recent price increases for many farm commodities. In response, global agricultural production increases in 2011, particularly for grains. Production adjustments are made in the livestock sector during the first several years of the projections in response to high grain and soybean meal prices in 2011. Longrun developments for global agriculture reflect a resumption of steady world economic growth following the global recession and continued demand for biofuels, which combine to support increases in consumption, trade, and prices. Thus, after near-term declines from 2011 record levels, the value of U.S. agricultural exports and net farm income each rise through the rest of the decade. U.S. retail food prices increase faster than the overall rate of inflation rate in 2011 and 2012, reflecting higher food commodity prices and energy costs. Food prices rise less than the general inflation rate over the remainder of the projections, largely reflecting production increases in the livestock sector which limit meat price increases.

Chapter 2- U.S. agricultural exports, imports, and the agricultural trade surplus are expected by the U.S. Department of Agriculture (USDA) to reach record levels in FY2011. FY2011 U.S. farm exports are forecast by the U.S. Department of Agriculture to reach $137 billion, while agricultural imports are expected to reach $93 billion. The agricultural trade surplus is projected to be $44 billion. Exports of high-value products (e.g., fruits, vegetables, meats, wine and beer) have increased since the early 1990s and now account for 60% of total U.S. agricultural exports. Exports of bulk commodities (e.g., soybeans, wheat, and feed grains) remain significant.

Leading markets for U.S. agricultural exports are China, Canada, Mexico, Japan, the European Union (EU), South Korea, and Taiwan. The United States in 2011 is forecast to be the world's leading exporter of corn, wheat, soybeans, and cotton. The U.S. share of world beef exports, which declined after the 2003 discovery of a case of "mad cow disease" in the United States, is recovering as more countries have re-opened their markets to U.S. product. The United States, European Union, Australia, and New Zealand are dominant suppliers of dairy products in global agricultural trade. New Zealand and the United States are the main suppliers of nonfat dry milk to world markets, while the EU is the leading supplier of cheeses.

China has been among the fastest-growing markets for U.S. agricultural exports. Agricultural exports to Canada and Mexico, both partners of the United States in the North American Free Trade Agreement (NAFTA), have also grown rapidly.

In: Global Agriculture
Editors: Christopher R. Fisher and Wade P. Ellis
ISBN: 978-1-61942-859-1

Chapter 1

USDA AGRICULTURAL PROJECTIONS TO 2020*

United States Department of Agriculture

ABSTRACT

This report provides projections for the agricultural sector through 2020. Projections cover agricultural commodities, agricultural trade, and aggregate indicators of the sector, such as farm income and food prices. The projections are based on specific assumptions about macroeconomic conditions, policy, weather, and international developments, with no domestic or external shocks to global agricultural markets. Provisions of current law are assumed to remain in effect through the projection period. The projections are one representative scenario for the agricultural sector for the next decade. The projections in this report were prepared during October through December 2010, reflecting a composite of model results and judgment-based analyses.

Prospects for the agricultural sector in the near term reflect market adjustments to the supplyand-demand conditions underlying recent price increases for many farm commodities. In response, global agricultural production increases in 2011, particularly for grains. Production adjustments are made in the livestock sector during the first several years of the projections in response to high grain and soybean meal prices in 2011. Longrun developments for global agriculture reflect a resumption of steady world economic growth following the global recession and continued demand for biofuels, which combine to support increases in consumption, trade, and prices. Thus, after near-term declines from 2011 record levels, the value of U.S. agricultural exports and net farm income each rise through the rest of the decade. U.S. retail food prices increase faster than the overall rate of inflation rate in 2011 and 2012, reflecting higher food commodity prices and energy costs. Food prices rise less than the general inflation rate over the remainder of the projections, largely reflecting production increases in the livestock sector which limit meat price increases.

Keywords: Projections, crops, livestock, biofuel, ethanol, trade, farm income, food prices, U.S. Department of Agriculture, USDA

* This is an edited, reformatted and augmented version of The United States Department of Agriculture, Office of the Chief Economist, World Agricultural Outlook Board, U.S. Department of Agriculture publication,. prepared by the Interagency Agricultural Projections Committee. Long-term Projections Report OCE-2011-1, dated February 2011.

A Note to Users of USDA Long-term Projections

USDA's long-term agricultural projections presented in this report are a Departmental consensus on a longrun scenario for the agricultural sector. These projections provide a starting point for discussion of alternative outcomes for the sector.

The scenario presented in this report is not a USDA forecast about the future. Instead, it is a conditional, longrun scenario about what would be expected to happen under a continuation of current farm legislation and specific assumptions about external conditions. Critical long-term assumptions are made for U.S. and international macroeconomic conditions, U.S. and foreign agricultural and trade policies, and growth rates of agricultural productivity in the United States and abroad. The report assumes that there are no domestic or external shocks that would affect global agricultural supply and demand. Normal weather is assumed. Changes in any of these assumptions can significantly affect the projections, and actual conditions that emerge will alter the outcomes.

The report uses as a starting point the short-term projections from the November 2010 *World Agricultural Supply and Demand Estimates* report. The macroeconomic assumptions were completed in October 2010.

The projections analysis was conducted by interagency committees in USDA and reflects a composite of model results and judgment-based analyses. The Economic Research Service had the lead role in preparing the departmental report.

The projections and the report were reviewed and cleared by the Interagency Agricultural Projections Committee, chaired by the World Agricultural Outlook Board. USDA participants in the projections analysis and review include the World Agricultural Outlook Board; the Economic Research Service; the Farm Service Agency; the Foreign Agricultural Service; the Agricultural Marketing Service; the Office of the Chief Economist; the Office of Budget and Program Analysis; the Risk Management Agency; the Natural Resources Conservation Service; and the National Institute of Food and Agriculture.

Introduction and Projections Overview

This report provides longrun projections for the agricultural sector through 2020. Major forces and uncertainties affecting future agricultural markets are discussed, such as prospects for long-term global economic growth and population trends. Projections cover production and consumption for agricultural commodities, global agricultural trade and U.S. exports, commodity prices, and aggregate indicators of the sector, such as farm income and food prices.

The projections are a conditional scenario based on specific assumptions about the macroeconomy, agricultural and trade policies, the weather, and international developments. The report assumes that there are no domestic or external shocks that would affect global agricultural markets. Normal weather is assumed. Provisions of current law are assumed to remain in effect through the projection period, including the Food, Conservation, and Energy Act of 2008 (the 2008 Farm Act), the Energy Independence and Security Act of 2007, and the Energy Improvement and Extension Act of 2008. Thus, the projections are not intended to be a forecast of what the future will be, but instead are a description of what would be expected to happen under these very specific external circumstances and assumptions. As such, the projections provide a neutral, reference scenario that can serve as a point of departure for discussion of alternative farm sector outcomes that could result under different domestic or international assumptions.

The projections in this report were prepared during October through December 2010 and reflect a composite of model results and judgment-based analyses. Short-term projections used as a starting point in this report are from the November 2010 *World Agricultural Supply and Demand Estimates* report. The macroeconomic assumptions were completed in October 2010.

Prospects for the agricultural sector in the near term reflect market adjustments to the supply-anddemand conditions underlying recent high prices for many farm commodities. In response, global agricultural production increases in 2011, particularly for grains.

Production adjustments are made in the livestock sector during the first several years of the projections in response to high grain and soybean meal prices in 2011. The high prices underlie record projected levels of U.S. agricultural exports and U.S. net farm income in 2011.

Longrun developments for global agriculture reflect a resumption of steady world economic growth following the global recession and continued demand for biofuels, particularly in the United States and the European Union (EU).

These factors combine to support longer run increases in consumption, trade, and prices for agricultural products. Thus, after near-term reductions from 2011 records, the value of U.S. agricultural exports and net farm income each rise through the rest of the decade. U.S. retail food prices increase faster than the general inflation rate in 2011 and 2012, reflecting higher food commodity prices and energy costs.

Food prices rise less than the overall rate of inflation over the remainder of the projections, largely reflecting production increases in the livestock sector which limit meat price increases.

KEY ASSUMPTIONS AND IMPLICATIONS

Major Assumptions Underlying the Projections and Selected Implications Include

Economic Growth

- U.S. and world economic growth reflect a movement back toward long-run steady growth in the aftermath of the global financial crisis and economic recession.
- Global economic growth is assumed at a 3.4-percent average growth rate for 2011-2020. Continued high growth rates in emerging market countries, such as China and India, and a return to strong growth in other developing countries underpin world macroeconomic gains.
- The U.S. economy is projected to grow at an average rate of 2.6 percent over the next decade. With slower growth in the United States than in the world economy, the U.S. share of global gross domestic product (GDP) falls from over 26 percent currently to less than 25 percent at the end of the projection period. Employment gains are projected to be slow, with high rates of unemployment lasting for a number of years.

- In the longer run, the return to steady global economic growth supports longer term gains in world food demand, global agricultural trade, and U.S. agricultural exports. Economic growth in developing countries is especially important because food consumption and feed use are particularly responsive to income growth in those countries, with movement away from staple foods and increased diversification of diets.

Population

- Stronger global economic growth over the next decade contributes to the continued slowing of population gains around the world as birth rates decline. Growth in global population is assumed to average about 1 percent per year over the projection period compared with average annual rates of 1.7 percent in the 1980s, 1.4 percent in the 1990s, and 1.2 percent in the last decade.
- Population growth rates in most developing countries remain above those in the rest of the world. As a consequence, the share of world population accounted for by developing countries increases to 82 percent by 2020, up from 74 percent in 1980 and 77 percent in 1990.
- Population gains in developing countries along with increased urbanization and expansion of the middle class are particularly important for the projected growth in global food demand. Developing countries' populations, in contrast to those of more developed countries, are dominated by younger population cohorts who consume larger quantities of food of increasingly diverse types.

The Value of the U.S. Dollar

- The U.S. dollar is assumed to depreciate somewhat over the next decade. Although there has been a recent depreciation of the euro due to the sovereign debt problems in the EU, the longer term depreciation of the dollar relative to the euro and yen is part of an ongoing global rebalancing of international currency portfolios.
- The weaker dollar will remain a facilitating factor in projected gains in U.S. agricultural exports. Although trade competition will continue to be strong, the United States will remain competitive in global agricultural markets, with export gains contributing to increases in cash receipts for U.S. farmers.

Oil Prices

- Crude oil prices are assumed to increase over the next decade as global economic activity improves. Increases are expected to be faster than the general inflation rate, with the nominal refiner acquisition cost for crude oil imports projected to exceed $110 per barrel by the end of the projection period.
- These increases in crude oil prices raise production costs in the agricultural sector.

U.S. Agricultural Policy

- Provisions of current law, particularly the 2008 Farm Act, are assumed to remain in effect through the projection period.
- Under the 2008 Farm Act, the maximum acreage enrolled in the Conservation Reserve Program (CRP) was reduced from 39.2 million acres to 32 million acres, beginning on October 1, 2009. Acreage enrolled in the program has fallen from more than 36 million acres to about 31.4 million acres and is projected to remain close to its legislated maximum throughout the projections. This reduction in CRP acreage provides some additional cropland for potential use in production.
- With high prices for many crops, price-dependent farm program benefits have become less important in overall Government payments to the U.S. agricultural sector. The CRP and fixed direct payments represent most payments to the sector throughout the projection period. As a consequence, Government payments have a smaller role and the sector relies on the market for more of its income.

U.S. Biofuels

- The projections assume that the 45-cents-per-gallon tax credit available to blenders of ethanol and the 54-cents-per-gallon tariff on imported ethanol used as fuel are in effect through the projection period. The $1.00-per-gallon tax credit for blending biodiesel, which had expired at the end of 2009, was not assumed to be available since its retroactive reinstatement and extension through 2011 occurred after these projections were completed.
- Expansion in the U.S. ethanol industry is projected to continue. However, growth is projected to be slower than the rapid gains during 2005-09, despite some potential to increase into the E15 (15-percent ethanol blend) market for some vehicles. The projections reflect the October 2010 approval by the U.S. Environmental Protection Agency (EPA) of E15 for use in model year 2007 and newer passenger vehicles (including cars, sport utility vehicles, and light pickup trucks), but were completed before the more-recent EPA announcement of E15 approval for model years 2001-06.
- Corn is expected to remain the primary feedstock for U.S. ethanol production during the projection period, with about 36 percent of total corn use going to ethanol production over the next decade. Nonetheless, smaller gains for corn-based ethanol are projected, reflecting only moderate growth in overall gasoline consumption in the United States, limited potential for further market penetration of ethanol into the E10 (10-percent ethanol blend) market, constraints in the E15 market, and the small size of the E85 (85-percent ethanol blend) market. By the end of the projection period, corn-based ethanol production represents more than 10 percent of annual gasoline consumption.

- Biodiesel production in the United States is assumed to increase to 1 billion gallons by 2012. Almost half of this volume is assumed to be from domestic first-use vegetable oils, with animal fats and recycled vegetable oil accounting for the remainder.

Livestock and Meat Trade

- The projections assume continued policies in Russia that build toward self sufficiency in their poultry and pork sectors.
- Beef exports from competitor countries of Argentina, Australia, and Canada increase slowly as those countries rebuild breeding herds.
- The projections were completed before the recent outbreak of food and mouth disease in South Korea.

International Policy

- Trade projections assume that countries comply with existing bilateral and multilateral agreements affecting agriculture and agricultural trade. The report incorporates effects of trade agreements and domestic policies in place in November 2010.
- Domestic agricultural and trade policies in individual foreign countries are assumed to continue to evolve along their current paths, based on the consensus judgment of USDA's regional and commodity analysts. In particular, long-term economic and trade reforms in many developing countries are assumed to continue.

International Biofuels

- Demand for biofuel feedstocks is projected to continue growing in a number of countries. The largest markets—the United States, Brazil and the EU—will grow at a slower pace than in recent years. Continued expansion is largely due to biofuel policies, mainly use mandates and tax incentives.
- The projections assume that 60 percent of the EU 2020 mandate, that renewable fuels provide 10 percent of the energy used in the transportation sector, is achieved from annual agricultural crop feedstocks. Biodiesel accounts for 60 percent of total biofuel use in 2020 and ethanol accounts for 40 percent, compared with 69 percent for biodiesel and 31 percent for ethanol estimated for 2010.
- To boost biodiesel production, the EU is projected to increase oilseed production as well as imports of oilseeds and vegetable oil from countries in the former Soviet Union and non-EU Europe. EU wheat provides the feedstock for EU ethanol expansion in the early years but corn used as an ethanol feedstock grows more rapidly toward the end of the projections.
- The EU imports biodiesel from Argentina and ethanol from Brazil, and is the world's largest importer of both throughout the projection period. Overall, biofuel imports become increasingly important in the EU, rising to about one-fourth of total use.

Prices

- Prices for major crops are projected to decline in the near term as production globally responds to current high prices. Nonetheless, after near-term price declines, long-term growth in global demand for agricultural products, in combination with the continued presence of U.S. ethanol demand for corn and EU biodiesel demand for vegetable oils, holds prices for corn, oilseeds, and many other crops at historically high levels.
- Adjustments in the U.S. livestock sector to high feed costs continue in the near term, lowering production of total meat and poultry and raising livestock and meat prices. Improving net returns provide economic incentives for expansion later in the decade, with nominal livestock prices rising moderately over most of the rest of the projection period.
- Although farm income initially declines from a projected 2011 record, strengthening global food demand and sustained biofuel demand keep net farm income historically high.
- U.S. retail food prices rise faster than the general inflation rate in 2011 and 2012, reflecting higher food commodity prices, rising energy costs, and improved demand as the economic recovery continues. Food prices rise less than the overall rate of inflation over the remainder of the projections, largely reflecting production increases in the livestock sector which limit meat price increases.

Macroeconomic Assumptions

The United States and much of the developed world are moving to steady growth following the most serious worldwide economic downturn since the end of World War II. Given the depth and widespread nature of the recession, the transition has been characterized by slow economic growth and slow employment gains, and is likely to result in high rates of unemployment lasting a number of years.

Thus, macroeconomic assumptions underlying USDA's long-term projections reflect this slow transition back toward longrun sustainable growth in 2011 and beyond. Implicit in this baseline is the assumption that the U.S. Federal Reserve Board and other major central banks around the world continue to take aggressive action, as needed, to counter the continuing financial problems lingering from the recession. Even with these actions, evolving situations will affect the recovery and provide risks for the longer term outlook. (See boxes, *Financial Crisis in the Eurozone: Implications for U.S. Agricultural Exports*, page 9; and *Macroeconomic Risks in the Projections*, page 10.) The macroeconomic assumptions were completed in October 2010.

After averaging 2.9-percent growth between 2001 and 2008, overall global real gross domestic product (GDP) fell by 2.1 percent in 2009. World economic growth for 2010 is estimated to be 3.3 percent. From 2011 through 2020, world growth is projected to increase at an annual average rate of 3.5 percent. Most of these economic gains reflect continued high growth rates in emerging market countries such as China and India and a return to strong growth in other developing countries. While developed countries' share of global real GDP is still more than 60 percent at the end of the projection period, that is down from 80 percent in 1970 and almost 70 percent in 2007.

Following a contraction of about 2.6 percent in 2009, the U.S. economy is expected to grow by 2.4 to 2.5 percent in 2010 and 2011, 2.8 percent in 2012, and then settle at a longer term rate of 2.6 percent in 2013 and beyond. With U.S. GDP growing more slowly than the world economy throughout the projections period, the U.S. share of global GDP falls below 25 percent by 2020.

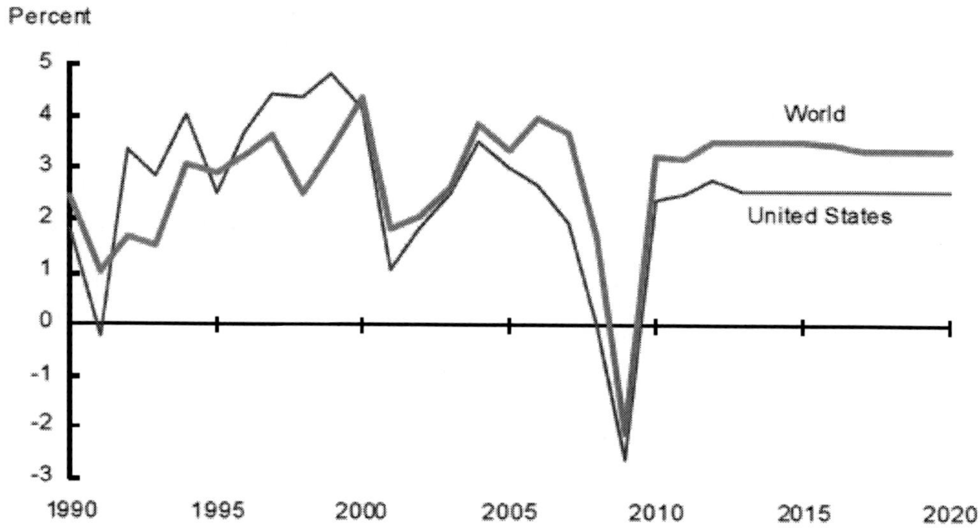

U.S. and World Gross Domestic Product (GDP) Growth.

Agricultural Implications

The return of global economic growth beginning in 2010 and the continuation of population gains are expected to boost food demand. This is particularly true since world growth is concentrated in emerging markets and developing countries with high income-related propensities for consumption of food and agricultural products. In addition, growing biofuel demand will remain an important factor shaping the projections for world trade, U.S. agricultural exports, and commodity prices. Also supporting the outlook for U.S. agricultural exports is the cumulative effect of the depreciated U.S. dollar since 2002 and its continued decline through the projection period. The declining dollar makes U.S. agricultural exports increasingly competitive in international markets.

Developed economies are projected to grow at an average annual rate of 2.2 percent in 2011-20, more than half a percentage point lower than the 1970-2008 historical average. Both the European Union (EU) and Japan experienced more severe recessions than the United States, with prospects for both countries growing more slowly than the U.S. economy in coming years.

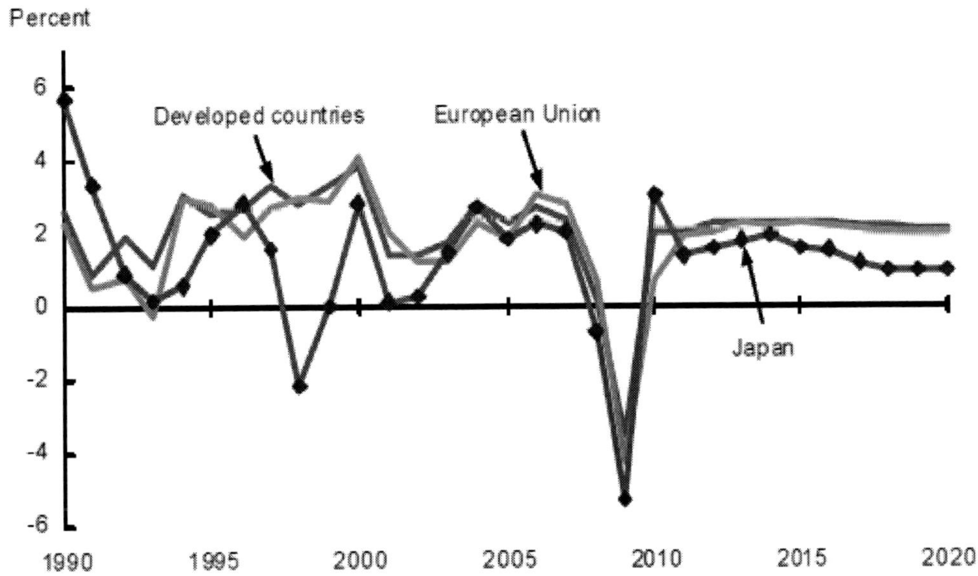

GDP Growth for Developed Countries, European Union, and Japan.

- Economic growth rates for the EU remain about 2 percent per year in the projection period, somewhat less than their historical average. The EU was less aggressive in combating the impact of the global financial crisis than was the United States. The Eurozone crisis of 2010 further set back growth prospects for the EU (see box, *Financial Crisis in the Eurozone: Implications for U.S. Agricultural Exports*). Lingering structural rigidities, particularly inflexible labor laws and a very expensive social security system, impinge on growth and the EU financial system. Political difficulties also limit the benefits of economic integration, particularly with continued restrictions on labor mobility between EU countries and the cumbersome EU Commission decisionmaking process. Unemployment rates are expected to decline from double-digit rates in the projection period.
- The projections assume economic growth in Japan averages around 1.4 percent per year, a continuation of the slow growth and deflationary environment that Japan has experienced since the 1990s. Japan continues to face constraints to economic growth, largely the result of long-term structural rigidities (such as legal constraints on new business entry), a difficult political process for economic reform, and a rapidly aging population. Japan's labor market liberalization partly eases these constraints, aiding some productivity growth. Increasing integration with the other economies of Asia, especially China, will mitigate some of the growth constraints in the Japanese economy. Nonetheless, while Japan is a heavily trade-dependent country, its trade-dependent sectors have declined significantly. The yen has continued to appreciate against the dollar in spite of the interventions of Japan's central bank to moderate the appreciation. Slow growth prospects in Japan relative to high growth in other major Asian countries suggest that the importance of Japan in the global economy will diminish throughout the projection period.

Financial Crisis in the Eurozone: Implications for U.S. Agricultural Exports

The Eurozone Crisis of 2010 was the result of the evolution of large current account imbalances between Eurozone countries. The large fiscal debt accumulation in Greece, Ireland, Spain, Portugal, and Italy became unsustainable. The resulting dramatic increase in the market cost of credit to those countries precipitated the crisis.

The creation of a European Financial Stabilization Facility to support the sovereign debt of Eurozone deficit countries put a short-term halt to the threat of default.

The facility, largely funded by Germany, is also based on commitments by the deficit countries to institute austerity measures to substantially reduce Government deficits. The longer term outcome will depend largely on whether the programs put in place to address the imbalances in trade and Government finances are effective.

One potential outcome of the crisis would be a sustained long-term depreciation of the euro against the dollar and other currencies. In this case, Eurozone products would become more competitive in world markets. On the other hand, some investment that would have gone to the Eurozone would instead go to other countries. This investment would strengthen global growth and demand for agricultural products, particularly in developing economies, and thus benefit U.S. agricultural exports. On balance, even with near-term appreciation relative to the euro, the U.S. dollar still depreciates overall and remains relatively low compared with currencies of most of its export markets. This depreciation facilitates continued strength in U.S. agricultural exports over the projection period.

Macroeconomic Risks in the Projections

Macroeconomic assumptions behind the projections in this report include a modest recovery in the U.S. economy, with a return to steady long-term growth and a pickup in job growth in late 2011. Economic gains in the rest of the developed world, which have been uneven in the early part of the recovery, are expected to pick up in late 2011. Developing economies overall are now in an expansion phase starting in China and India (whose economies showed no signs of an overall recession) joined by much of Latin America and almost all of Asia in 2010.

Thus, the overall world economy is expected to return to near longer term trend growth rates by mid 2011 although, unlike many previous recovery periods, no sharp short-term bounce back with accelerated growth is assumed. Nonetheless, even with this return to sustained world economic growth, there has been a dramatic change in the underlying macroeconomic policy environment and an increased risk of downside scenarios from multiple sources.

Labor Market Risks in Developed Economies. The potential for a noticeable slowing of world and U.S. growth in 2011-20 is substantial. Relatively slow growth in the United States and other developed countries implies continuing high levels of unemployment. The U.S. unemployment rate is projected to remain persistently high and to stay above 6 percent until 2018-20.

Prolonged weakness in U.S. labor markets would have important implications for trend productivity and output growth due to both supply side and demand side risks. On the supply side, relatively high unemployment could substantially curtail growth in the capacity of the U.S. economy.

Larger unemployment would imply substantial risks to labor incomes, potentially dampening consumption and causing aggregate demand growth to stagnate. Similar risks are present in the European economies.

Financial Market Risks. There remain notable risks to U.S. and world economic growth because of continuing problems in financial markets. The potential for a substantial decline in the euro due to problems with the internal Eurozone structural debt could be confined to European financial markets or could affect U.S. and other financial markets with uncertain consequences for world growth.

Additionally, due to increased economic and financial market uncertainty, consumers in developed economies could decide to add to savings, thereby shrinking consumer spending growth. Such a reduction in consumer spending could weaken corporate profits and cause a decline in stock markets, further increasing uncertainty. In this climate, the rise in savings and reduction in consumer spending could lower trend growth in developed economies and thereby dampen growth in developing economies.

U.S. Business Confidence Risks. The recovery of business confidence in the United States is a prerequisite to achieving sustained employment gains and economic growth. Businesses are now keeping record-high levels of cash and, while they are replenishing inventories and replacing old equipment, they are generally not starting many new major business projects. For the domestic economy to have sustained growth and move toward full employment, business confidence needs to improve so that new business projects can move forward. As a business cycle matures, business confidence typically rises, leading to job growth and increasing demand for capital as new business projects are started. Thus, a weaker recovery of business confidence represents a major risk to domestic GDP growth, employment gains, and consumer spending increases.

U.S. Dollar Risks. If the U.S. economy were to undergo a longer and deeper recession due to some combination of the factors above, one low-probability outcome could be a weakening of the U.S. dollar as the default reserve currency in the world. Such an outcome would imply a substantial decline in the dollar's value and a potential decline in U.S. living standards. In turn, this would lead to lower U.S. demand for raw materials and manufactured goods from developing countries, lowering their growth as well. For agriculture, implications would depend on how weaker economic growth and demand gains in the developing economies would balance against agricultural trade effects of a sharply lower dollar.

China's Inflation Risks. China may face a more difficult problem in constraining inflation in the next decade than in the last, as industrial commodity and wage inflation speed up. Consumer price inflation went above 3 percent in the fall of 2010, despite a 2 to 3 percent appreciation of the yuan, a modest tightening of credit, and a Government edict to prevent provincial hoarding of coal and oil. Bank reserve requirements were raised six times in 2010, and short-term interest rates were increased as well. However, as inflation in China continued to rise, many analysts suggested that the increases in bank reserve requirements, interest rates, and the yuan were too modest. A medium-term risk is that fighting inflation may sharply limit bank credit expansion and thus slow GDP growth. The yuan may be allowed to appreciate more rapidly than projected to keep Chinese inflation in check.

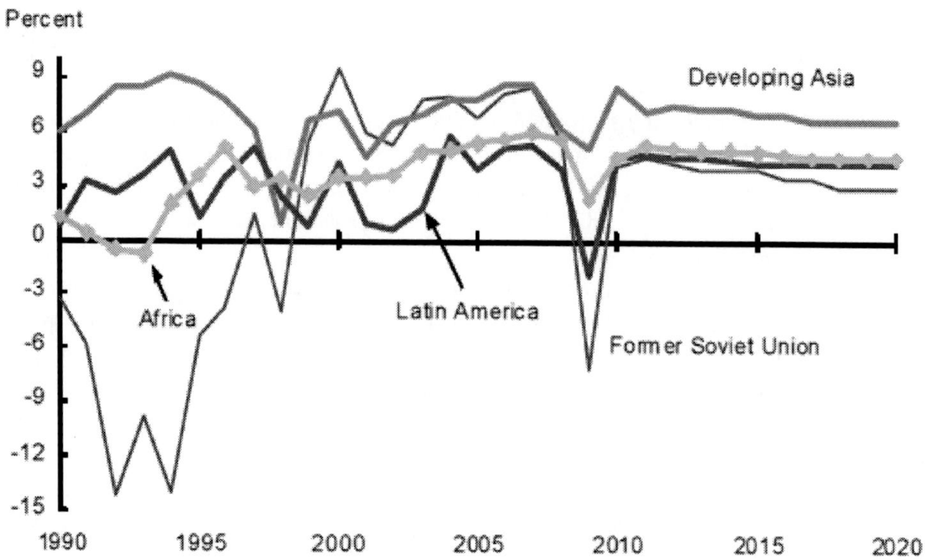

GDP Growth for Developing Economies and the Former Soviet Union.

Economic growth in developing countries is projected to average close to 6 percent annually during 2011-20. These countries were much less affected by the global recession than were the developed countries. The pattern of developing countries producing and consuming a larger share of world output, relative to developed countries, strengthens in the projections.

- Developing countries will play an increasingly important role in the global economy and growth in food demand, and will become a more important destination for U.S. agricultural exports. High income growth, along with high responsiveness of consumption and imports of food and feed, drives this result. As incomes rise in developing countries, consumers tend to diversify their diets, increasing their relative consumption of meat, dairy products, fruits, vegetables, and processed foods (including vegetable oils). These shifts increase import demand for feedstuffs and high-value food products.
- Continued strong growth in China, India, and the rest of Asia make this region an increasingly important part of the global economy, with developing Asia's share of world GDP rising to 22 percent by the end of the projection period. Projected growth for Southeast Asia is 5.2 percent for the next decade while growth in developing countriesof East Asia is projected to be more than 7 percent.
- China's economic growth has been consistently the strongest in Asia, averaging almost 10 percent between 2001 and 2010. While some slowing is expected, China's growth is expected to average more than 8 percent over the next decade and will account for almost 12 percent of the world economy. India's projected average economic growth of almost 8 percent per year puts it in the top tier of high-growth countries. Nonetheless, India remains a low-income country, with real (inflation-adjusted) 2005-based per capita income of $962 in 2010, compared with $2,800 in China. Continued strong income growth in India and China is expected to bring their

real per capita income to $1,800 and nearly $6,000 by 2020. This continued rapid growth in per capita income is expected to move a significant number of people out of poverty.

- Latin America sustains projected growth of about 4.4 percent per year. An overall improvement in macroeconomic policieshas attracted foreign capital inflows (particularly foreign direct investment to Chile, Colombia, and Brazil) and sustained growth in the region.
- Economic growth in the countries of the former Soviet Union (FSU) is projected to average 3.6 percent annually for the next decadeas these countries return to sustainable growth after their shift to more market-oriented economies. Russia and other energy-rich FSU countries also benefit from relatively high oil prices.

World population growth continues to slow over the next decade, rising about 1 percent per year for the projection period compared to an annual rate of 1.7 percent in the 1980s.

- Developed countries have very low projected rates of population growth, at 0.4 percent over 2011-20. Projected annual average population growth rates for the United States in the 0.8 to 0.9 percent range over the period are the highest among developed countries, in part reflecting large immigration. Japan's population is projected to decline by an average of 0.4 percent over the projection period.
- Overall, population in the FSU is projected to decline moderately. Population growth rates in developing economies are projected to be sharply lower than rates in the 1980s and 1990s, but remain above those in developed countries and the FSU. As a result, the share of world population accounted for by developing countries increases to 82 percent by 2020, compared to 74 percent in 1980.
- China and India together account for 37 percent of the world's population. China's population growth rate slows from 1.5 percent per year in 1981-90 to 0.4 percent in 2011-20. The population growth rate in India, the world's second most populous nation, is projected to decline from 2.0 percent to 1.2 percent per year over the same period.
- Brazil's population growth rate falls from 2.1 percent per year in 1981-90 to 1 percent annually in 2011-20. Although Sub-Saharan Africa's population growth rate declines from 2.9 percent to 2.3 percent per year between the same periods, this region continues to have the highest population growth rate of any region in the world.
- There are a number of countries with declining populations, including Germany, Italy, Spain, Russia, Ukraine, some other countries in Western and Central Europe, and Japan. South Africa is projected to have a declining population resulting from the continuing AIDS epidemic.

The U.S. dollar is projected to depreciate moderately through the projection period and thus continue to facilitate growth in U.S. agricultural exports. Among agricultural products, U.S. exports of bulk commodities and horticultural products tend to be the most sensitive to movements in the U.S. dollar's value, because they face more global trade competition. The dollar depreciation is part of a global rebalancing of trade and financial markets in the aftermath of the global financial crisis and recession.

- Strong GDP growth in the United States relative to the EU and Japan will tend to mitigate the continued appreciation of the euro and yen to the U.S. dollar. The immediate effect of the debt crisis in Greece was a depreciation of the euro relative to the dollar, with the euro depreciating by about 25 percent between December 2009 and June 2010. In the longer term, a depreciation of the dollar relative to the euro and yen is likely as part of the global rebalancing of international currency portfolios.
- China initiated a process for appreciating its currency in 2005 after a long period of maintaining a fixed nominal exchange rate and an undervalued currency. However, that process was halted in 2008. After nearly two years of maintaining a constant nominal exchange rate of the yuan to the dollar, the Chinese Central Bank announced in June 2010 that they will allow increased flexibility in the bilateral exchange rate. Since then, there has been a very modest 2-3 percent nominal appreciation of the yuan. The projections assume that China allows its real exchange rate to continue to appreciate modestly. The real appreciation of yuan also leads to some appreciation of other Asian currencies. These developments will strengthen U.S. agricultural exports to Asian countries.

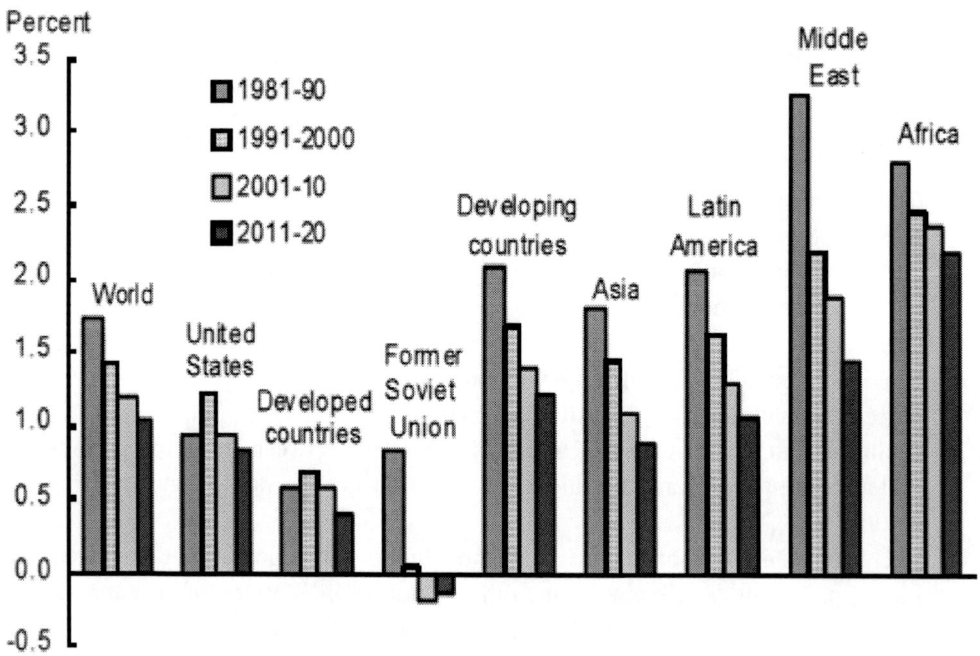

Sou rce: U.S. Department of Commerce, U.S. Censu s Bu reau a nd U.S. Department of Agriculture, Economic Research Se rvice.

Population Growth Continues to Slow.

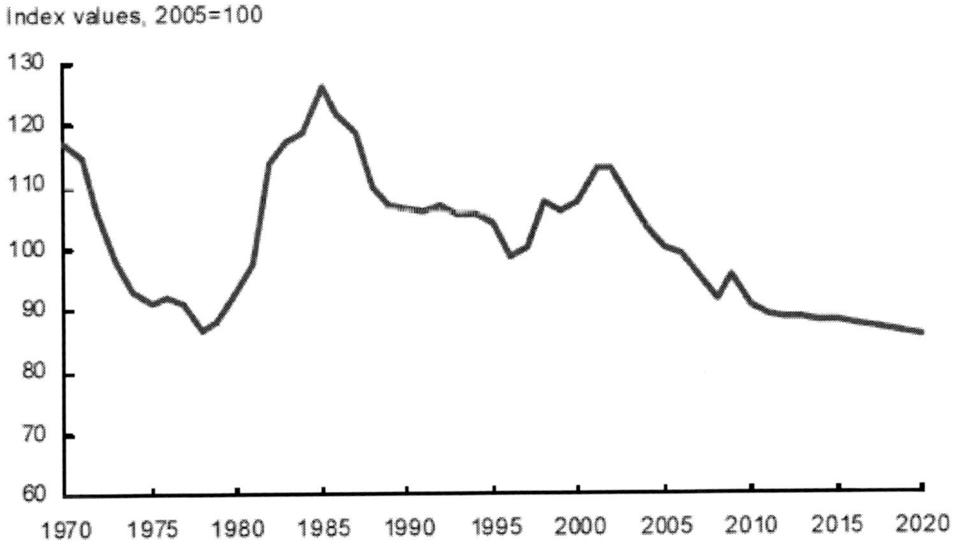

1/ Real U.S. agricultural trade-weighted dollar exchange rate, using U.S. agricultural export weights, based on 192 countries.

U.S. Agricultural Ttrade-Weighted Dollar Continues Depreciation 1/.

Crude oil prices are assumed to increase over the projection period as global economic activity picks up.

From 2011 through 2020, crude oil prices are expected to rise somewhat faster than the general inflation rate. By the end of the projection period, the nominal refiner acquisition cost for crude oil imports is projected to be around $110 per barrel.

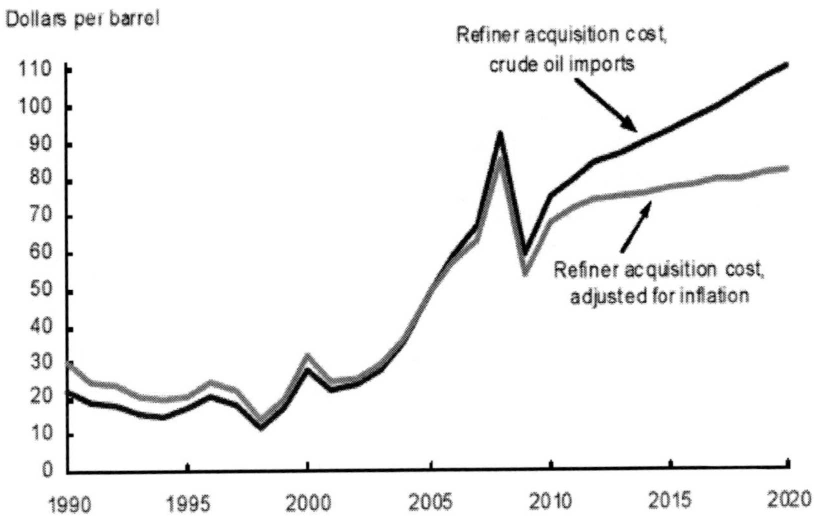

U.S. Crude Oil Prices.

AGRICULTURAL TRADE

Renewed economic growth following the global recession began in 2010. During the 2011-2020 projection period, income growth is projected to continue and to be slightly above the historical average long-term rate during the last half of the period.This growth provides a foundation for gains in world demand and trade for agricultural products. Consequently, agricultural product prices are projected to remain historically high.

Historical Background for Trade Projections

Since the beginning of 2002, fluctuations in production, trade, and stocks of agricultural commodities have been unusually large, and have been contributing factors to wide price fluctuations.

Between January 2002 and June 2008, an index of monthly-average world prices of wheat, rice, corn, and soybeans rose 226 percent and then declined 40 percent in the following 6 months.

By June 2010, the index had fallen another 11 percent. The price index then rose 55 percent by December 2010 and stood at about 172 percent above the January 2002 level, although still 17 percent below the June 2008 peak.

The 55-percent increase between June and December 2010 raised concerns about another major food-commodity price spike as in 2007-08.

The main factors contributing to this recent increase in staple food prices was a series of weather events, beginning with a severe drought in Russia and parts of Ukraine and Kazakhstan that reduced production of all crops, but particularly wheat. In late summer 2010, yield prospects for U.S. corn declined due to high temperatures during pollination. About the same time, rain on the nearly mature wheat crops in Canada and northwestern Europe reduced the quality of much of the crop to feed-grade wheat. Continued drought in the former Soviet Union significantly reduced winter wheat plantings. Since November 2010, drought and periodic high temperatures associated with a La Niña weather pattern have reduced prospects for the corn and soybean crops in central Argentina. Dry fall and winter weather also affected the U.S. hard red winter wheat crop in the western Great Plains. Additionally, rains in Australia in late 2010-early 2011 downgraded much of the Australian wheat crop to feed quality, further reducing global supplies of food-quality wheat.

Other factors contributing to the recent rise in prices include resurgent global economic growth and increasing energy prices. The run-up in crop prices during the last half of 2010 is expected to stimulate increased plantings and more intensive use of production inputs in 2011. Assuming average weather in major producing regions in 2011, global production and world stocks of grains and oilseeds are projected to increase. However, even with the projected increases in world crop production and stocks, world market prices are expected to remain well above historical levels for the next decade.

Table 1. U.S. Macroeconomic Assumptions

tem	2009	2010	2011	2012	2013	2014	2015	2016	2017	2018	2019	2020
GDP, billion dollars												
Nominal	14,119	14,574	15,118	15,758	16,492	17,293	18,133	19,013	19,937	20,905	21,921	22,985
Real 2005 chained dollars	12,881	13,190	13,519	13,898	14,259	14,630	15,010	15,401	15,801	16,212	16,634	17,066
percent change	-2.6	2.4	2.5	2.8	2.6	2.6	2.6	2.6	2.6	2.6	2.6	2.6
Disposable personal income												
Nominal (billion dollars)	11,035	11,344	11,741	12,246	12,834	13,475	14,149	14,856	15,599	16,379	17,198	18,058
percent change	0.7	2.8	3.5	4.3	4.8	5.0	5.0	5.0	5.0	5.0	5.0	5.0
Nominal per capita, dollars	35,888	36,567	37,517	38,792	40,307	41,964	43,694	45,498	47,381	49,346	51,396	53,535
percent change	-0.1	1.9	2.6	3.4	3.9	4.1	4.1	4.1	4.1	4.1	4.2	4.2
Real (billion 2005 chained dollars)	10,100	10,302	10,539	10,845	11,148	11,460	11,781	12,111	12,450	12,799	13,157	13,526
percent change	0.6	2.0	2.3	2.9	2.8	2.8	2.8	2.8	2.8	2.8	2.8	2.8
Real per capita, 2005 chained dollars	32,848	33,209	33,676	34,353	35,013	35,690	36,382	37,091	37,816	38,559	39,320	40,098
percent change	-0.3	1.1	1.4	2.0	1.9	1.9	1.9	1.9	2.0	2.0	2.0	2.0
Consumer spending												
Real (billion 2005 chained dollars)	9,154	9,364	9,589	9,839	10,084	10,337	10,595	10,860	11,131	11,410	11,695	11,987
percent change	-1.2	2.3	2.4	2.6	2.5	2.5	2.5	2.5	2.5	2.5	2.5	2.5
Inflation measures												
GDP price index, chained, 2005=100	109.6	110.5	111.8	113.4	115.7	118.2	120.8	123.5	126.2	128.9	131.8	134.7
percent change	2.2	0.8	1.2	1.4	2.0	2.2	2.2	2.2	2.2	2.2	2.2	2.2
CPI-U, 1982-84=100	214.5	217.1	220.6	224.8	230.4	236.2	242.1	248.1	254.3	260.7	267.2	273.9
percent change	-0.4	1.2	1.6	1.9	2.5	2.5	2.5	2.5	2.5	2.5	2.5	2.5
PPI, finished goods 1982=100	172.5	181.0	188.2	192.0	195.6	199.3	203.1	207.0	210.9	214.9	219.0	223.1
percent change	-2.6	4.9	4.0	2.0	1.9	1.9	1.9	1.9	1.9	1.9	1.9	1.9
PPI, crude goods 1982=100	175.2	210.3	218.7	223.0	225.3	227.5	229.8	232.1	234.4	236.8	239.1	241.5
percent change	-30.4	20.0	4.0	2.0	1.0	1.0	1.0	1.0	1.0	1.0	1.0	1.0
Crude oil price, $/barrel												
EIA refiner acq. cost, imports	59.0	74.9	80.1	84.0	87.0	90.0	93.2	96.5	99.9	103.4	107.0	110.8
percent change	-36.2	26.8	6.9	4.9	3.6	3.4	3.5	3.5	3.5	3.5	3.5	3.6
Real 2005 chained dollars	53.9	67.8	71.6	74.1	75.2	76.1	77.1	78.1	79.1	80.2	81.2	82.3

tem	2009	2010	2011	2012	2013	2014	2015	2016	2017	2018	2019	2020
GDP, billion dollars												
percent change	-36.8	25.8	5.6	3.5	1.5	1.2	1.3	1.3	1.3	1.3	1.3	1.3
Labor compensation per hour												
nonfarm business, 2005=100	113.5	116.0	118.9	122.0	125.4	128.9	132.5	136.2	140.0	143.9	147.9	152.0
percent change	1.9	2.2	2.5	2.6	2.8	2.8	2.8	2.8	2.8	2.8	2.8	2.8
Interest rates, percent												
3-month Treasury bills	0.2	0.4	2.8	4.0	4.6	4.8	4.8	4.8	4.8	4.8	4.8	4.8
3-month commercial paper	0.3	1.8	3.0	4.2	5.1	5.3	5.3	5.3	5.3	5.3	5.3	5.3
Bank prime rate	3.3	4.0	5.4	6.8	7.7	8.2	8.2	8.2	8.2	8.2	8.2	8.2
10-year Treasury bonds	3.3	3.5	5.2	5.2	5.6	5.7	5.7	5.7	5.7	5.7	5.7	5.8
Moody's Aaa bond yield index	5.3	4.8	5.4	5.7	6.3	6.2	6.2	6.2	6.2	6.2	6.2	6.2
Labor and population												
Civilian unemployment												
rate, percent	9.3	9.7	9.3	8.5	8.0	7.5	7.0	6.5	6.2	6.0	6.0	6.0
Nonfarm payroll emp., millions	130.9	130.3	131.6	133.2	134.5	135.9	137.2	138.6	139.8	141.0	142.1	143.2
percent change	-4.3	-0.5	1.0	1.2	1.0	1.0	1.0	1.0	0.9	0.8	0.8	0.8
Total population, millions	307.5	310.2	313.0	315.7	318.4	321.1	323.8	326.5	329.2	331.9	334.6	337.3
percent change	0.9	0.9	0.9	0.9	0.9	0.9	0.8	0.8	0.8	0.8	0.8	0.8

Domestic macroeconomic assumptions w ere completed in October 2010. CPI-U is the consumer price index for all urban consumers. PPI is the producer price index. EIA is the Energy Information Administration, U.S. Department of Energy.

Table 2. Global real GDP growth assumptions

		Share of world GDP	**Per capita income,**								**Average**	
Region/country	GDP, 2009	2007-2009	2009	2009	2010	2011	2012	2013	2014	1991-2000	2001-2010	2011-2020
	Bil. 2005		*2005*									
	dollars	*Percent*	*dollars*					*Percent change*				
World	48,350	100.0	7,164	-2.1	3.3	3.2	3.5	3.6	3.6	2.7	2.4	3.4
Less United States	35,469	73.1	5,506	-1.9	3.6	3.5	3.8	3.9	3.9	2.5	2.7	3.7
North America	14,128	29.5	41,436	-2.6	2.5	2.6	2.9	2.7	2.6	3.4	1.7	2.7
Canada	1,248	2.6	37,262	-2.5	3.5	3.8	3.5	3.3	3.0	2.9	2.0	3.2

Table 2. (Continued)

		Share of world GDP	Per capita income,								Average	
Region/country	GDP, 2009	2007-2009	2009	2009	2010	2011	2012	2013	2014	1991-2000	2001-2010	2011-2020
	Bil. 2005		*2005*									
	dollars	*Percent*	*dollars*					*Percent change*				
United States	12,881	26.9	41,890	-2.6	2.4	2.5	2.8	2.6	2.6	3.4	1.6	2.6
Latin America	3,085	6.3	5,281	-2.0	4.6	4.7	4.6	4.6	4.4	3.1	3.0	4.4
Mexico	787	1.7	7,075	-6.5	4.5	4.7	4.3	4.2	4.1	3.5	1.6	4.0
Caribbean & Central America	318	0.7	3,911	-0.5	1.9	3.4	4.5	4.5	4.4	3.1	2.7	4.1
South America	1,980	4.0	5,056	-0.2	5.0	4.9	4.8	4.7	4.5	3.0	3.6	4.5
Argentina	221	0.4	5,411	0.9	4.5	4.3	4.0	3.8	3.8	4.4	4.1	3.8
Brazil	1,072	2.3	5,656	-0.2	6.5	5.4	5.2	5.1	4.8	2.6	3.4	4.7
Other	635	1.3	4,176	-0.7	2.6	4.2	4.3	4.4	4.3	3.3	3.8	4.3
Europe	14,775	31.1	27,169	-4.1	1.0	1.6	2.0	2.2	2.2	2.1	1.2	2.1
European Union-27	13,936	29.4	27,340	-4.2	0.7	1.9	2.0	2.2	2.2	2.1	1.2	2.1
Other Europe	839	1.7	24,601	-1.8	1.5	2.2	2.3	2.5	2.6	1.8	1.8	2.3
Former Soviet Union	1,178	2.5	4,267	-7.1	4.1	4.6	4.2	4.0	3.9	-4.0	5.3	3.6
Russia	896	1.9	6,401	-7.9	4.0	4.3	3.8	3.8	3.5	-3.6	4.8	3.4
Ukraine	85	0.2	1,859	-15.1	3.6	5.8	6.9	5.7	5.4	-7.7	4.5	5.1
Other	197	0.4	2,179	1.0	4.9	5.1	4.7	4.2	4.9	-3.8	8.3	4.0
Asia and Oceania	12,493	25.2	3,342	1.1	6.2	5.0	5.2	5.3	5.4	3.7	4.2	5.1
East Asia	9,139	18.5	5,962	0.3	6.3	4.7	5.0	5.1	5.3	3.4	4.0	4.9
China	3,385	6.4	2,557	8.7	10.8	8.6	8.6	8.6	8.8	10.5	9.9	8.3
Hong Kong	196	0.4	27,848	-2.8	5.6	5.1	5.6	5.3	4.8	4.5	4.0	4.4
Japan	4,203	9.0	33,074	-5.3	3.0	1.4	1.6	1.8	1.9	1.2	0.8	1.4
South Korea	956	1.9	19,702	0.2	5.3	3.8	4.0	4.1	4.0	6.2	4.0	3.8
Taiw an	383	0.8	16,651	-1.9	6.6	4.5	5.9	5.0	4.5	6.5	3.5	4.2
Southeast Asia	1,131	2.3	1,887	1.1	6.1	5.6	5.8	5.6	5.4	5.2	4.7	5.2
Indonesia	371	0.7	1,546	4.5	6.0	6.3	6.5	6.3	6.0	4.4	5.2	5.7
Malaysia	156	0.3	5,610	-1.7	6.7	5.1	5.8	5.2	5.0	7.2	4.4	5.0
Philippines	124	0.3	1,267	0.9	5.0	5.3	5.0	4.8	4.7	3.1	4.4	4.7

		Share of world GDP	Per capita income,								Average	
Region/country	**GDP, 2009**	**2007-2009**	**2009**	**2009**	**2010**	**2011**	**2012**	**2013**	**2014**	**1991-2000**	**2001-2010**	**2011-2020**
	Bil. 2005		***2005***									
	dollars	***Percent***	***dollars***					***Percent change***				
Thailand	207	0.4	3,111	-2.3	5.0	5.3	5.5	5.3	5.0	4.6	4.1	4.8
Vietnam	69	0.1	775	5.3	6.5	7.0	7.2	6.9	6.4	7.4	7.2	6.9
South Asia	1,308	2.5	832	7.1	7.5	7.7	7.8	7.7	7.5	5.2	7.0	7.4
Bangladesh	68	0.1	444	5.9	5.5	6.0	6.3	6.1	6.1	4.8	5.7	5.9
India	1,043	2.0	902	7.6	8.1	8.2	8.4	8.2	8.0	5.5	7.5	7.9
Pakistan	141	0.3	779	3.7	4.1	4.4	4.6	4.9	4.4	4.0	5.2	4.3
Oceania	915	1.9	26,337	1.1	2.9	3.2	3.3	3.4	3.3	3.5	2.9	3.2
Australia	779	1.6	36,659	1.3	2.9	3.3	3.4	3.5	3.3	3.6	3.0	3.2
New Zealand	104	0.2	24,651	-0.5	2.5	2.3	3.1	3.1	2.9	2.9	2.5	2.7
Middle East	1,542	3.1	5,420	-1.0	4.1	5.0	5.0	4.9	4.7	3.6	4.0	4.4
Iran	223	0.5	2,932	-2.2	3.2	5.2	4.4	4.3	4.4	2.6	5.1	4.1
Iraq	85	0.2	2,920	5.6	7.5	7.9	7.3	6.9	6.0	9.5	11.9	6.1
Saudi Arabia	350	0.7	13,828	0.6	3.2	4.5	5.2	5.3	4.9	2.6	3.6	4.3
Turkey	367	0.8	4,775	-4.7	5.7	5.0	4.9	4.8	4.5	3.6	3.6	4.5
Other	517	1.0	6,687	0.1	3.4	4.7	4.9	4.6	4.5	4.8	4.3	4.3
Africa	1,149	2.3	1,170	2.2	4.6	5.2	5.0	5.0	5.0	2.2	4.6	4.8
North Africa	381	0.8	2,366	3.4	4.6	4.8	4.7	4.4	4.3	3.5	4.6	4.0
Algeria	111	0.2	3,246	2.0	4.0	3.5	3.6	3.6	3.6	1.7	3.9	3.0
Egypt	125	0.2	1,590	4.7	5.2	5.8	5.0	4.2	4.0	4.5	5.0	4.3
Morocco	65	0.1	7,361	4.9	3.8	4.8	5.2	5.1	5.0	2.4	4.7	4.5
Tunisia	34	0.1	2,065	3.1	4.2	4.6	5.2	5.9	5.5	4.8	4.6	4.9
Sub-Saharan Africa	767	1.5	935	1.6	4.7	5.4	5.2	5.2	5.3	1.6	4.7	5.2
South Africa	248	0.5	5,063	-1.8	3.1	3.5	3.9	3.8	4.2	1.8	3.2	4.4
Other Sub-Saharan Africa	519	1.0	673	3.2	5.5	6.3	5.8	5.8	5.8	1.5	5.4	5.5

International macroeconomic assumptions w ere based on information available in July 2010.

Table 3. Population Growth Assumptions

Region/country	Population in 2009	2009	2010	2011	2012	2013	2014	1991-2000	2001-2010	2011-2020
	Millions				Percent change					
World[1]	6,749	1.1	1.1	1.1	1.1	1.1	1.1	1.4	1.2	1.0
Less United States	6,442	1.1	1.1	1.1	1.1	1.1	1.1	1.4	1.2	1.0
North America	341	0.9	0.9	0.9	0.9	0.9	0.8	1.2	0.9	0.8
Canada	33	0.8	0.8	0.8	0.8	0.8	0.8	1.1	0.8	0.8
United States	307	0.9	0.9	0.9	0.9	0.9	0.9	1.2	0.9	0.8
Latin America	584	1.2	1.2	1.2	1.1	1.1	1.1	1.6	1.3	1.1
Mexico	111	1.1	1.1	1.1	1.1	1.1	1.1	1.6	1.2	1.0
Caribbean & Central America	81	1.3	0.9	1.1	1.1	1.1	1.1	1.7	1.3	1.1
South America	392	1.2	1.2	1.2	1.2	1.1	1.1	1.6	1.3	1.1
Argentina	41	1.1	1.1	1.0	1.0	1.0	1.0	1.2	1.0	0.9
Brazil	199	1.2	1.2	1.2	1.1	1.1	1.1	1.6	1.3	1.0
Other	152	1.3	1.3	1.2	1.2	1.2	1.2	1.8	1.4	1.1
Europe	544	0.2	0.2	0.2	0.2	0.2	0.2	0.2	0.3	0.1
European Union-27	510	0.2	0.2	0.2	0.2	0.2	0.2	0.3	0.3	0.1
Other Europe	34	0.1	0.1	0.0	0.0	0.0	0.0	0.0	0.3	0.0
Former Soviet Union	276	-0.1	-0.1	-0.1	-0.1	-0.1	-0.1	0.0	-0.2	-0.1
Russia	140	-0.5	-0.5	-0.5	-0.5	-0.5	-0.5	-0.1	-0.5	-0.5
Ukraine	46	-0.6	-0.6	-0.6	-0.6	-0.6	-0.6	-0.5	-0.8	-0.6
Other	90	0.7	0.7	0.7	0.7	0.7	0.7	0.6	0.6	0.7
Asia and Oceania	3,738	1.0	1.0	1.0	1.0	0.9	0.9	1.4	1.1	0.9
East Asia	1,533	0.4	0.4	0.4	0.4	0.4	0.4	0.9	0.5	0.3
China	1,324	0.5	0.5	0.5	0.5	0.5	0.5	1.0	0.5	0.4
Hong Kong	7	0.5	0.5	0.5	0.4	0.4	0.4	1.6	0.6	0.3
Japan	127	-0.2	-0.2	-0.3	-0.3	-0.3	-0.4	0.3	0.0	-0.4
South Korea	49	0.3	0.3	0.2	0.2	0.2	0.2	0.9	0.4	0.1
Taiw an	23	0.2	0.2	0.2	0.2	0.2	0.1	0.9	0.4	0.1
Southeast Asia	600	1.3	1.3	1.2	1.2	1.2	1.1	1.8	1.4	1.1
Indonesia	240	1.2	1.1	1.1	1.1	1.0	1.0	1.6	1.3	1.0
Malaysia	28	1.7	1.6	1.6	1.6	1.5	1.5	2.6	2.0	1.4
Philippines	98	2.0	2.0	1.9	1.9	1.9	1.8	2.2	2.1	1.8
Thailand	67	0.7	0.7	0.6	0.6	0.6	0.6	1.2	0.8	0.5

Region/country	Population in 2009	2009	2010	2011	2012	2013	2014	1991-2000	2001-2010	2011-2020
	Millions				**Percent change**					
Vietnam	89	1.2	1.1	1.1	1.1	1.0	1.0	1.6	1.2	1.0
South Asia	1,571	1.5	1.5	1.4	1.4	1.4	1.4	1.9	1.6	1.3
Bangladesh	154	1.6	1.6	1.6	1.6	1.6	1.6	1.6	1.7	1.6
India	1,157	1.4	1.4	1.4	1.3	1.3	1.3	1.8	1.5	1.2
	Millions				Percent change					
Pakistan	181	1.7	1.6	1.6	1.6	1.5	1.5	2.5	1.9	1.5
Oceania	35	1.4	1.3	1.3	1.3	1.2	1.2	1.4	1.4	1.2
Australia	21	1.2	1.2	1.2	1.1	1.1	1.1	1.2	1.2	1.1
New Zealand	4	1.0	0.9	0.9	0.9	0.9	0.8	1.1	1.1	0.8
Middle East	284	1.8	1.7	1.6	1.5	1.4	1.5	2.2	1.9	1.5
Iran	76	1.3	1.3	1.3	1.3	1.2	1.2	1.7	1.1	1.2
Iraq	29	2.6	2.5	2.5	2.4	2.3	2.3	2.3	2.7	2.2
Saudi Arabia	25	1.7	1.6	1.6	1.5	1.5	1.5	2.9	1.9	1.5
Turkey	77	1.3	1.3	1.3	1.2	1.2	1.1	1.8	1.5	1.1
Other	77	2.4	2.3	2.1	1.5	1.3	1.7	3.1	2.8	1.8
Africa	982	2.3	2.3	2.3	2.3	2.3	2.2	2.5	2.4	2.2
North Africa	161	1.6	1.6	1.6	1.6	1.5	1.5	1.7	1.7	1.5
Algeria	34	1.2	1.2	1.2	1.2	1.2	1.2	1.9	1.3	1.1
Egypt	79	2.1	2.0	2.0	2.0	1.9	1.9	1.7	2.1	1.8
Morocco	31	2.2	2.2	2.1	2.1	2.0	1.9	2.1	2.3	1.8
Tunisia	10	1.1	1.1	1.1	1.1	1.1	1.0	1.6	1.2	1.0
Sub-Saharan Africa	820	2.5	2.4	2.4	2.4	2.4	2.4	2.6	2.5	2.3
South Africa	49	0.6	0.1	-0.2	-0.4	-0.4	-0.5	1.6	0.9	-0.1
Other Sub-Saharan Africa	771	2.6	2.6	2.6	2.6	2.6	2.5	2.7	2.6	2.5

[1]/ Totals for the w orld and w orld less United States include countries not otherw ise listed in the table.

Source: U.S. Department of Commerce, U.S. Census Bureau and U.S. Department of Agriculture, Economic Research Service.

The population assumptions w ere completed in July 2010 based on the June 2010 update from the U.S. Census Bureau.

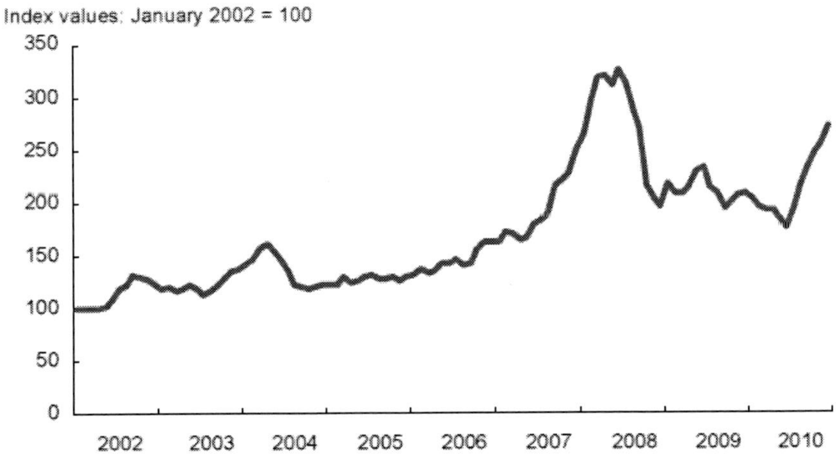

1/ ERS calculations based on International Monetary Fund (IMF) average monthly world price quotes for wheat, corn, soybeans, and rice; aggregated by IMF's fixed historical exports weights.

Trade Projections Overview

Developing countries are the main source of growth in world agricultural demand and trade. Food consumption and feed use are particularly responsive to income growth in developing countries, with movement away from staple and/or traditional foods and toward more diversified diets. Agricultural demand in developing countries is further reinforced by population growth rates that are nearly twice those of developed countries.

General International Assumptions

Trade projections to 2020 are founded on assumptions concerning trends in foreign area, yields, and use and on the assumption that countries comply with existing bilateral and multilateral agreements affecting agriculture and agricultural trade. The projections incorporate the effects of trade agreements and domestic policies in place or authorized by November 2010. International macroeconomic assumptions were completed in October 2010.

Domestic agricultural and trade policies in individual foreign countries are assumed to continue to evolve along their current paths, based on the consensus judgment of USDA's analysts. In particular, long-term economic and trade reforms in many developing countries are assumed to continue. Similarly, the development and use of technology and changes in consumer preferences are assumed to continue evolving based on past performance and analysts' judgments regarding future developments.

In particular, Africa and the Middle East as a combined region is projected to have some of the strongest growth in food demand and agricultural trade over the coming decade. Both poultry imports and beef imports have their largest increases in the countries of Africa and the Middle East. With these projected gains, in 2020 the region accounts for about 45 percent of poultry imports and 20 percent of beef imports by the major importers of the world. Strong policy support for domestically produced meat also motivates growth in feed-grain imports, especially where land constraints or agroclimatic conditions limit an expansion of domestic crop production. As a result, the region accounts for about 35 percent of the projected growth in world coarse grain imports over the next 10 years. Strong import growth by Africa and the Middle East over the projection period also accounts for 58 percent of the increase in wheat imports, 35 percent of the growth in rice imports, and 27 percent of rise in soybean oil trade.

Mexico is projected to be another large growth market for meat imports. Large increases in Mexican meat demand provide incentives to expand livestock production as well as to import more meat. Imports of beef, pork, and poultry each rise by 50 percent or more.

Agricultural prices are projected to remain above pre-2006 levels during the coming decade as a result of increasing world demand for grains, oilseeds, and livestock products; a devaluation of the U.S. dollar; continuing high energy prices; and some further growth in biofuels production.

Prices for vegetable oils are projected to rise relative to prices for protein meals. Oilseed prices rise slightly more than grain prices, and meat prices rise relative to the costs of feedstuffs, both for protein meals and grains.

World agricultural production rises in response to high prices and technology enhancements. However, a number of factors are expected to slow production growth in the future. Many countries have a limited ability to expand planted area. And, in many regions, the expansion that does occur takes place on land with lower productive capacity. The growth rate in world average crop yields has been slowing for nearly two decades, to some extent as a result of reduced research and development funding. Water constraints in some countries are impeding the expansion in irrigation. Where irrigation water is pumped from deep wells, the energy cost of pumping is projected to continue to increase. Other costs of production such as fertilizers and chemicals are also likely to increase.

Traditional exporters of a wide range of agricultural commodities, such as Argentina, Australia, Canada, the European Union (EU), and the United States, remain important in global trade in the coming decade. But countries that are making significant investments in their agricultural sectors and increasingly pursuing policies to encourage agricultural production, including Brazil, Russia, Ukraine, and Kazakhstan, are expected to have an increasing presence in export markets for basic agricultural commodities.

Global trade in soybeans and soybean products has risen rapidly since the early 1990s, and has surpassed not only wheat—the traditional leader in agricultural commodity trade—but also total coarse grains (corn, barley, sorghum, rye, oats, millet, and mixed grains). Continued strong growth in global demand for vegetable oil and protein meal, particularly in China and other Asian countries, is expected to maintain soybean and soybean-product trade well above wheat and coarse grains trade throughout the next decade.

- In most countries, the projected growth in total harvested area of all crops rises less than a half-percent per year. Area expands more rapidly in countries with a reserve of available land and policies that enable farmers to respond to higher prices. Such countries include Brazil, Russia, Ukraine, Argentina, and some other countries in South America and Eastern Europe. About two-thirds of the projected growth in global production is derived from rising yields. However, growth in crop yields has slowed during the last several decades and is projected to continue doing so.
- The market impact of slower crop yield growth is partially offset by slower growth in world population. Nonetheless, increasing population is a significant factor driving overall growth in demand for agricultural products. Additionally, rising per

capita income in many countries supplements population gains in the demand for vegetable oils, meats, horticultural products, and coarse grains. World per capita use of vegetable oils is projected to rise 15 percent over the next 10 years, compared with 9 percent for meat and 5 percent for total coarse grains. Per capita use is projected to be flat for wheat and to decline nearly 2 percent for rice.

- Wheat, coarse grains, oilseeds, and other crops compete for limited cropland. Higher prices for vegetable oils, as a result of increased demand for food use, biodiesel production, and other industrial uses, are bringing previously uncropped land in Brazil, Argentina, Indonesia, and Malaysia into soybean and palm oil production.
- In the coming decade, overall gains in global grain trade come from a broad range of countries, but particularly from countries in Africa and the Middle East.

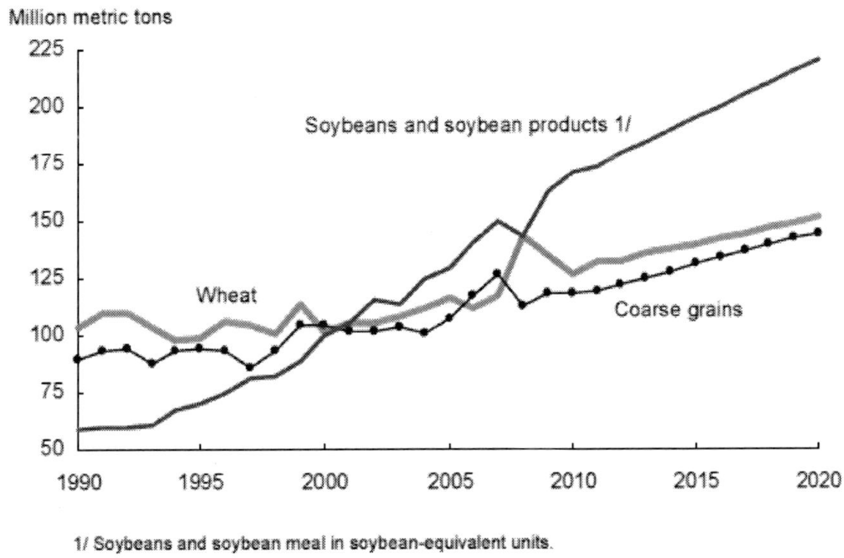

Global Trade: Wheat, Coarse Grains, and Soybeans and Soybean Products.

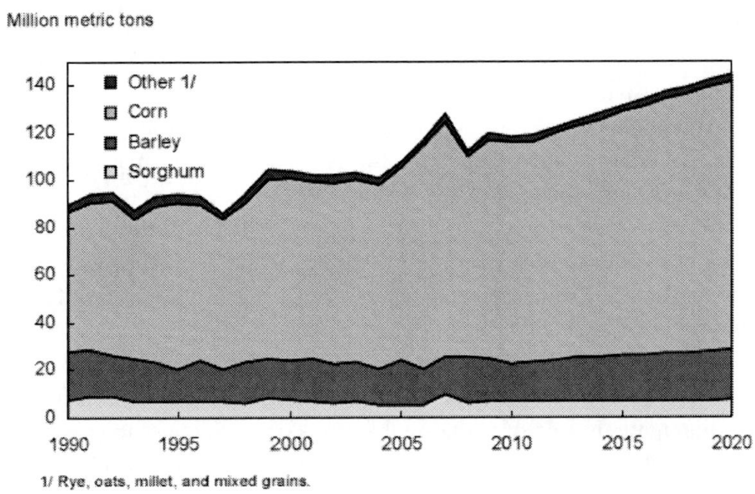

Global Coarse Grain Trade.

Demand for Biofuel Feedstocks

The demand for biofuel feedstocks is projected to continue growing in a number of countries, although at a slower pace than in recent years. Expansion continues to depend on policy support, mainly tax incentives and use mandates which is motivated by environmental concerns and a goal to reduce energy dependence.

Six countries and regions (United States, Brazil, European Union (EU), Argentina, Canada, and China) accounted for 87 percent of world biodiesel production and 98 percent of ethanol production in 2009. Over the next 10 years, production in these countries is projected to rise 20 percent for biodiesel and nearly 25 percent for ethanol.

Country Assumptions

EU. The EU is the world's largest importer of both ethanol and biodiesel throughout the projection period. Two key pieces of legislation impacting the biofuel market are the Renewable Energy Directive and the amended Fuel Quality Directive that require by 2020 at least 10 percent of the energy used for transportation be from renewable sources and a 6-percent cut in greenhouse gas emissions by fuel suppliers. To boost biodiesel production, the EU increases its internal oilseed production and its imports of oilseeds and vegetable oil, mainly from Ukraine and Russia. Biodiesel production increases 22 percent by 2020. During the same period, ethanol production is projected to increase more than 40 percent. Internally produced wheat provides the growth for ethanol in the early years but corn used as a feedstock grows more rapidly toward the end of the projections. Ethanol's share of total biofuel use grows from 31 percent to about 40 percent. Ethanol imports rise to nearly one-third of domestic use by 2020. Nevertheless, in 2020 only 60 percent of the EU's mandate is achieved from annual-crop feedstocks.

Brazil. Sugarcane-based ethanol production is projected to rise 45 percent during the coming decade and a growing share of ethanol production is exported in response to demand from Europe and the United States. The rate of growth in soybean-oil-based biodiesel production is faster than for sugarcane-based ethanol, although rising from a much smaller base. However, most of the biodiesel is used domestically.

Canada. Ethanol production is projected to increase 17 percent, with corn imports accounting for an increasing share of the feedstock. Biodiesel production climbs 30 percent, most of it using rapeseed (canola) oil as a feedstock. Some of the rapeseed-meal byproduct is exported to the United States.

Argentina. Argentina's production of biodiesel is assumed to expand 16 percent during the projection period. Although some of the biodiesel is used to meet a mandated increase in the domestic blend rate, exports continue to rise and the country continues to be the world's largest biodiesel exporter. Argentina's ethanol production increases faster, but from a small base.

China. About 4 million tons of corn were used to produce fuel ethanol in 2010. China has implemented policies to limit the expansion of grain-based ethanol production for transportation fuel use, and is now emphasizing the use of nongrain feedstocks such as cassava.

Non-EU Europe and the former Soviet Union (FSU). This region is assumed to respond to the EU's increasing demand for biodiesel by expanding rapeseed production. In the FSU, rapeseed production more than doubles during the projections. Some of the production gains are destined for export to the EU, either as rapeseed oil or as rapeseed for crushing in the EU.

World coarse grain trade expands 25 million metric tons (21 percent) from 2011 to 2020. The share of global coarse grain production used as animal feed trended downward from 66 percent a decade ago to about 60 percent in 2010, and is projected to remain just below 60 percent during the coming decade. Industrial uses, such as starch, ethanol, and malt production, are much smaller than feed use but are increasing more than twice as fast.

- Corn is the dominant feed grain traded in international markets. Corn's share of total world coarse grain trade continues to rise slowly and averages 78 percent through the projection period. Barley has the next largest share (15 percent), followed by sorghum (5 percent). The trade share of the other coarse grains, mostly oats and rye, continues declining slowly to about 2 percent by 2020.
- Corn's increasing share of world production and trade is attributable to yield growth that is more rapid than for other grains, to new varieties that enable it to be competitive in a wider range of climatic regions, and to its preferred qualities for feed, biofuels, and other industrial uses.
- Commercialization of livestock feeding has been a driving force behind the growing dominance of corn in international feed grain markets. Hogs and ruminants, such as cattle and sheep, are capable of digesting a broad range of feedstuffs, making demand relatively price-sensitive across alternate feed sources. However, as global pork and poultry production becomes increasingly commercialized, higher quality feeds are used, boosting the demand for corn and soybean meal.

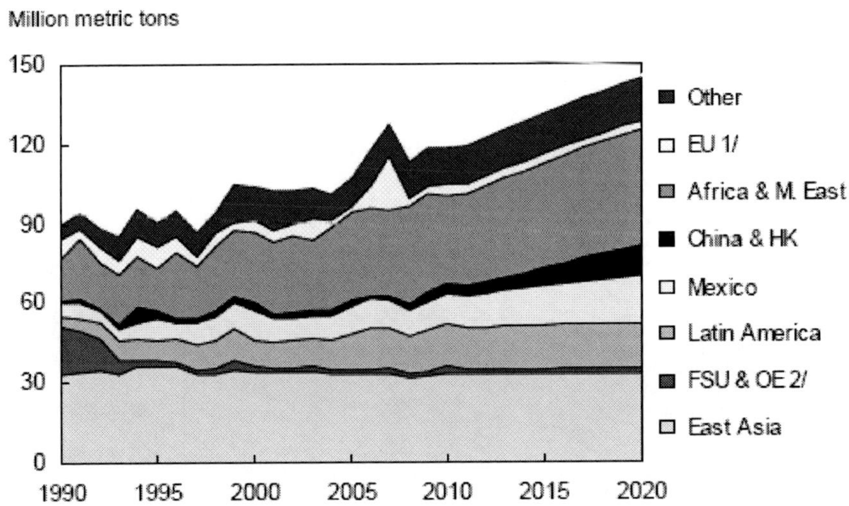

1/ Excludes intra-EU trade.
2/ Former Soviet Union and other Europe; prior to 1999, includes Czech Republic, Estonia, Hungary, Latvia, Lithuania, Malta, Poland, Slovakia, and Slovenia.

Global Coarse Grain Imports.

Growth in coarse grain imports is strongly linked to expansion of livestock production in regions unable to meet their own feed needs. Key growth markets include North Africa and the Middle East, China, Mexico, and Southeast Asia. Japan and South Korea are large but mature markets for coarse grain imports.

- Coarse grain imports by Africa and the Middle East did not decline during the recent global economic slowdown. The region accounts for more than 34 percent of growth in world trade through 2020 as rising populations and increasing incomes sustain strong demand growth for animal products. In Egypt, Government policy has shifted toward allowing more poultry meat imports. Still, poultry production is projected to increase, boosting corn imports 14 percent to more than 6 million tons.
- Mexico's corn imports are projected to rise from 9 million tons in 2011/12 to more than 14 million in 2020/21. Mexico's sorghum imports increase by one-third to more than 3.7 million tons, but do not surpass the 2000 record. Altogether, the growth in Mexico's coarse grain imports represents almost 25 percent of the increase in global coarse grain trade. This reflects increased demand for meat in Mexican diets that stimulates an expansion in meat production as well as increased meat imports.
- In East Asia (Japan, South Korea, Taiwan, and Hong Kong), environmental constraints on expanding livestock production and increasing imports of selected meat cuts contribute to very little growth in coarse grain imports.
- Southeast Asian corn imports rise nearly 1 million tons (29 percent) by 2020 as increased demand for livestock products exceeds the capacity to grow more feed grains.
- China is projected to become a net importer of 8 million tons of corn by the end of the projections as imports grow slowly while exports remain small. China's strengthening domestic demand for corn is driven by its expanding livestock and industrial sectors. The increase in China's imports account for one-third of the growth in world corn trade.

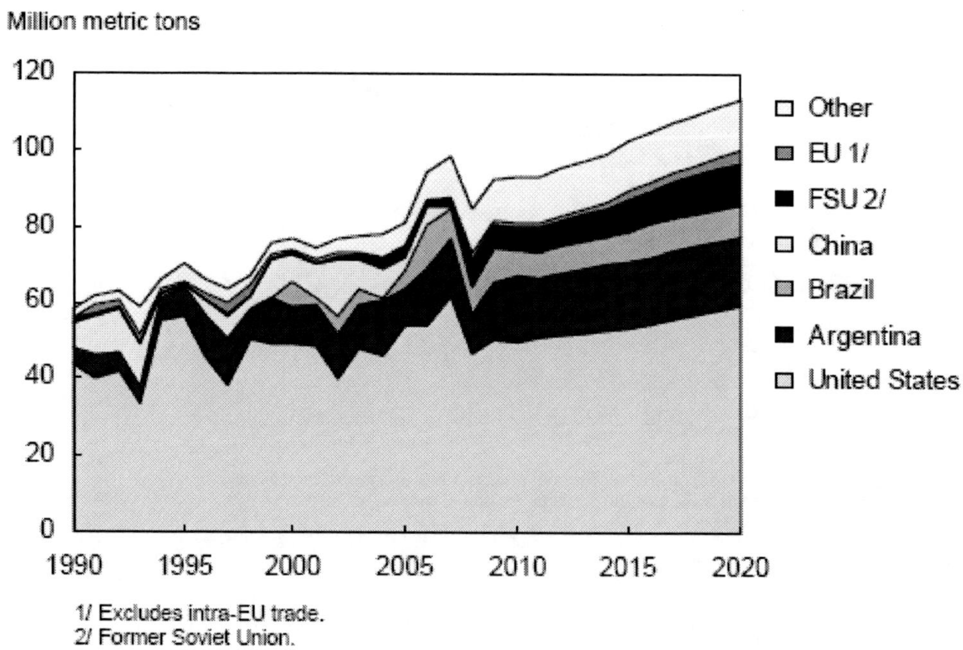

Global Corn Exports.

U.S. corn exports are projected to grow over the next decade and approach record levels by 2020. However, large world supplies of feed-quality wheat compete with U.S. corn exports at the beginning of the projection period. The U.S. share of world corn trade declines slowly from an average of nearly 60 percent during the last half decade to less than 53 percent by 2020 as exports rise from the FSU, Brazil, the EU, and Argentina.

- Brazil's corn exports have been large during the last few years as Brazil has targeted the EU's demand for grain that has not been genetically modified (GM). However, this marketing situation has diminished as Brazil continues to expand production of GM corn varieties. Also, strong growth in demand for corn in Brazil's livestock and poultry sectors and the profitability of growing soybeans limit the country's production and exports of corn.
- Argentina, with a small domestic market, remains the world's second-largest corn exporter. Due to continued quantitative controls on exports, corn area is expected to stagnate.
- In the EU, increases in area and yields enable it to increase corn production. Although more corn is allocated to ethanol production, exports more than double during the projections. The Eastern EU countries have a transportation advantage to parts of North Africa and the Middle East. Exports from other European countries are also projected to rise.
- Corn exports from the FSU, mostly Ukraine, rise more than 80 percent to 11 million tons by 2020. Favorable resource endowments, increasing economic openness, wider use of hybrid seed, and greater investment in agriculture stimulate corn production in these countries.

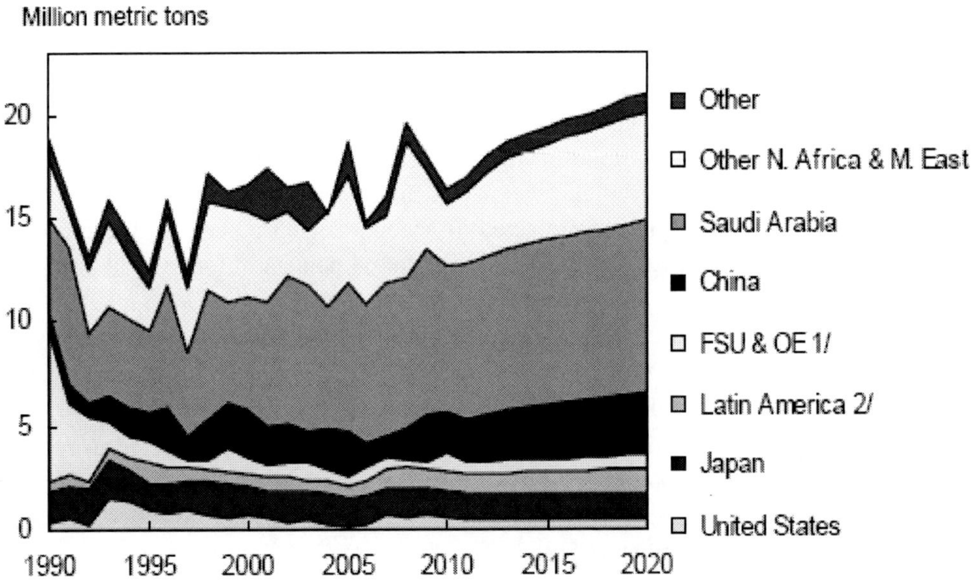

1/ Former Soviet Union and other Europe; prior to 1999, includes Czech Republic, Estonia, Hungary, Latvia, Lithuania, Malta, Poland, Slovakia, and Slovenia.
2/ Includes Mexico.

Global Barley Imports.

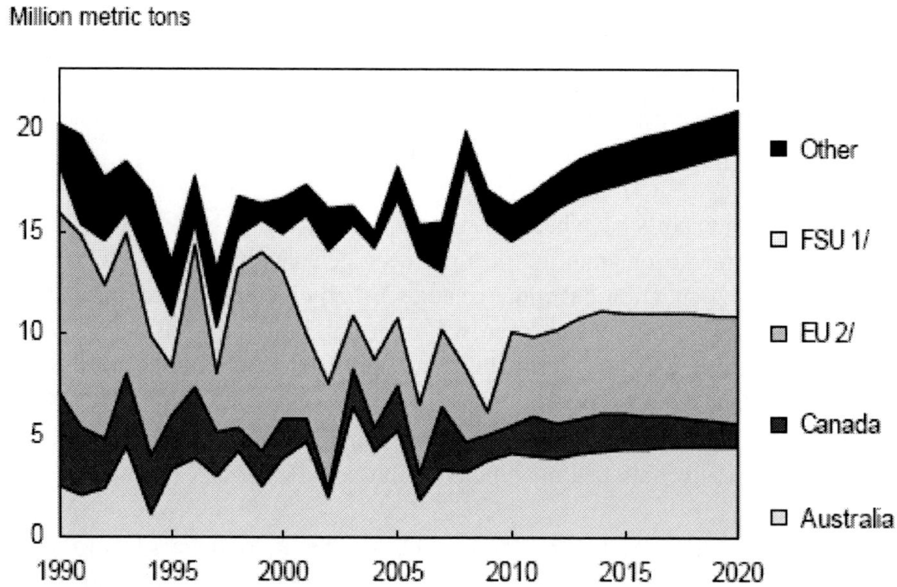

1/ Former Soviet Union and other Europe; prior to 1999, includes Czech Republic, Estonia, Hungary, Latvia, Lithuania, Malta, Poland, Slovakia, and Slovenia.
2/ Excludes intra-EU trade.

Global Barley Exports.

Global barley trade expands 4 million tons (24 percent) during the projection period. Rising demand for both malting and feed barley underpin the increased trade.

- Feed barley imports by North African and Middle Eastern countries grow steadily over the next decade. In the mid-1990s, corn overtook barley as the principal coarse grain imported by these countries, due mainly to rising poultry production. This pattern is expected to continue through the projection period. However, the North Africa and Middle East region is expected to remain the world's largest barley-importing area. The region is projected to account for 65 percent of the growth in world imports during the coming decade, and for 64 percent of total world imports in 2020.
- Saudi Arabia—the world's foremost barley-importing country—accounts for over 40 percent of world barley trade through the coming decade. Saudi Arabia's barley imports are used primarily as feed for sheep, goats, and camels.
- Iran is another Middle East country whose barley imports are projected to increase rapidly. Although the total imports by other countries in the North Africa and Middle East region are projected to grow more slowly, they still account for about a third of the increase in world barley trade.
- The international market for malting barley is boosted by strong growth in beer demand in some developing countries, most notably in China—the world's largest malting-barley importer. China's beer demand is rising steadily due to income and population growth. Expansion in China's brewing capacity is being aided by foreign investment.

- China's domestic malting barley production is increasing, but imports also rise during the projection period. Australia and Canada are China's main sources of malting barley imports.

Historically, global barley exports have originated primarily from Australia, the EU, and Canada. However, Ukraine and, to a lesser extent, Russia have emerged as important competitors in international feed-barley markets and remain so throughout the projection period.

- The FSU continues to be a major barley exporter throughout the coming decade with annual exports around 8 million tons. Ukraine became the world's largest barley exporter in 2009 and is projected to remain so throughout the projection period. Russia's barley exports also increased in the 2 years prior to the 2010 drought. Together, their share of world barley trade has been over 50 percent in some recent years. The drought-induced sharp drop in FSU production in 2010 reflects the variability of production and exports that can be expected in the FSU. However, assuming normal weather, exports are projected to recover over the next few years and then trend slowly upward. FSU exports are projected to rise 2.8 million tons by 2020 and to account for 70 percent of the increase in world exports.
- Australia's barley exports are projected to rise slowly, and the country is expected to maintain its role as the world's third-largest exporter.
- EU barley exports are projected to climb modestly during the projection period, but remain well below the levels of the late 1990s.
- Malting barley commands a substantial price premium over feed barley. This quality premium is expected to influence planting decisions in Canada and Australia. In both countries, malting barley's share of total barley area is expected to rise during the projection period. Canada's area planted to barley continues to decline gradually as canola remains more profitable.

World sorghum trade projected to trend upward from about 6.5 million tons to 7.3 million tons by 2020. Sorghum trade is driven mostly by U.S. exports to Mexico and Japan.

- Mexico's sorghum imports are projected to increase about 1 million tons to 3.7 million tons by 2020. Many Mexican livestock producers have a slight preference for feeding sorghum, while U.S. livestock feeders increasingly prefer corn, thus facilitating U.S. sorghum shipments to Mexico. Mexico generally accounts for about half of world sorghum imports.
- Sorghum imports by Japan, the world's second-largest importer, have trended slowly downward during the past decade. After a small rebound in the last 2 years, imports are projected to renew the downward trend. Slow growth in imports by Sub-Saharan Africa offsets declining imports by Japan.
- EU imports of sorghum are projected to be modest as it normally imports only small quantities of sorghum as part of the Spain-Portugal Accession Agreement.

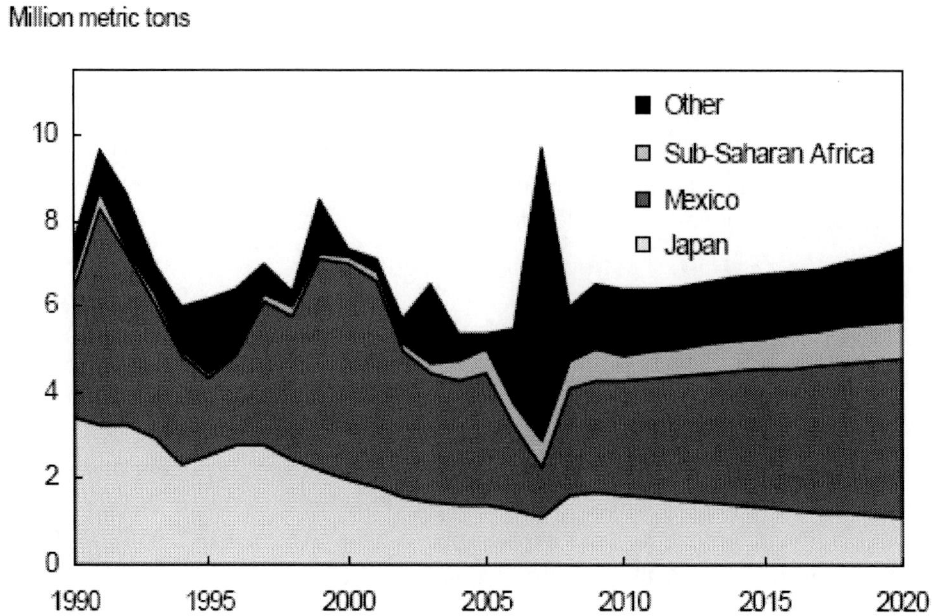

Global Sorghum Imports.

- The United States is projected to remain the largest exporter of sorghum. However, during the last decade, U.S. sorghum acreage and production have declined because of lower net returns compared with corn and soybeans. As a result, exportable supplies have generally tightened. Nonetheless, U.S. sorghum exports are projected to gradually recover, but remain slightly below historical highs. The U.S. share of world sorghum trade also recovers but remains well below that of the last decade.
- Sorghum exports by Argentina, the world's second-largest exporter, and Australia have risen sharply over the last several years. Both countries are expected to continue being prominent exporters during the coming decade although exports from both countries remain relatively flat. Argentina and Australia retain a larger share of world trade than during the previous decade. The primary sorghum markets for Argentina are Japan, Chile, and Europe.

World wheat trade (including flour) expands by 20 million tons (15 percent) between 2011 and 2020 to nearly 152 million tons. Growth in wheat imports is concentrated in those developing countries where income and population gains drive increases in demand.

- In many developing countries, almost no change in per capita wheat consumption is expected, but imports are projected to expand modestly because of population growth and limited potential to expand production. Rising per capita consumption of wheat in Indonesia, Vietnam, and some other Asian countries, reflects a dietary shift from rice as incomes rise. Nonetheless, overall global per capita wheat consumption is projected to decline slightly during the coming decade.

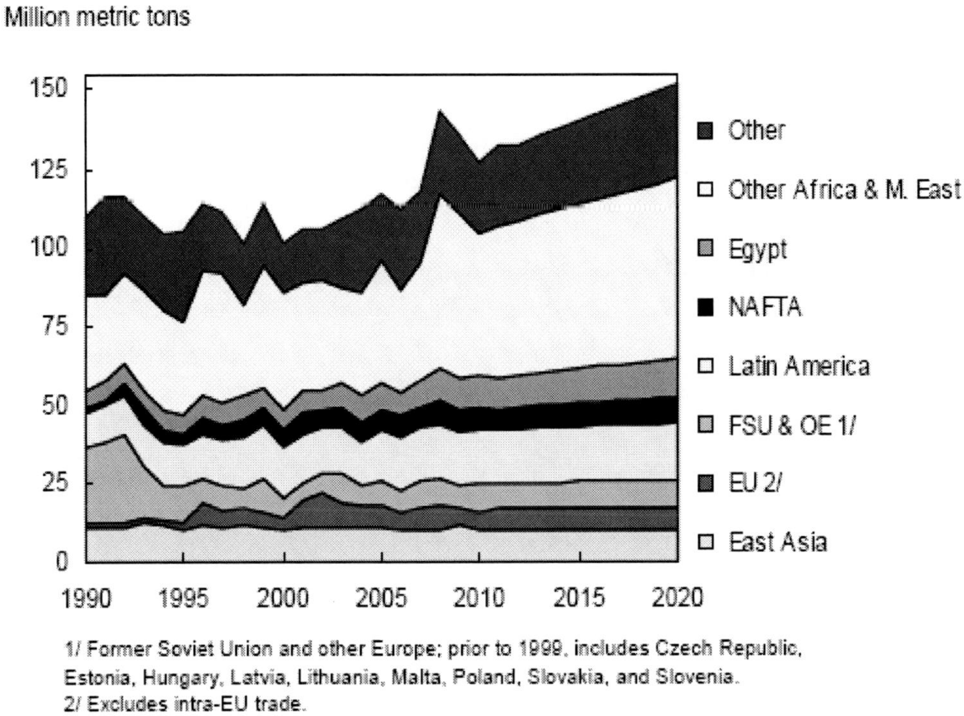

Global Wheat Imports.

The largest growth markets include Sub-Saharan Africa, Egypt, Indonesia, Algeria, Saudi Arabia, and other countries in the Africa and Middle East region.

- Egypt maintains its position as the world's largest wheat importing country, as its imports climb to more than 12 million tons. Imports by the EU, Algeria, Brazil, and Indonesia are each projected to exceed 6 million tons by 2020.
- Imports by countries in Africa and the Middle East rise 11.6 million tons and account for nearly 60 percent of the total increase in world wheat trade. Saudi Arabia has adopted a policy to phase out wheat production by 2016 because of water scarcity concerns, and imports are projected to rise to more than 3 million tons by 2020.
- China's imports remain small as per capita consumption of wheat is expected to continue to decline.
- EU wheat used to produce ethanol is projected to continue rising rapidly during the first half of the projection period, especially in the United Kingdom.
- Abundant quantities of feed quality wheat in a number of countries enable wheat to compete effectively with corn for feed use in the early years of the projection period. Europe is expected to continue to account for nearly half of global wheat feeding.

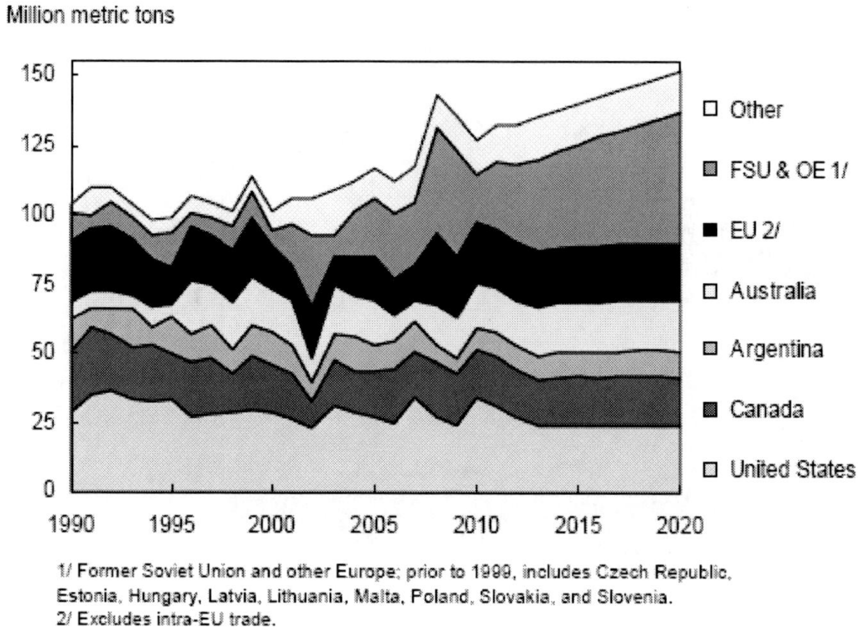

Global Wheat Exports.

The traditional five largest wheat exporters (the United States, Australia, the EU, Argentina, and Canada) are projected to account for almost 60 percent of world trade in 2020, compared with 70 percent during the last decade. This decrease in share is mostly due to increased exports from the Black Sea area. U.S. wheat exports are projected to account for less than 16 percent of global wheat trade at the end of the projection period, down from about 22 percent in the past 5 years. Although world wheat stocks are projected to continue increasing from their 2008 low during the next several years, prices are projected to remain above their pre-2006 average levels.

- Argentina is the only traditional exporter whose market share is not projected to decline. The shares of world wheat exports are projected to increase for Russia, Ukraine, Kazakhstan, and China, as well as for Argentina.
- Russia, Ukraine, and Kazakhstan have become significant wheat exporters in recent years. Low costs of production, new investments in agriculture production and marketing infrastructure, and generally favorable weather between 2001 and 2009 enabled their combined share of global wheat trade to rise to 36 percent in the 2 years before the 2010 drought caused exports to drop sharply. Exports from the former Soviet Union are expected to recover in the coming years and to account for about 30 percent of world exports by 2020. However, increasing wheat use for domestic feed is expected to restrain even more rapid export growth. Year-to-year volatility in production and trade, as occurred during the past year, can be expected because of the region's highly variable weather and yields.
- EU wheat exports decline slowly over the next decade as more wheat is used for ethanol. EU exports drop to about 21 million tons in 2020, down about 18 percent from the 2008/09 peak.

- In Canada, increased global demand for vegetable oils (especially rapeseed oil) and for barley is expected to reduce wheat area and limit any growth in wheat exports.
- Wheat exports by the smaller exporters change little during the projection period.

Global rice trade is projected to grow 2.7 percent per year from 2011 to 2020. In 2020, global rice trade reaches 41 million tons, 30 percent above the 2006 record. The main factors driving this expansion in global trade are a steady growth in demand—largely due to population growth in developing countries—and the inability of several key importers to significantly boost production. World trade as a share of world consumption, currently about 7 percent, remains substantially smaller than for other grains and oilseeds.

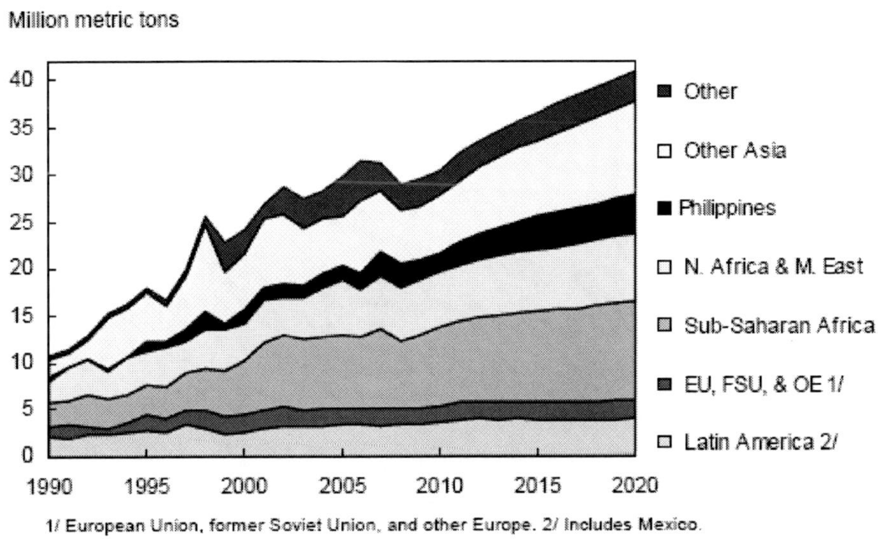

Global Rice Imports.

- Long-grain varieties account for around three-fourths of global rice trade and are expected to account for the bulk of trade growth over the next decade. Medium- and short-grain varieties account for 10-12 percent of global trade, with Northeast Asia the largest market. Aromatic rice, primarily basmati and jasmine, makes up most of the rest of global rice trade.
- The Philippines, Indonesia, the EU, and Bangladesh become the largest individual rice-importing countries by the end of the projection period. By 2020, each country is projected to import 1.4 million tons of rice or more. These countries have limited ability to expand production and are expected to account for more than one-third of the increase in global rice imports over the next decade.
- In Africa and the Middle East, strong demand growth is driven by rapidly expanding population and income, while production growth is limited. In North Africa and the Middle East, production is primarily limited by climate. In Sub-Saharan Africa, expanding production is constrained by infrastructure deficiencies and resource constraints. Altogether, the entire Africa and Middle-East region accounts for more than one-third of the increase in world rice trade between 2011 and 2020. Africa

accounts for most of this region's rising imports, but Iran, Iraq, and Saudi Arabia remain large importing countries.

- Rice imports by the Central America and Caribbean region are projected to increase by 0.4 million tons over the next decade and to surpass 2.1 million by 2020. Population growth and rising per capita incomes boost rice consumption and raise imports in this region.
- In the EU, Canada, and the United States, immigration is the driving force for rising per capita consumption and modest import growth. In Mexico, higher incomes contribute to higher per capita consumption and moderate gains in imports.
- Imports by the FSU are projected to decline slightly as a result of strong production growth and declining population that more than offsets slowly rising per capita consumption.

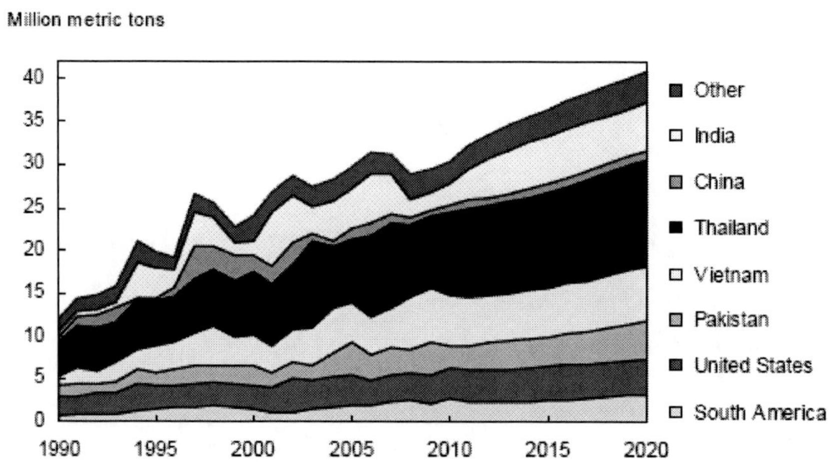

Global Rice Exports.

Asia continues to be the source of most of the world's exports throughout the projection period.

- Rice exports from Thailand and Vietnam, the world's largest rice-exporting countries, account for more than 45 percent of world trade and for nearly 30 percent of the growth in world exports in the coming decade. Thailand's exports increase 2.1 million tons, to more than 12 million by 2020. Rice area and yields are projected to increase in Thailand. Vietnam's export expansion is smaller, rising from 5.8 to 6.4 million tons. Per capita consumption declines slowly for both exporters as incomes rise.
- India has typically been the third- or fourth-largest rice exporter since the mid-1990s, but its export levels have been volatile, primarily due to fluctuating stock levels and Government policies. India's exports have been well below previous levels for the last several years as exports of non-basmati rice have largely been banned since the spike in world prices in early 2008. The export ban is assumed to be lifted once stocks are rebuilt, enabling India's rice exports to rise to about 5.6 million tons by 2020, making it the third-largest exporter.

- Pakistan has been exporting slightly more than 3 million tons in recent years and the United States about 3.5 million tons. Both exporters are projected to raise their exports to around 4.3 million tons over the next decade. Pakistan has expanded its rice area and production in recent years although production declined in 2010 due to devastating floods. Some rehabilitation of irrigation systems will be required as a result of the 2010 floods, and in the coming decade, Pakistan's agricultural sector will be confronted by a growing water shortage and a deteriorating infrastructure, limiting production and export gains.
- U.S. expansion in rice exports is attributable to a slight area expansion after 2012, continued yield growth, and only modest growth in domestic use.
- Rice exports from China, the sixth-largest rice-exporting country, have declined in recent years but are projected to begin rising again and to reach 1.1 million tons by 2020, nearly double the level shipped in 2009. Little change in production or total disappearance is expected. Higher yields are projected to offset declining area as China allows the use of genetically modified rice. Reductions in per capita consumption, a result of continued diet diversification resulting from higher incomes, are expected to offset population growth. China also builds rice stocks during the projection period.
- Australian exports are projected to recover only modestly from extremely low levels shipped during much of the past decade. Exports still will be limited by competing demands for irrigation water.

Economic growth and population increases in developing countries are projected to boost demand for vegetable oils for food consumption and for protein meals used in livestock production. Vegetable oil used for biodiesel production is also projected to increase. As demand for vegetable oils increases faster than for protein meals, vegetable oil prices rise more rapidly than for oilseeds and protein meals, particularly for rapeseed oil compared with rapeseed meal.

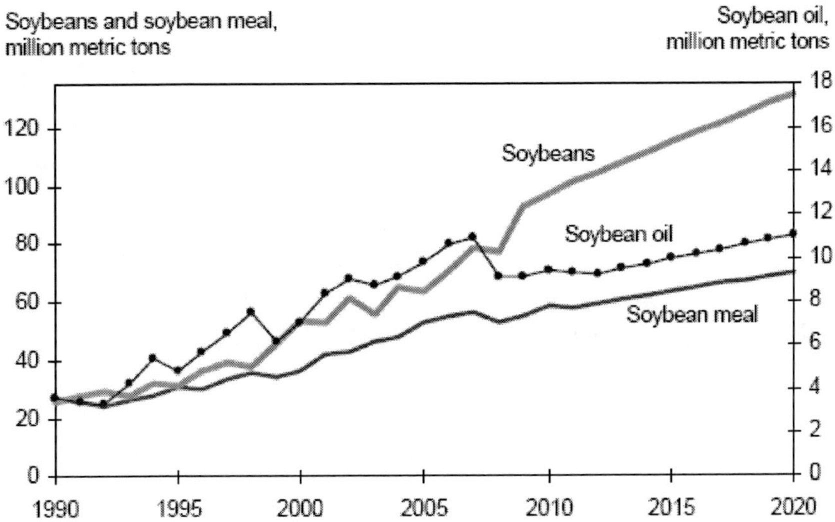

Global Exports: Soybeans, Soybean meal, and Soybean Oil.

- Many countries with limited opportunity to expand oilseed production, such as China and some countries in North Africa, the Middle East, and South Asia, have invested heavily in crushing capacity in recent years. As a result, import demand for oilseeds has grown rapidly and should continue. Global trade in soybeans is projected to increase 30 percent, soymeal by 21 percent, and soyoil by 19 percent.
- In China, increasing per capita income is projected to continue a rapid expansion of consumer demand for livestock products and vegetable oils. Feed rations are expected to include an increasing percentage of protein meal to improve rates of weight gain for meat-producing animals. China will mostly import oilseeds for crushing rather than large amounts of oilseed meals and oils. This changes the composition of world trade by raising global import demand for soybeans and other oilseeds rather than for oilseed products.
- Argentina, Brazil, and the United States continue to account for about 89 percent of the world's aggregate exports of soybeans, soybean meal, and soybean oil during the coming decade. In Argentina, uncertainties about grain policies cause farmers to shift some land to soybean production. Also, some pasture land is converted to crops, especially to soybean production. This enables Argentina to increase its soybean production, and its share of world exports of soybeans and products remains above 30 percent. Brazil's soybean area continues to increase, but an increasing share of soybean production is crushed for domestic feed and food use and its share of exports remains in the 25-31 percent range. The U.S. share of world soybean and soybean meal trade declines from 29 percent to less than 26 percent by 2020.
- The EU is expected to expand biodiesel production using rapeseed oil as the primary feedstock. Rapeseed area increases early in the projections. Although EU imports of soybeans are projected to decline, imports of soybean meal and soybean oil increase.

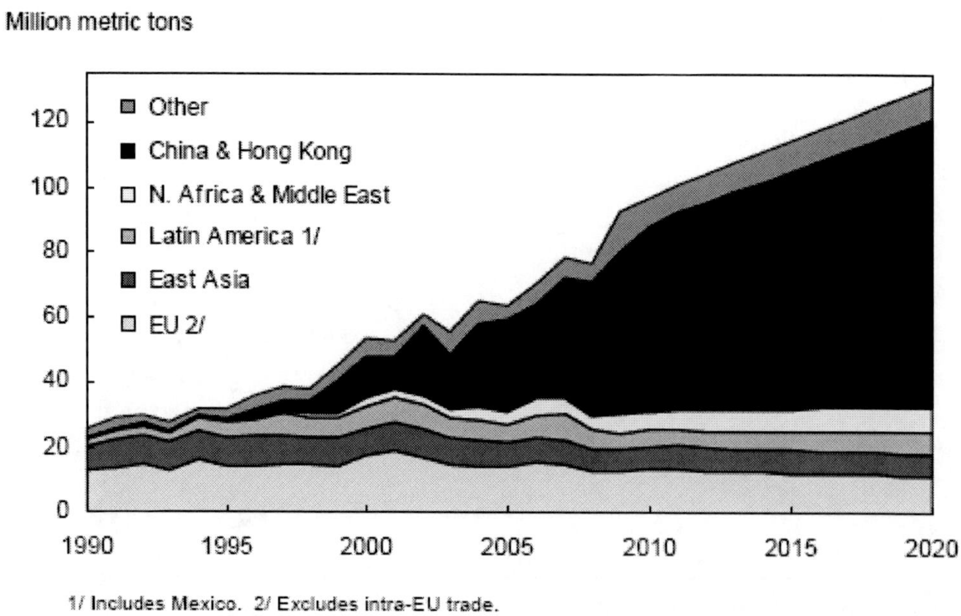

Global Soybean I mports.

World soybean trade is projected to rise rapidly, but at a slower pace than in recent years, climbing nearly 30 million tons (nearly 30 percent) during the next decade.

- The EU was the world's leading importer of soybeans until 2002. However, increases in grain and rapeseed meal feeding and rising imports of soybean meal have resulted in declining soybean imports since then. These trends are projected to continue.
- China's soybean imports have risen sharply and now account for more than 50 percent of world trade. China will face policy decisions regarding trade-offs in producing or importing corn and soybeans. The projections assume that Chinese policies will pursue self-sufficiency for domestic corn production and let soybean imports increase. Thus, China accounts for more than 90 percent of the projected 30-million-ton growth in global soybean imports over the next 10 years. China's underutilized oilseed crushing capacity drives strong gains in soybean imports as China seeks to capture the value added from processing oilseeds into protein meal and vegetable oil. The use of vegetable oils for biodiesel productionis assumed to have a negligible impact on China's total vegetable oil use.
- Imports of soybeans and meal by East Asia (Japan, South Korea,and Taiwan) are dominated by a continuing shift from importing feedstuffs to importing meat and other livestock products. As a result, this region's imports of soybeans do not change much during the coming decade. Small increases in soymeal imports support slowly rising meat production.
- Mexico's soybean imports are projected to increase by more than 20 percent during the projection period. These imports will support the production of soybean meal for the Mexican poultry and pork industries and soybean oil for domestic food consumption.

In recent years, Argentina has imported more than a million tons of soybeans to enable its crushing plants to operate at full capacity. However, changes in Argentine policy provide disincentives to import in the future.

The policy impediment to importing soybeans supports more rapid expansion in Argentine soybean area in order to supply the needs of the country's crushers.

The three leading soybean exporters—the United States, Brazil, and Argentina—have accounted for nearly 90 percent of world trade in recent years. Although exports from other countries, such as Uruguay, Paraguay, and Bolivia increase during the projections, the share held by the traditional exports remains near 90 percent.

- With continuing area gains, Brazil strengthens its position as a leading exporter of soybeans and soybean products. Combating soybean rust disease increases production costs.

  However, as world oilseed prices rise relative to the price of grains, soybeans remain more profitable than other crops in most areas of Brazil. With increasing soybean plantings in the Cerrados region and expansion extending into the Legal Amazon region, the growth rate for Brazil's soybean planted area is projected to average nearly 2.5 percent per year during the coming decade. During the next 10 years, soybean exports are projected to rise about 47 percent.

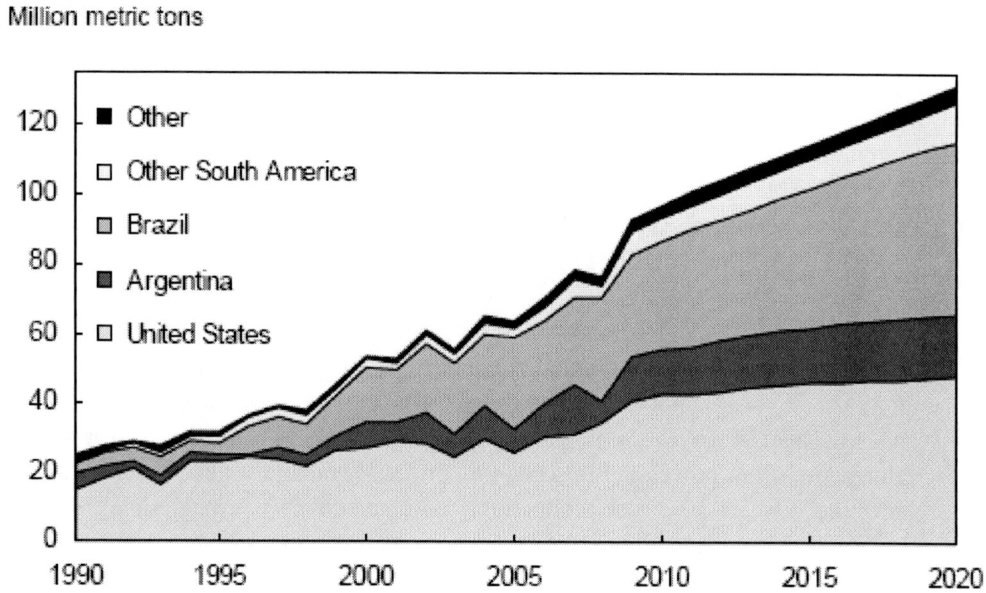

Global Soybean Exports.

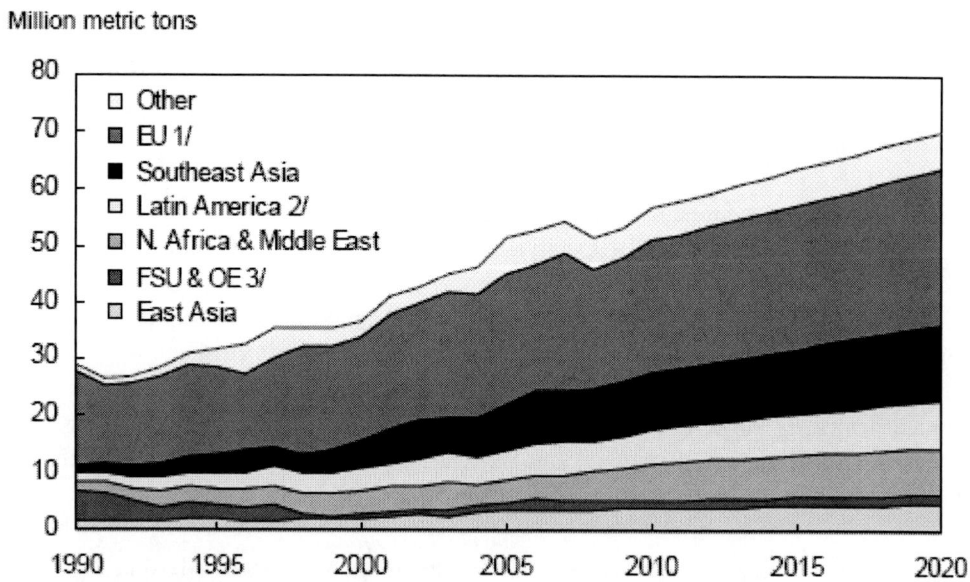

1/ Excludes intra-EU trade.
2/ Includes Mexico. 3/ Former Soviet Union and other Europe; prior to 1999, includes Czech Republic, Estonia, Hungary, Latvia, Lithuania, Malta, Poland, Slovakia, and Slovenia.

Global Soybean Meal Imports.

- Argentina's export tax rates are higher for soybeans than for soybean products, which favors domestic crushing of whole seeds and exporting the products. However, in response to world demand for soybeans for crushing, Argentina's soybean exports have risen sharply and are projected to continue doing so, rising about 30 percent to nearly 18 million tons by 2020. Most of the soybeans exported by Argentina go to China.

- Other South American countries, principally Uruguay, Paraguay, and Bolivia, respond to higher oilseed prices by expanding the area planted to soybeans. Exports rise more than 50 percent to nearly 11 million tons.
- Canada is the next largest soybean exporter, although its export volume and growth are well below those of the above-mentioned exporters.
- Ukraine responds to higher international market prices for oilseeds by increasing production of rapeseed and soybeans. Soybean exports from Ukraine are projected to rise rapidly (32 percent), but from a small base.

World trade in soybean meal climbs by more than 12 million tons (about 21 percent) in the projections to 2020. Continued growth in the demand for livestock products, limited capability to increase oilseed production, and relatively lower world prices for protein meals boost demand for soybean meal in a number of countries with rising middle-income populations. Lower import prices for soybean meal relative to soybeans and grains provide incentives for countries to use imported soybean meal at a higher rate in livestock feed rations.

- The EU remains the world's largest destination for soybean meal throughout the projection period, despite increased domestic feeding of grains and rapeseed meal. Although there will be abundant supplies of low-cost rapeseed meal available for feed as a result of the EU biofuels expansion, there are technical limits on the amount of rapeseed meal that can be incorporated in livestock rations. As a result, growth in EU soybean meal imports is expected to continue to increase and to account for more than one-fourth of the increase in world soybean meal trade.
- The regions of Southeast Asia, Latin America, and North Africa and the Middle East all become larger importers of soybean meal due to increasing demand for livestock feed and low oilseed meal prices.
- Russia is projected to experience rapid growth in soybean meal imports, although from a small base. Increased livestock production, especially from larger, more modern Russian facilities, will boost the demand for soybean meal.
- Mexico's strong growth in demand for protein feed and vegetable oils is projected to continue.
- Although the projected growth rate for China's use of soybean meal is one of the highest in the world, most of the meal will be supplied by domestic crush, either using domestically-produced or imported soybeans.

Argentina, Brazil, and the United States remain the three major exporters in international soybean meal markets. Together, their share of world exports rises slightly to 90 percent during the next 10 years. Argentina, the world's largest soybean meal exporter, increases its share of the world market from less than 50 percent in recent years to about 57 percent. Trade shares held by all other major exporters decline.

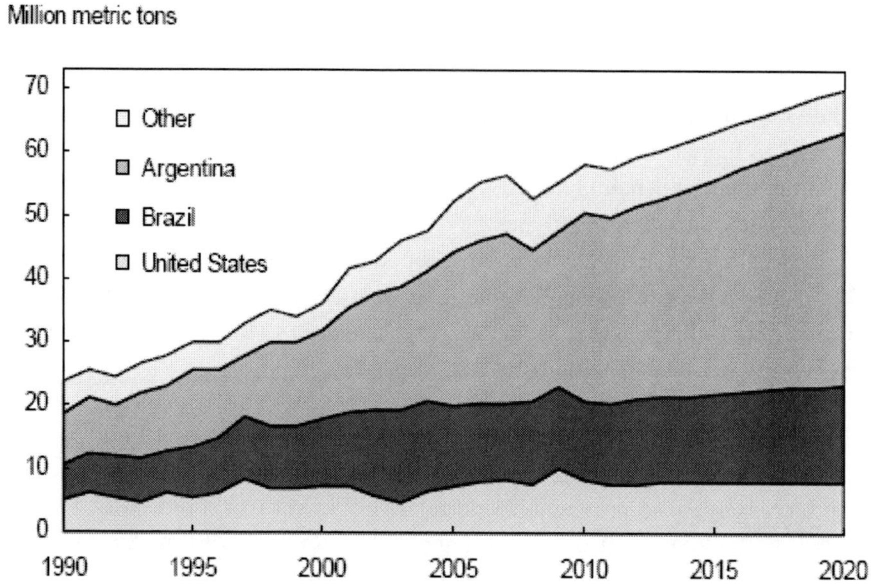

Global Soybean Meal Exports.

- Argentina imposes higher export taxes on soybeans than on soybean products. This has provided an incentive for the country to developa large oilseed crushing capacity. With Argentina's low cost of soybean production and the trade policy incentives to export soy products, soybean meal exports are projected to continue their robust growth.
- In Brazil, strong growth in domestic meal consumption due to rapid expansion of the poultry and pork sectors limits increases in soybean meal exports. Also, domestic soybean crushing capacity is not expected to grow as fast due to heavy competition from Argentina. Brazil's share of world exports declines from about 25 percent in recent years to less than 19 percent by 2020.
- U.S. soybean meal exports remain at about 8 million tons during the next 10 years. The U.S. share of world exports declines steadily from about 15 percent in most recent years to less than 12 percent by 2020.
- The volume of India's soybean meal exports declines from more than 3.5 million tons in most recent years to 1.5 million by 2020 as rapidly increasing poultry, egg, and milk production absorbs more of India's soybean meal supplies.
- The EU continues to be a small but steady exporter of soybean meal to Russia and other East European countries where livestock production is expected to increase significantly.

World soybean oil imports climb 1.8 million tons (19 percent) in the projection years, bolstered by rising food use and increased demand for use in biofuel production. China and India are the world's two largest soybean oil importers, primarily for food use. In recent years, their combined imports have been more than a third of total world trade. The growth in soybean oil trade will be constrained by competition with palm oil, which claims the top ranking in world vegetable oil trade.

- Income and population growth in Latin America, North Africa, and the Middle East contribute to gains in soybean oil demand and imports. Although rising international prices for soybean oil will temper consumption, especially in developing countries, imports by the North Africa and the Middle East region are projected to be exceeded only by those of Latin America.
- India remains the world's largest soybean oil importing country. Factors that contribute to continued growth in imports include burgeoning domestic demand for vegetable oils and limited capacity to expand domestic production of oilseeds. Low yields, associated with erratic rainfed growing conditions and low input use, inhibit growth of oilseed production. India sharply reduced its edible oil import tariffs to zero in 2008 in response to high world prices. It is assumed that during the next decade, the soybean oil tariff gradually rises toward the prior rate of 45 percent, but that tariffs for the other major imported oils—palm and sunflower—remain below their historical highs of 75-85 percent.
- China experiences a growing demand for vegetable oils, and land-use competition from other crops constrains the expansion in area planted to oilseed crops. However, with the rapid increase in soybean imports for crush, China is able to slowly decrease its imports of soybean oil during the coming decade.

Argentina's and Brazil's combined share of world soybean oil exports dropped from 84 percent in 2005/06 to 65 percent in 2009/10 due poor harvests. However, these countries are projected to recover partially during the next 5 years to about 75 percent of world trade.

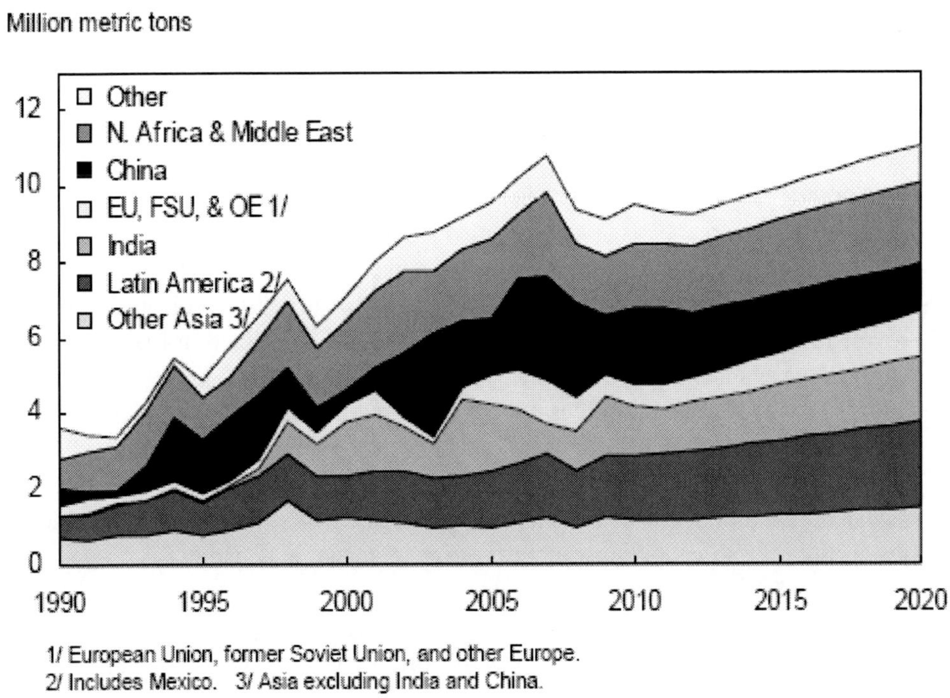

Global Soybean Oil imports.

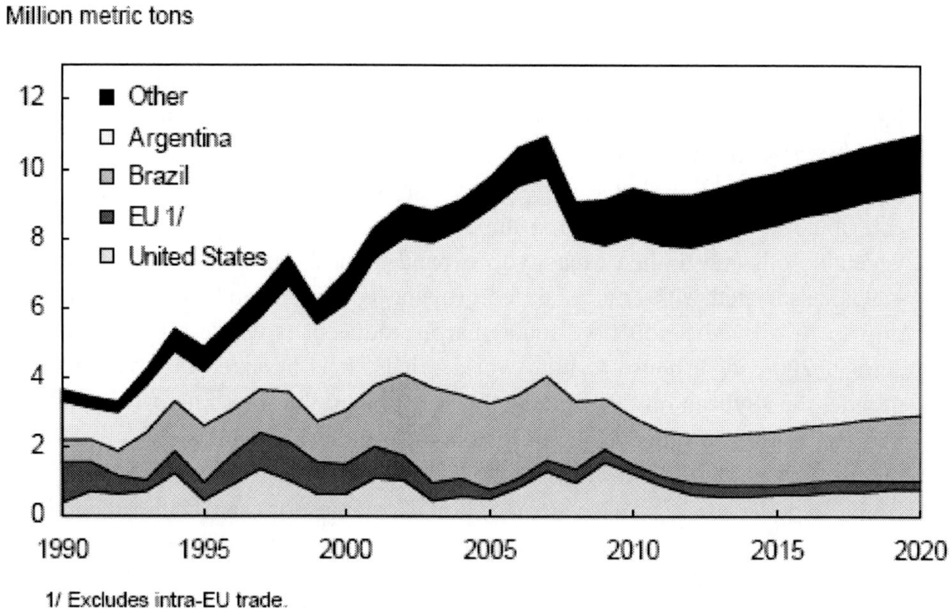

Global Soybean Oil Exports.

- Argentina is the leading exporter of soybean oil, reflecting the country's large crushing capacity, its small domestic market for soybean oil, and an export tax structure that favors exports of soybean products rather than soybeans. Gains in Argentine soybean production due to extensive double cropping, further adjustments in crop-pasture rotations, and the addition of marginal lands in the northwest part of the country, contribute to increased soybean production and crush. Argentina's soyoil exports are projected to continue increasing even though more soybean oil is expected to be used as a feedstock for biodiesel production—with most of the biodiesel destined for export. The projected 2011-2020 growth in soybean oil exports account for 60 percent of the increase in world soyoil trade.
- Brazil's projected increase in soybean oil exports accounts for most of the rest of global increases in soybean oil trade. Although Brazil is also projected to use more soyoil for biodiesel production, expansion of soybean production into new areas of cultivation enables it to increase its volume of soybean oil exports from its 2009/2010 reduced level. It does not however, recover to the large volumes exported between 2002 and 2007.
- The United States remains the world's third-largest soybean oil exporter. U.S. soybean oil exports will be constrained by increased use of soybean oil for biodiesel production. U.S. canola oil imports from Canada and palm oil imports from Southeast Asia are projected to continue to grow strongly, and augment the U.S. edible oil supply.
- In the EU, exportable supplies of vegetable oils are limited by the growth in biodiesel production.

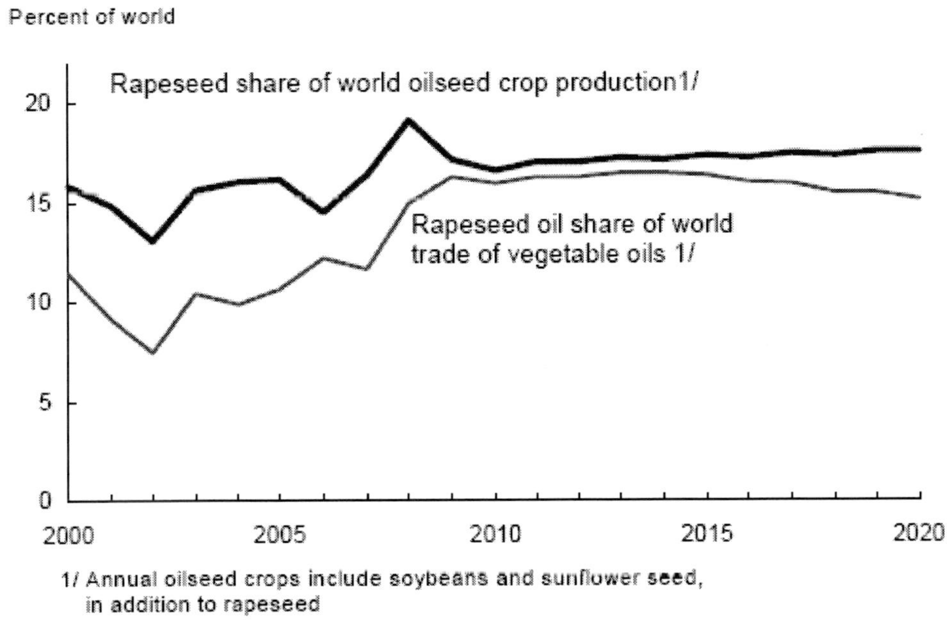

Rapeseed Production and Rapeseed Oil Trade.

In the last 10 years, rapeseed and rapeseed oil have captured an increasing share of world oilseed production and the trade in vegetable oils produced from annual oilseed crops.

- Global demand for vegetable oils has been strong, trending up more than 5 percent a year for more than a decade. A higher oil content for rapeseed (40 percent) compared to soybeans (19 percent) and other annual oilseed crops has enhanced the demand for rapeseed over other oilseeds. Rapeseed oil has also become a major feedstock for producing biodiesel in the EU and Canada.
- Between 2000 and 2010, the growth rate in world average rapeseed yields (2.4 percent) rose more than twice as rapidly as for soybeans (0.8 percent) and in recent years world-average rapeseed yields have been higher than for soybeans. Faster yield growth combined with higher oil content, and more oil produced per hectare, provided economic incentives to produce more rapeseed. The rate of increase in area planted to rapeseed (3.4 percent) was higher than for soybeans (2.8 percent), and was considerably higher than the rate for all other oilseeds, and the rate for all field crops.
- The major rapeseed importers are Japan, EU, China, and Mexico. A second tier of importers includes Pakistan, the United States, Turkey, and Bangladesh. Canada is by far the largest exporter, followed by Ukraine and Australia.

In the projections, the rate of growth in world rapeseed production continues to outpace that of soybeans, although the growth gap narrows. The projected growth rates for world rapeseed and rapeseed oil trade are also higher than the rates for soybeans and soybean oil. In Canada, rapeseed oil exports go mainly to the United States but start to slow as more oil is used for Canadian biodiesel production. Increasing exports from other countries, especially Russia and Ukraine, are assumed to partially offset slower growth in Canadian exports.

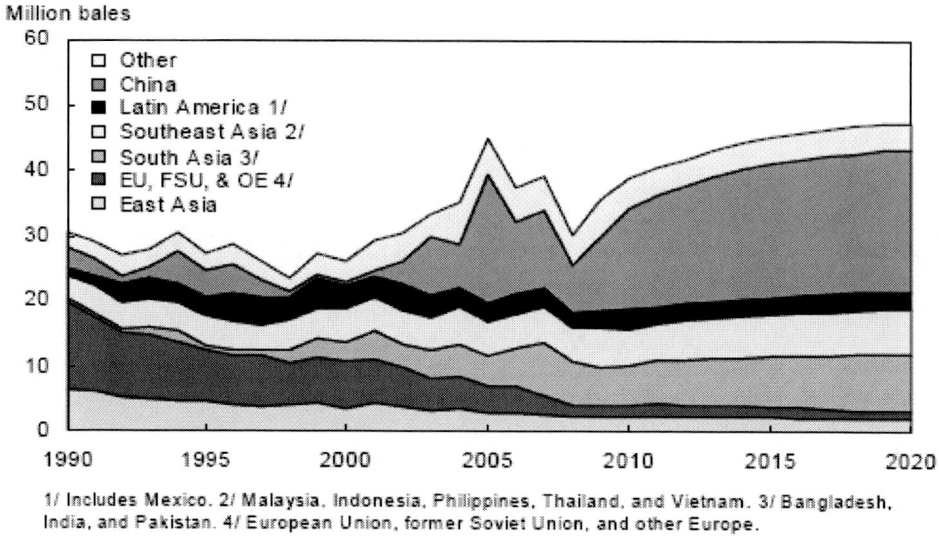

Global Cotton Imports.

World cotton trade is projected to trend upward at 1.8 per cent a year until 2020, but does not surpass the 2005 record until half way through the projection period. There continue to be geographical shifts in mill use and trade of cotton but not as dramatic as those associated with the elimination of the Multifiber Arrangement (MFA) quotas in 2005. Asia's share of world cotton imports has risen from less than 50 percent in the late 1990s to more than 70 percent in 2010 and is projected to reach more than 83 percent by 2020.

- The textile industries in China, India, and Pakistan were the major beneficiaries of textile trade liberalization as a result of the elimination of the MFA quotas in 2005. However, imports have risen in other Asian countries as well, most notably Bangladesh and Vietnam.
- China's textile industry and its cotton imports are expected to grow during the projection period, but more slowly than the rapid increases from 2001 to 2005 after joining the World Trade Organization (WTO). Nonetheless, during the coming decade, China is projected to account for more than two-thirds of the global increase in cotton imports.
- Bangladesh has become a major importer in recent years and as imports continue rising, the country is projected to become the world's second-largest importer by 2020.
- Pakistan has also become a significant importer in recent years but import growth slows in the projections as new *Bacillus thuringiensis* (*Bt*) cotton varieties specific to Pakistan's cotton production conditions prove more productive and reduce the need for imports.
- Until several years ago, Turkey's textile industry benefited from favorable trade access to the EU, its major market for textile and apparel exports. However, the end of the MFA quotas gave lower cost competitors more favorable access to EU

markets. Turkey's cotton imports have fallen and are projected to continue declining over the next 10 years.

- The EU, Japan, Taiwan, and South Korea all reduce their cotton imports as textile trade reforms or higher wages in these countries, or both, drive textile production to countries with lower wagesand other costs.

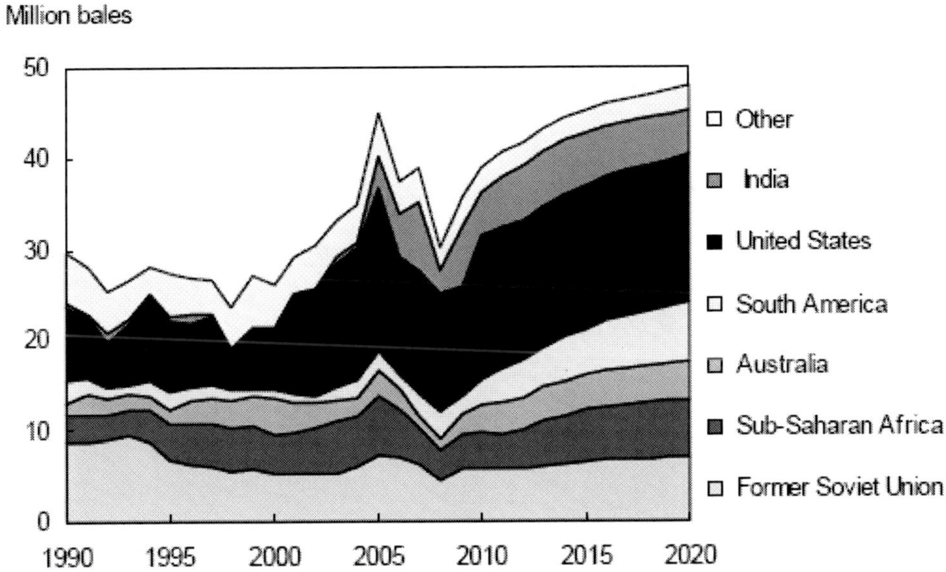

Global Cotton Exports.

Globalization is expected to continue to move raw cotton production to countries with favorable resource endowments and technology. Traditional producers with large land bases suitable for cotton production continue to benefit from post-MFA trade patterns, including the United States, Brazil, and Sub-Saharan Africa. The importance of technology has been highlighted by the impact of India's rapid adoption of genetically modified cotton, nearly all *Bt* cotton.

- The United States continues as the world's leading cotton exporter throughout the projections. U.S. exports rise slightly to about 16 million bales by 2020. The U.S. share of world exports declines slightly from 35 percent in recent years, to 34 percent by 2020.
- Brazil's cotton exports double during the coming decade as the area planted to cotton and soybeans expands. Exports from Brazil rise more than from any other country or region, surpassing exports from India and Australia, and enable Brazil to become the world's second-largest cotton exporter.
- Sub-Saharan Africa's exports are projected to rise rapidly during the coming decade as these economies develop and as *Bt* cotton is adopted by the region's producers. The region's exports are projected to rise about 60 percent during the next 10 years and to account for one third of world trade growth.

- Government policies in the Central Asian countries of the FSU promoting investment in textiles have contributed to more exports of textile products rather than exports of raw cotton. However, the continued increase in cotton exports account for 17 percent of the increase in world exports.
- Improved cotton yields in India, largely due to the adoption of *Bt* cotton containing the *Bt* gene, have raised India's production and exports in recent years. Yield growth is projected to continue as the area planted to *Bt* cotton expands and cultivation practices improve. The increase in cotton output is expected to enable India to increase textile production and maintain exports.

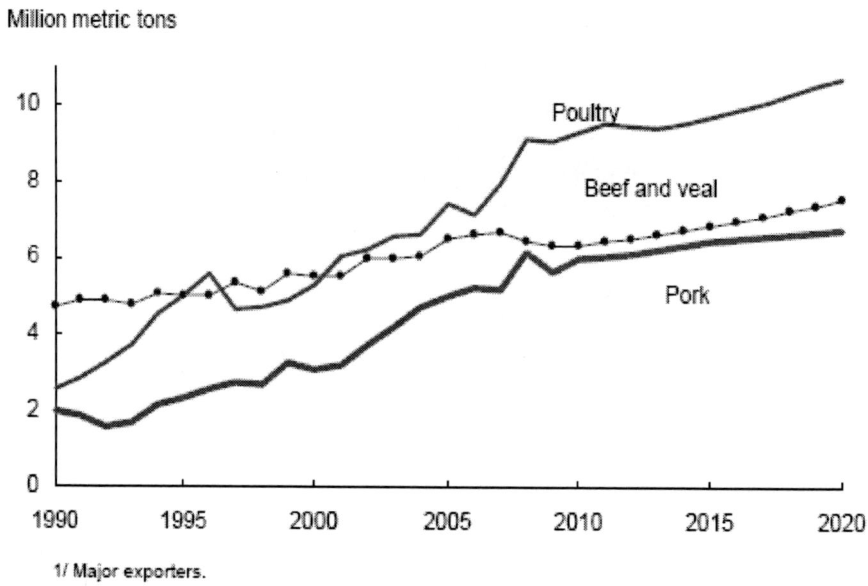

Meat Exports 1/.

The growth in world per capita meat consumption is expected to slow during the 2011-20 projection period to less than two-thirds of 1 percent per year. Still, meat shipments from major exporters trend upwards at 1.4 percent per year. The projected growth rates of exports from major exporters of beef, pork, and poultry meat are 1.7, 1.3, and 1.2 percent per year, respectively. During this period, exports rise 1.1 million tons for beef, 1.2 million for pork, and 0.9 million for poultry. Rising per capita incomes combined with population growth in a number of countries are the driving forces behind the projected growth in global meat demand.

- Russia's net imports of meat decline slowly during the coming decade in response to the country's policies to reduce imports and to stimulate meat production. Pork and poultry meat account for most of the decline in meat imports.
- Canadian beef exports and imports are each projected to rise slowly after 2012 with net exports remaining stable but well below the 2004 record. Canada's cow herd contracted significantly during 2006-10 and rebuilding beef herds is expected to progress slowly.

- EU beef exports, after steadily declining for more than a decade, stabilize at the current low level as policies continue to discourage beef production and limit the EU's competitiveness in international markets.
- Argentine beef exports declined sharply after the 2005 peak as export restrictions on beef and changes in other policies made Argentina's exports less competitive. Beef exports are projected to decline further during the next several years as Argentine producers begin to rebuild their herds. Beef exports then begin to rise slowly, but are constrained by reduced beef imports by Russia, which has been a major market for Argentine beef.
- The projections assume no changes in the set of countries that recognize all regions within Brazil as free of foot-and-mouth disease (FMD), thus limiting Brazil's ability to compete in some markets for pork and beef. However, exports from Brazil's expanding pork sector are expected to be competitive in price-sensitive markets such as Russia and Asian countries other than Japan and South Korea.
- During the coming decade, Brazil is expected to continue as the largest exporter of poultry products, as a result of low production costs and competitive export prices.

Beef imports by major importers declined in 2009. The most significant declines occurred in South Asian countries, the United States, Russia, and Mexico.

In 2010, import growth renewed in the regions of North Africa, the Middle East, and Asia, but was offset by stagnant trade or continuing declines in most of the rest of the world.

Between 2011 and 2020, beef imports by major importers resume growth and expand nearly 0.7 million metric tons (14 percent).

Traditionally, developed countries have been the primary importers of beef.

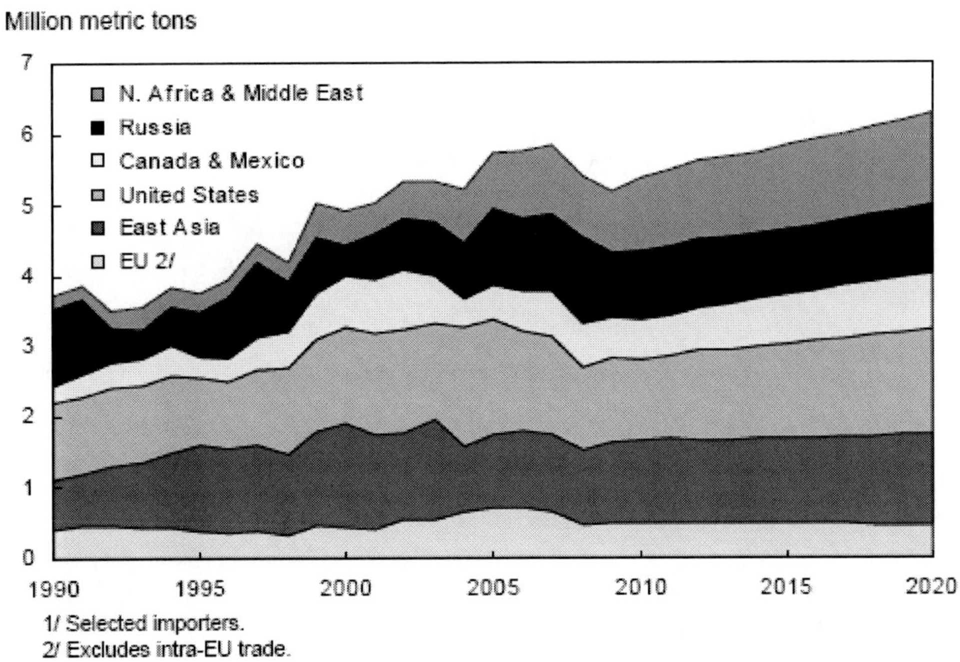

Beef Imports 1/.

However, imports by a number of low- and middle-income income countries are projected to increase, especially imports of lower priced, grass-fed beef from Brazil.

- During the next 10 years, Russian beef imports are projected to fluctuate around 0.9 million tons as rising consumer demand is offset by expanding Russian beef production and import restrictions. Russia remains a significant market for EU and South American beef exports.
- Imports of grain-fed beef by higher-income countries are projected to rise slowly. U.S. beef exports to these countries are projected to increase somewhat over the next 10 years although they will have to compete with exports from other suppliers.
- U.S. beef imports, primarily of grass-fed, lean beef from Australia and New Zealand for use in ground beef and processed products, rise during the projection period. Also, strong Asian imports of beef enable Australia and New Zealand to maintain significant levels of exports over the projection period.
- Strong growth in Mexican beef imports is projected to resume over the next several years. Much of Mexico's imports consist of higher valued, grain-fed beef from the United States.

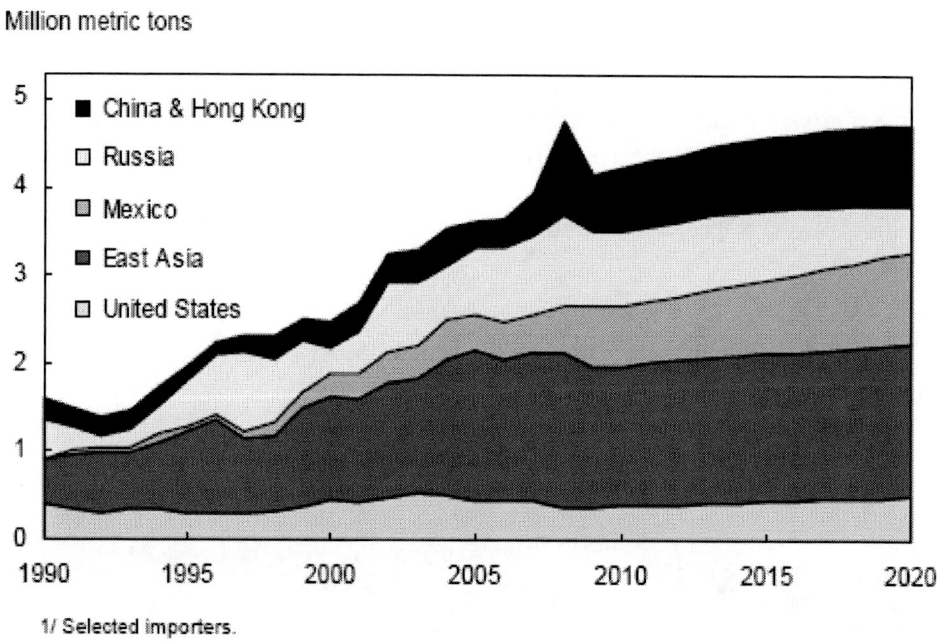

Pork Imports 1/.

Global pork trade declined in 2009 in response to the global economic recession.

Imports fell the most in China, Russia, Ukraine, other countries of the FSU, Japan, and South Korea.

Although world imports partially recovered in 2010, import levels for many countries remained below the 2008 peak.

In the projections for 2011 to 2020, world pork imports are expected to resume growth, and to increase by more than 0.66 million tons (11 percent).

- Russia's policies to stimulate livestock production are expected to cause pork imports to decline steadily during the next 10 years. Although Russia's TRQ on pork imports is assumed to cease after 2012, other trade barriers may constrain growth in Russian pork imports.
- Mexican pork imports increase the most of any country in the world, rising more than 350,000 tons (52 percent) between 2011 and 2020. Increases in income and population are the primary drivers of Mexico's increasing demand for pork. Mexico accounts for more than one-half of the growth in global pork trade during the coming decade.
- Some higher income countries in East Asia increase pork imports to satisfy demand for selected cuts of pork, especially pork bellies. Japan is by far the world's largest pork importer, but as a mature market with declining population, its imports are not projected to rise significantly. South Korea is Asia's fastest growing pork importer and its imports account for one-fourth of the increase in world pork imports during the projection period.
- China's pork imports rose sharply in 2008 and it became a net importer. Since then, the country's pork imports have declined significantly but it remains a net importer. In the projections, pork exports rise slightly more than imports, but the country remains a small net importer in 2020. Hong Kong's pork imports are expected to continue rising during the coming decade.

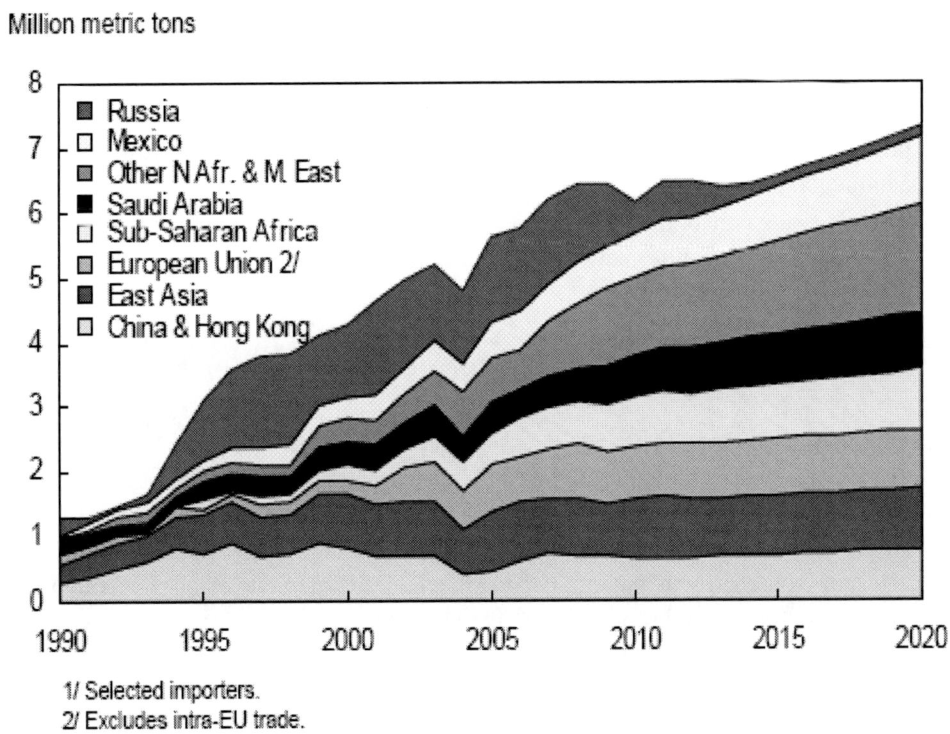

Poultry Imports 1/.

Poultry meat imports by major importers are projected to increase by more than 1 million tons (20 percent) between 2011 and 2020.

The projections indicate strong poultry import growth throughout much of the world except, most notably, for Russia, Europe, and Japan.

- Poultry imports by Africa and the Middle East now account for about 40 percent of imports by the major importers. Income and population growth boosts demand in the projections. In addition, ongoing animal disease concerns in a number of countries are expected to slow growth in production and to increase demand for imports. As a result, the region's imports grow more than the rest of the world combined.
- Rising consumer incomes increase poultry demand and imports in Mexicoand the Central America and Caribbean region. Poultry products remain less expensive than beef or pork, further stimulating demand. Mexico's domestic poultry production continues to increase during the projection period, but rises at a slower rate than consumption, with the result that imports rise by 0.35 million tons (50 percent).
- Russia's poultry imports are projected to decline sharply during the next 5 years. Policies that make the poultry TRQ regime more restrictive will restrain poultry imports and stimulate domestic poultry production. Higher prices and slower growth in income and per capita poultry consumption also inhibit import growth.
- In South Korea, increasing per capita consumption, combined with environmental concerns that limit production growth, boost imports 16 percent during the next decade.
- Because of avian influenza, some major poultry-exporting countries such as Thailand and China have shifted most of their exports to fully cooked products, and are projected to continue to do so. Because of higher production costs, these cooked products will be marketed to higher income countries in Asia, Europe, and the Middle East.
- China's rising consumption of poultry meat is met by expanding domestic production and the country's poultry net exports climb by about 55,000 tons.

U.S. Crops

Near-term adjustments in the U.S. crops sector reflect market responses to relatively high prices that have resulted from the 2010 global wheat production shortfall (largely in Russia), reduced U.S. corn yields, and strong global demand for soybeans and cotton. Over the longer run, global economic recovery with steady growth provides an improved foundation for crop demand. Despite some growth potential from the E15 (15-percent ethanol blend) market, increases in corn-based ethanol production in the United States are projected to slow.

Table 4. U.S. Macroeconomic Assumptions

	2009/10	2010/11	2011/12	2012/13	2013/14	2014/15	2015/16	2016/17	2017/18	2018/19	2019/20	2020/21
				Imports, million metric tons								
Importers												
Former Soviet Union[1]	0.5	2.3	1.0	1.0	1.1	1.2	1.2	1.3	1.3	1.4	1.5	1.5
Other Europe	0.7	0.7	0.7	0.7	0.7	0.6	0.6	0.6	0.6	0.6	0.6	0.6
European Union[2]	3.0	5.0	3.8	3.5	3.3	3.2	3.5	3.6	3.6	3.4	3.4	3.3
North Africa and Middle East	33.6	31.3	32.8	34.2	35.3	36.0	37.0	37.8	38.6	39.2	39.8	40.2
Sub-Saharan Africa[3]	3.1	2.2	2.2	2.3	2.4	2.5	2.7	2.8	2.9	3.0	3.2	3.3
Japan	19.2	19.2	19.0	19.0	18.9	18.8	18.8	18.7	18.6	18.5	18.5	18.4
South Korea	8.5	9.0	9.0	9.1	9.1	9.2	9.3	9.3	9.4	9.5	9.6	9.6
Taiw an	4.8	4.9	5.0	5.1	5.1	5.1	5.1	5.2	5.2	5.1	5.1	5.2
China	3.8	3.1	3.4	4.2	5.0	5.8	6.8	7.6	8.7	9.5	10.5	11.1
Other Asia and Oceania	6.4	6.2	6.5	6.9	7.0	7.2	7.5	7.7	7.9	8.0	8.2	8.3
Mexico	11.2	12.0	12.2	12.9	13.6	14.0	14.5	15.2	15.9	16.6	17.4	18.2
Central America and Caribbean	4.9	5.0	5.0	5.0	5.0	5.0	5.1	5.2	5.3	5.3	5.3	5.3
Brazil	1.1	1.4	1.4	1.4	1.4	1.4	1.4	1.5	1.5	1.5	1.5	1.6
Other South America	9.9	9.3	9.4	9.6	9.7	9.9	10.1	10.1	10.2	10.2	10.2	10.1
Other foreign[4]	5.5	4.8	5.2	5.2	5.2	5.2	5.2	5.2	5.1	5.2	5.2	5.3
United States	2.6	2.3	2.7	2.6	2.5	2.5	2.5	2.5	2.5	2.5	2.5	2.5
Total trade	118.7	118.4	119.4	122.5	125.5	127.8	131.3	134.1	137.2	139.6	142.4	144.4
Exporters				**Exports, million metric tons**								
European Union[2]	3.0	6.0	5.6	6.5	7.0	7.3	7.6	7.8	8.2	8.3	8.6	8.8
China	0.2	0.3	0.3	0.3	0.3	0.3	0.3	0.2	0.2	0.2	0.2	0.2
Argentina	16.9	19.7	18.3	18.8	19.4	19.6	19.9	20.1	20.2	20.1	20.1	19.9
Australia	4.6	5.1	5.0	4.7	5.0	5.1	5.1	5.1	5.1	5.2	5.2	5.2
Canada	3.1	3.1	4.2	3.9	3.8	3.9	3.8	3.7	3.5	3.3	3.1	3.0
South Africa	2.5	2.5	2.5	2.5	2.7	2.7	2.7	2.6	2.7	2.6	2.7	2.6

Other Europe	1.8	2.7	2.5	2.5	2.6	2.7	2.8	2.9	2.8	2.9	2.8	2.8
Former Soviet Union[1]	14.9	10.5	11.7	12.6	13.0	13.3	15.0	15.6	16.7	17.8	19.0	19.8
Other foreign	16.7	14.6	14.0	14.7	15.0	15.4	15.9	16.5	16.8	16.6	16.7	16.8
United States	54.8	53.9	55.3	56.0	56.8	57.5	58.3	59.7	61.1	62.5	63.9	65.3
						Percent						
U.S. trade share	46.2	45.5	46.3	45.7	45.3	45.0	44.4	44.5	44.5	44.8	44.9	45.2

[1]/ Covers FSU-12, includes intra-FSU trade.

[2]/ Covers EU-27, excludes intra-EU trade.

[3]/ Includes South Africa.

[4]/ Includes unaccounted.

The projections w ere completed in November 2010.

Table 5. Corn Trade Long-Term Projections

2009/10		2010/11	2011/12	2012/13	2013/14	2014/15	2015/16	2016/17	2017/18	2018/19	2019/20	2020/21
						Imports, million metric tons						
Importers												
European Union[1]	2.9	4.5	3.4	3.0	2.8	2.7	3.0	3.0	3.0	2.8	2.8	2.6
Former Soviet Union[2]	0.3	1.2	0.5	0.5	0.6	0.7	0.7	0.8	0.8	0.9	0.9	0.9
Egypt	5.5	5.4	5.4	5.4	5.5	5.5	5.6	5.8	6.0	6.1	6.1	6.2
Algeria	2.3	2.3	2.4	2.4	2.5	2.6	2.7	2.7	2.8	2.8	2.9	2.9
Morocco	1.7	1.8	1.9	2.0	2.1	2.2	2.2	2.3	2.4	2.4	2.5	2.5
Iran	4.2	3.2	3.4	3.6	3.8	3.9	4.1	4.2	4.3	4.3	4.4	4.4
Saudi Arabia	1.8	1.8	1.9	2.0	2.1	2.2	2.3	2.4	2.5	2.6	2.7	2.8
Turkey	0.6	0.7	0.8	0.8	0.9	0.9	1.0	1.0	1.0	1.1	1.1	1.2
Other N. Africa & Middle East	5.6	6.0	6.0	6.1	6.1	6.2	6.3	6.3	6.4	6.4	6.5	6.5
Japan	16.0	16.1	16.0	16.0	16.0	15.9	15.9	15.9	15.9	15.9	15.8	15.8
South Korea	8.5	9.0	9.0	9.0	9.1	9.1	9.2	9.3	9.3	9.4	9.5	9.5
Taiw an	4.6	4.7	4.9	4.9	4.9	4.9	5.0	5.0	5.0	5.0	5.0	5.0
China	1.3	1.0	1.2	1.8	2.5	3.2	4.1	4.9	5.8	6.6	7.5	8.0
Indonesia	1.2	0.8	0.9	0.9	1.0	1.1	1.1	1.2	1.2	1.3	1.4	1.4
Malaysia	2.8	2.8	2.9	3.0	3.0	3.1	3.2	3.2	3.3	3.3	3.4	3.4
Other Asia & Oceania	2.3	2.5	2.7	2.9	3.0	3.1	3.2	3.3	3.4	3.4	3.4	3.5
Canada	2.1	1.8	1.8	1.9	1.9	1.9	1.8	1.8	1.8	1.9	1.9	1.8
Mexico	8.4	9.1	9.2	9.9	10.4	10.8	11.1	11.8	12.3	13.0	13.6	14.3

2009/10		2010/11	2011/12	2012/13	2013/14	2014/15	2015/16	2016/17	2017/18	2018/19	2019/20	2020/21
						Imports, million metric tons						
Central America & Caribbean	4.9	5.0	5.0	5.0	5.0	5.0	5.1	5.2	5.3	5.3	5.3	5.3
2009/10		**2010/11**	**2011/12**	**2012/13**	**2013/14**	**2014/15**	**2015/16**	**2016/17**	**2017/18**	**2018/19**	**2019/20**	**2020/21**
						Imports, million metric tons						
Brazil	0.7	1.0	1.0	1.0	1.0	1.0	1.0	1.0	1.0	1.0	1.0	1.0
Other South America	8.6	8.1	8.1	8.3	8.4	8.5	8.6	8.6	8.7	8.6	8.6	8.6
Sub-Saharan Africa[3]	2.3	1.5	1.5	1.6	1.6	1.7	1.8	1.9	2.0	2.1	2.2	2.3
Other foreign[4]	4.0	2.7	3.0	3.0	3.0	3.0	3.0	3.0	3.0	3.0	3.0	3.0
United States	0.2	0.3	0.3	0.3	0.3	0.3	0.3	0.3	0.3	0.3	0.3	0.3
Total trade	92.6	93.2	93.0	95.2	97.4	99.3	102.3	104.8	107.5	109.4	111.6	113.2
Exporters						*Exports, million metric tons*						
European Union[1]	1.5	1.0	1.3	1.5	1.7	1.9	2.2	2.3	2.6	2.7	2.9	3.1
China	0.2	0.2	0.2	0.2	0.2	0.2	0.2	0.2	0.1	0.1	0.1	0.1
Argentina	15.0	17.5	16.0	16.5	17.0	17.2	17.5	17.7	17.8	17.7	17.7	17.4
Brazil	9.0	7.0	6.5	7.0	7.2	7.5	8.0	8.5	8.8	8.5	8.5	8.5
South Africa	2.5	2.5	2.5	2.5	2.6	2.6	2.6	2.6	2.6	2.6	2.7	2.6
Other Europe	1.8	2.7	2.4	2.4	2.6	2.7	2.8	2.8	2.8	2.9	2.8	2.8
Former Soviet Union[2]	5.5	5.6	6.1	6.4	6.6	7.1	8.3	8.5	9.2	10.0	10.8	11.1
Other foreign	6.6	7.1	7.1	7.2	7.3	7.4	7.4	7.5	7.6	7.7	7.8	7.9
United States	50.5	49.5	50.8	51.4	52.1	52.7	53.3	54.6	55.9	57.2	58.4	59.7
						Percent						
U.S. trade share	54.5	53.2	54.6	54.1	53.5	53.1	52.1	52.1	52.0	52.3	52.3	52.7

[1]/ Covers EU-27, excludes intra-EU trade.

[2]/ Covers FSU-12, includes intra-FSU trade.

[3]/ Includes South Africa.

[4]/ Includes unaccounted.

The projections were completed in November 2010.

Table 6. Barley Trade Long-Term Projections

2009/10		2010/11	2011/12	2012/13	2013/14	2014/15	2015/16	2016/17	2017/18	2018/19	2019/20	2020/21
					Imports, million metric tons							
Importers												
Former Soviet Union[1]	0.2	0.8	0.4	0.4	0.5	0.5	0.5	0.5	0.5	0.5	0.6	0.6
Japan	1.4	1.4	1.4	1.3	1.4	1.4	1.3	1.3	1.4	1.4	1.4	1.3
South Korea	0.0	0.0	0.0	0.0	0.0	0.0	0.0	0.0	0.0	0.1	0.1	0.1
Taiw an	0.1	0.1	0.1	0.1	0.1	0.1	0.1	0.1	0.1	0.1	0.1	0.1
China	2.3	2.0	2.1	2.3	2.4	2.5	2.6	2.7	2.7	2.8	2.9	3.0
European Union[2]	0.1	0.2	0.2	0.2	0.2	0.2	0.2	0.2	0.3	0.3	0.3	0.3
Latin America[3]	0.9	0.9	0.9	0.9	0.9	1.0	1.0	1.0	1.0	1.1	1.1	1.1
Algeria	0.1	0.0	0.0	0.0	0.0	0.0	0.1	0.2	0.2	0.2	0.2	0.2
Saudi Arabia	7.9	7.0	7.5	7.7	7.8	7.9	8.0	8.0	8.1	8.2	8.2	8.3
Morocco	0.3	0.2	0.3	0.5	0.6	0.7	0.7	0.7	0.8	0.8	0.9	0.9
Tunisia	0.1	0.4	0.4	0.4	0.4	0.4	0.4	0.4	0.4	0.4	0.4	0.4
South Africa	0.1	0.1	0.1	0.1	0.1	0.1	0.1	0.1	0.1	0.1	0.1	0.1
Iran	0.9	0.4	0.6	0.7	0.9	0.9	0.9	0.9	0.9	1.0	1.0	1.0
Other N. Africa & M. East	2.4	1.8	2.0	2.2	2.3	2.4	2.4	2.5	2.5	2.5	2.6	2.6
Other foreign[4]	-0.2	0.6	0.6	0.6	0.6	0.6	0.6	0.6	0.6	0.6	0.6	0.6
United States	0.7	0.5	0.4	0.4	0.4	0.4	0.4	0.4	0.4	0.4	0.4	0.4
Total trade	17.1	16.3	17.0	18.0	18.7	19.1	19.4	19.7	20.1	20.4	20.8	21.0
Exporters					**Exports, million metric tons**							
European Union[2]	1.1	4.6	3.9	4.6	4.9	5.0	5.0	5.0	5.1	5.2	5.2	5.2
Australia	3.8	4.1	4.0	3.9	4.2	4.3	4.3	4.4	4.4	4.5	4.5	4.5
Canada	1.3	1.4	1.9	1.8	1.7	1.8	1.8	1.6	1.5	1.4	1.2	1.1
Russia	2.7	0.3	0.5	0.5	0.4	0.4	0.5	0.5	0.6	0.7	0.9	1.0
Ukraine	6.2	4.0	4.2	4.7	4.9	4.8	5.1	5.3	5.4	5.5	5.6	5.7
Other Former Soviet Union[5]	0.4	0.2	0.6	0.7	0.8	0.8	0.8	0.9	1.1	1.2	1.3	1.4
Turkey	0.8	0.4	0.4	0.4	0.4	0.5	0.4	0.4	0.4	0.4	0.5	0.5
Other foreign	0.7	1.1	1.2	1.2	1.2	1.2	1.3	1.3	1.3	1.3	1.3	1.3
United States	0.1	0.2	0.2	0.2	0.2	0.2	0.2	0.2	0.2	0.2	0.2	0.2
					Percent							
U.S. trade share	0.7	1.3	1.3	1.2	1.2	1.1	1.1	1.1	1.1	1.1	1.0	1.0

[1]/ Covers FSU-12, includes intra-FSU trade. [2]/ Covers EU-27, excludes intra-EU trade.
[3]/ Includes Mexico. [4]/ Includes unaccounted.
[5]/ Covers FSU-12 except Russia and Ukraine, includes intra-FSU trade.
The projections w ere completed in November 2010.

Table 7. Sorghum Trade Long-Term Projections

	2009/10	2010/11	2011/12	2012/13	2013/14	2014/15	2015/16	2016/17	2017/18	2018/19	2019/20	2020/21
Importers					*Imports, million metric tons*							
Japan	1.7	1.6	1.6	1.5	1.5	1.4	1.3	1.3	1.2	1.2	1.1	1.1
Mexico	2.6	2.7	2.8	2.9	3.0	3.1	3.2	3.3	3.4	3.5	3.6	3.7
North Africa & Middle East	0.2	0.1	0.1	0.1	0.1	0.1	0.1	0.1	0.1	0.1	0.1	0.1
South America	0.8	0.8	0.8	0.8	0.8	0.9	0.9	0.9	0.9	0.9	0.9	0.9
Sub-Saharan Africa[1]	0.7	0.6	0.6	0.6	0.7	0.7	0.7	0.8	0.8	0.8	0.9	0.9
Other[2]	0.5	0.6	0.6	0.5	0.5	0.5	0.5	0.4	0.4	0.5	0.5	0.6
Total trade	6.5	6.4	6.4	6.5	6.6	6.7	6.8	6.8	6.9	7.0	7.2	7.3
Exporters					*Exports, million metric tons*							
Argentina	1.4	1.3	1.3	1.3	1.3	1.3	1.3	1.3	1.2	1.2	1.2	1.2
Australia	0.6	0.8	0.7	0.6	0.6	0.5	0.5	0.4	0.4	0.5	0.5	0.5
Brazil	0.0	0.0	0.0	0.0	0.0	0.0	0.0	0.0	0.0	0.0	0.0	0.0
Other foreign	0.3	0.2	0.2	0.3	0.3	0.3	0.3	0.3	0.3	0.3	0.3	0.3
United States	4.2	4.1	4.2	4.3	4.4	4.6	4.7	4.8	5.0	5.1	5.2	5.3
					Percent							
U.S. trade share	64.9	63.2	65.2	66.9	67.5	68.3	69.5	70.9	72.1	72.3	72.7	72.9

[1]/ Includes South Africa.

[2]/ EU-27 and the rest of the w orld. Excludes intra-EU trade. Includes unaccounted.

The projections were completed in November 2010.

Table 8. Wheat Trade Long-Term Projections

	2009/10	2010/11	2011/12	2012/13	2013/14	2014/15	2015/16	2016/17	2017/18	2018/19	2019/20	2020/21
					Imports, million metric tons							
Importers												
Algeria	5.2	5.3	5.7	5.8	5.9	6.1	6.2	6.3	6.4	6.5	6.6	6.7
Tunisia	1.5	1.8	1.7	1.7	1.8	1.8	1.8	1.9	1.9	1.9	1.9	2.0
Morocco	2.3	3.6	3.4	3.4	3.5	3.6	3.6	3.7	3.7	3.7	3.8	3.9
Egypt	10.3	9.8	10.0	10.1	10.4	10.7	10.9	11.1	11.3	11.6	11.8	12.1
Saudi Arabia	1.9	2.0	2.3	2.5	2.7	2.7	2.8	2.9	3.0	3.1	3.2	3.3
Iran	5.0	0.8	2.5	2.5	2.5	2.5	2.5	2.5	2.5	2.5	2.5	2.5
Iraq	3.9	3.6	3.2	3.5	3.6	3.7	3.8	3.9	4.1	4.2	4.3	4.4

	2009/10	2010/11	2011/12	2012/13	2013/14	2014/15	2015/16	2016/17	2017/18	2018/19	2019/20	2020/21
					Imports, million metric tons							
Other N. Africa & Middle East	15.2	13.1	13.7	13.6	13.9	14.0	14.1	14.2	14.4	14.5	14.5	14.6
Sub-Saharan Africa1	15.8	14.3	14.4	15.0	15.8	16.2	16.7	17.1	17.6	18.1	18.5	19.0
Mexico	3.2	3.3	3.4	3.4	3.5	3.6	3.7	3.7	3.8	3.9	3.9	4.0
Central America & Caribbean	3.5	3.5	3.5	3.6	3.7	3.7	3.7	3.7	3.8	3.8	3.8	3.8
Brazil	7.0	6.5	6.5	6.6	6.7	6.7	6.7	6.8	6.8	6.9	7.0	7.0
Other South America	6.6	6.5	6.5	6.6	6.8	6.8	6.8	6.9	6.9	7.0	7.0	7.0
European Union2	5.5	5.5	6.2	6.3	6.4	6.5	6.6	6.7	6.8	6.9	6.9	7.0
Other Europe	1.7	1.8	1.8	1.9	1.9	1.9	2.0	2.0	2.1	2.1	2.2	2.2
Former Soviet Union3	5.4	7.4	5.9	6.0	6.0	6.0	6.1	6.1	6.1	6.1	6.1	6.2
Japan	5.5	5.2	5.2	5.2	5.2	5.2	5.1	5.1	5.0	5.0	5.0	4.9
South Korea	4.5	3.6	4.0	3.9	3.9	4.0	4.0	4.0	4.0	4.0	4.0	4.0
Philippines	3.2	2.8	2.9	3.1	3.2	3.3	3.3	3.4	3.5	3.6	3.6	3.7
Indonesia	5.4	5.5	5.6	5.8	6.0	6.1	6.2	6.3	6.5	6.6	6.7	6.9
China	1.4	1.0	0.9	0.8	0.8	0.7	0.8	0.7	0.8	0.9	1.0	1.0
Bangladesh	3.3	2.5	2.6	2.6	2.7	2.8	2.9	3.0	3.0	3.1	3.2	3.3
Malaysia	1.3	1.3	1.3	1.3	1.4	1.4	1.4	1.4	1.4	1.4	1.4	1.5
Thailand	1.6	1.1	1.2	1.3	1.3	1.3	1.3	1.4	1.4	1.4	1.5	1.5
Vietnam	1.9	1.5	1.6	1.7	1.8	1.8	1.9	1.9	2.0	2.0	2.1	2.2
Pakistan	0.2	0.3	2.6	1.0	0.6	0.4	0.4	0.4	0.4	0.4	0.4	0.5
Other Asia & Oceania	7.7	7.2	7.4	7.6	8.1	8.4	8.7	9.0	9.3	9.6	9.9	10.2
Other foreign[4]	2.2	3.5	2.9	2.9	2.9	2.9	2.9	3.0	3.0	3.0	3.0	3.0
United States	3.2	3.0	3.0	3.0	3.0	3.1	3.1	3.3	3.3	3.4	3.4	3.5
Total trade	135.3	127.2	132.1	132.8	135.8	138.0	140.1	142.5	144.6	147.1	149.4	151.9
					Exports, million metric tons							
Exporters												
European Union[2]	22.1	22.0	21.2	20.5	20.4	20.1	20.0	20.4	20.2	20.1	19.9	20.8
Canada	19.0	17.5	17.9	17.2	16.3	17.1	17.2	17.2	17.2	17.3	17.3	17.3
Australia	14.5	16.0	16.5	17.0	17.8	18.0	18.0	18.0	18.1	18.2	18.2	18.2
Argentina	5.5	8.0	8.1	8.2	8.4	8.6	8.8	9.0	9.2	9.4	9.6	9.8
					Exports, million metric tons							
Russia	18.6	4.0	7.0	10.8	14.0	16.0	17.5	18.8	20.0	21.2	22.5	23.5
Ukraine	9.3	6.0	8.5	9.0	9.4	9.7	10.0	10.2	10.4	10.6	10.8	11.0
Other Former Soviet Union[5]	8.8	6.7	8.0	8.2	8.5	8.7	9.1	9.8	10.4	11.0	11.6	12.2
Other Europe	0.8	0.3	0.3	0.3	0.3	0.3	0.3	0.3	0.3	0.3	0.4	0.4
India	0.1	0.2	0.4	1.3	3.0	1.5	0.9	0.3	0.1	0.1	0.1	0.1

Table 8. (Continued)

	2009/10	2010/11	2011/12	2012/13	2013/14	2014/15	2015/16	2016/17	2017/18	2018/19	2019/20	2020/21
					Imports, million metric tons							
China	0.9	2.0	2.3	2.5	2.8	3.0	3.1	3.3	3.4	3.5	3.6	3.8
Turkey	4.4	3.0	3.0	2.9	2.8	2.8	2.8	2.8	2.8	2.8	2.7	2.7
Other foreign	7.3	7.5	7.6	7.7	7.7	7.8	7.8	7.9	8.0	8.1	8.2	8.2
United States	24.0	34.0	31.3	27.2	24.5	24.5	24.5	24.5	24.5	24.5	24.5	23.8
						Percent						
U.S. trade share	17.7	26.7	23.7	20.5	18.0	17.8	17.5	17.2	16.9	16.7	16.4	15.7

[1]/ Includes South Africa.

[2]/ Covers EU-27, excludes intra-EU trade.

[3]/ Covers FSU-12, includes intra-FSU trade.

[4]/ Includes unaccounted w hich can be negative.

[5]/ Covers FSU-12 except Russia and Ukraine, includes intra-FSU trade.

The projections w ere completed in November 2010.

Table 9. Rice Trade Long-Term Projections

	2009/10	2010/11	2011/12	2012/13	2013/14	2014/15	2015/16	2016/17	2017/18	2018/19	2019/20	2020/21
					Imports, million metric tons							
Importers												
Canada	0.36	0.34	0.35	0.35	0.36	0.36	0.37	0.37	0.38	0.38	0.38	0.39
Mexico	0.60	0.65	0.69	0.71	0.74	0.77	0.79	0.82	0.84	0.87	0.89	0.92
Central America/Caribbean	1.44	1.48	1.69	1.82	1.87	1.91	1.94	1.96	2.01	2.03	2.09	2.13
Brazil	0.90	0.65	0.94	0.87	0.84	0.88	0.82	0.72	0.61	0.60	0.61	0.61
Other South America	0.46	0.73	0.56	0.53	0.43	0.37	0.31	0.31	0.31	0.31	0.31	0.31
European Union[1]	1.24	1.35	1.29	1.32	1.35	1.37	1.39	1.41	1.43	1.45	1.47	1.49
Former Soviet Union[2]	0.37	0.34	0.35	0.36	0.35	0.35	0.35	0.35	0.34	0.34	0.33	0.32
Other Europe	0.13	0.12	0.13	0.13	0.13	0.13	0.13	0.13	0.13	0.13	0.13	0.13
Bangladesh	0.09	0.75	0.82	0.89	0.99	1.04	1.12	1.18	1.25	1.32	1.39	1.45
China	0.30	0.33	0.37	0.40	0.43	0.45	0.49	0.52	0.54	0.57	0.60	0.62
Japan	0.70	0.70	0.68	0.68	0.68	0.68	0.68	0.68	0.68	0.68	0.68	0.68
South Korea	0.30	0.33	0.35	0.39	0.41	0.41	0.41	0.41	0.41	0.41	0.41	0.41
Indonesia	0.80	0.65	0.80	0.93	1.05	1.11	1.17	1.25	1.34	1.43	1.51	1.57

	2009/10	2010/11	2011/12	2012/13	2013/14	2014/15	2015/16	2016/17	2017/18	2018/19	2019/20	2020/21
					Imports, million metric tons							
Malaysia	1.07	1.02	1.01	1.09	1.17	1.24	1.28	1.30	1.32	1.34	1.36	1.37
Philippines	2.20	2.00	2.50	2.70	3.00	3.30	3.50	3.70	3.85	3.97	4.08	4.22
Other Asia & Oceania	2.37	2.46	2.55	2.70	2.81	2.90	3.02	3.13	3.26	3.41	3.55	3.70
Iraq	1.10	1.15	1.17	1.20	1.23	1.25	1.27	1.29	1.32	1.34	1.36	1.37
Iran	1.15	1.20	1.24	1.32	1.35	1.36	1.35	1.36	1.37	1.37	1.37	1.36
Saudi Arabia	1.10	1.10	1.10	1.12	1.14	1.16	1.18	1.21	1.23	1.26	1.29	1.32
Other N. Africa & M. East	2.54	2.46	2.50	2.46	2.57	2.68	2.76	2.83	2.91	3.00	3.09	3.17
Sub-Saharan Africa[3]	6.90	7.41	7.75	8.19	8.38	8.55	8.73	8.91	9.08	9.25	9.42	9.59
South Africa	0.80	0.90	0.91	0.92	0.91	0.92	0.94	0.96	0.97	0.99	1.00	1.02
Other foreign[4]	2.02	1.75	1.80	1.81	1.81	1.84	1.90	1.96	2.00	2.03	2.03	2.04
United States	0.60	0.62	0.64	0.65	0.67	0.69	0.71	0.72	0.74	0.76	0.78	0.80
Total imports	29.54	30.47	32.20	33.54	34.66	35.72	36.60	37.47	38.33	39.22	40.12	41.00
Exporters					***Exports, million metric tons***							
Australia	0.04	0.33	0.18	0.15	0.15	0.15	0.15	0.15	0.15	0.15	0.15	0.15
Argentina	0.55	0.70	0.66	0.61	0.61	0.63	0.66	0.69	0.72	0.74	0.76	0.78
Other South America	1.57	1.95	1.64	1.69	1.74	1.79	1.82	1.91	2.00	2.15	2.30	2.46
European Union[1]	0.23	0.18	0.18	0.18	0.18	0.18	0.18	0.18	0.18	0.18	0.19	0.19
					Exports, million metric tons							
China	0.60	0.90	0.90	0.90	0.95	0.99	0.97	1.01	1.02	1.03	1.04	1.07
India	2.20	2.50	3.64	4.62	5.07	5.42	5.58	5.65	5.55	5.56	5.55	5.59
Pakistan	3.80	2.65	2.75	3.09	3.20	3.31	3.46	3.63	3.80	3.98	4.18	4.38
Thailand	8.50	9.70	10.37	10.43	10.69	10.83	11.13	11.36	11.80	12.03	12.30	12.43
Vietnam	6.20	5.80	5.80	5.60	5.62	5.71	5.77	5.86	5.94	6.09	6.23	6.40
Egypt	0.70	0.30	0.28	0.26	0.24	0.23	0.21	0.20	0.18	0.17	0.15	0.14
Other foreign	1.69	1.83	2.02	2.18	2.34	2.55	2.66	2.77	2.88	2.99	3.10	3.21
United States	3.47	3.64	3.79	3.82	3.88	3.94	4.01	4.05	4.10	4.15	4.18	4.21
Total exports	29.54	30.47	32.20	33.54	34.66	35.72	36.60	37.47	38.33	39.22	40.12	41.00
						Percent						
U.S. trade share	11.7	12.0	11.8	11.4	11.2	11.0 10.9		10.8	10.7	10.6	10.4	10.3

[1]/ Covers EU-27, excludes intra-EU trade.

[2]/ Covers FSU-12, includes intra-FSU trade.

[3]/ Excludes South Africa

[4]/ Includes unaccounted.

The projections were completed in November 2010.

Table 10. Soybean Trade Long-Term Projections

	2009/10	2010/11	2011/12	2012/13	2013/14	2014/15	2015/16	2016/17	2017/18	2018/19	2019/20	2020/21
					Imports, million metric tons							
Importers												
European Union[1]	12.9	13.5	13.5	13.1	12.9	12.7	12.5	12.3	12.1	11.9	11.7	11.5
Japan	3.4	3.5	3.6	3.4	3.3	3.3	3.3	3.2	3.2	3.1	3.1	3.0
South Korea	1.2	1.2	1.2	1.2	1.2	1.2	1.2	1.3	1.3	1.3	1.3	1.3
Taiwan	2.5	2.5	2.5	2.5	2.5	2.5	2.5	2.5	2.5	2.5	2.5	2.5
Mexico	3.5	3.6	3.7	3.8	3.9	4.0	4.1	4.1	4.2	4.3	4.4	4.5
Importers												
Former Soviet Union[2]	1.0	1.2	1.2	1.3	1.4	1.4	1.5	1.5	1.6	1.6	1.6	1.7
Other Europe	0.5	0.5	0.5	0.5	0.5	0.5	0.5	0.5	0.5	0.5	0.5	0.5
China	50.3	57.0	60.7	64.0	66.9	70.1	73.2	76.4	79.4	82.4	85.4	88.3
Malaysia	0.6	0.6	0.6	0.6	0.6	0.6	0.7	0.7	0.7	0.7	0.7	0.7
Indonesia	1.6	1.6	1.7	1.7	1.7	1.8	1.8	1.9	1.9	2.0	2.0	2.0
Other	15.2	11.9	12.1	12.4	12.8	13.1	13.5	13.9	14.2	14.6	15.0	15.3
Total imports	92.7	97.2	101.4	104.5	107.8	111.3	114.7	118.3	121.6	124.9	128.3	131.5
Exporters					Exports, million metric tons							
Argentina	13.0	13.0	13.7	14.8	15.1	15.6	16.1	16.7	17.1	17.5	17.5	17.9
Brazil	28.6	31.4	33.6	34.5	36.2	37.9	40.0	41.9	43.9	45.9	48.0	49.5
Other South America	7.3	6.4	7.2	7.4	7.8	8.0	8.5	8.9	9.4	9.9	10.5	11.1
China	0.2	0.5	0.5	0.5	0.5	0.5	0.5	0.5	0.5	0.5	0.5	0.5
Other foreign	2.8	3.2	3.6	3.6	3.7	3.8	3.9	3.9	4.1	4.2	4.3	4.4
United States	40.9	42.7	42.9	43.7	44.5	45.4	45.9	46.4	46.7	47.1	47.5	48.0
Total exports	92.7	97.2	101.4	104.5	107.8	111.3	114.7	118.3	121.6	124.9	128.3	131.5
						Percent						
U.S. trade share	44.1	44.0	42.3	41.8	41.3	40.8 40.0		39.2	38.4	37.7	37.0	36.5

[1]/ Covers EU-27, excludes intra-EU trade.

[2]/ Covers FSU-12, includes intra-FSU trade.

The projections w ere completed in November 2010.

Table 11. Soybean Meal Trade Long-Term Projections

	2009/10	2010/11	2011/12	2012/13	2013/14	2014/15	2015/16	2016/17	2017/18	2018/19	2019/20	2020/21
Importers					**Imports, million metric tons**							
European Union[1]	21.8	23.3	23.6	24.0	24.4	24.8	25.2	25.6	26.0	26.3	26.7	27.1
Former Soviet Union[2]	0.7	0.7	0.6	0.7	0.7	0.8	0.8	0.8	0.9	0.9	1.0	1.0
Other Europe	0.6	0.7	0.7	0.7	0.7	0.7	0.7	0.7	0.7	0.7	0.7	0.7
Canada	1.1	1.2	1.2	1.2	1.2	1.2	1.3	1.3	1.3	1.4	1.4	1.4
Japan	2.1	2.1	2.2	2.3	2.3	2.3	2.4	2.4	2.5	2.5	2.5	2.6
Southeast Asia	9.6	10.2	10.1	10.4	10.8	11.2	11.5	11.9	12.3	12.6	13.0	13.4
Mexico	1.2	1.4	1.4	1.5	1.5	1.6	1.6	1.6	1.7	1.7	1.7	1.8
Other Latin America	5.6	6.1	6.3	6.5	6.7	7.0	7.2	7.4	7.6	7.9	8.1	8.3
North Africa & Middle East	5.8	6.2	6.6	6.8	7.0	7.2	7.4	7.5	7.7	7.9	8.0	8.2
Other	4.6	5.1	5.0	5.1	5.2	5.3	5.3	5.5	5.5	5.6	5.7	5.7
Total imports	53.1	56.8	57.8	59.3	60.6	62.0	63.4	64.8	66.1	67.5	68.8	70.1
Exporters					**Exports, million metric tons**							
Argentina	24.7	29.6	29.5	30.5	31.4	32.7	33.8	34.9	36.2	37.5	38.7	40.0
Brazil	13.0	12.8	12.6	13.3	13.6	13.8	14.1	14.3	14.5	14.8	15.0	15.3
Other South America	2.3	2.3	2.3	2.4	2.4	2.4	2.4	2.5	2.5	2.6	2.6	2.7
China	1.2	1.2	1.2	1.2	1.2	1.2	1.3	1.3	1.3	1.3	1.4	1.4
India	3.0	3.5	3.4	3.1	3.1	2.9	2.8	2.5	2.3	2.0	1.8	1.5
European Union[1]	0.5	0.5	0.5	0.5	0.5	0.5	0.5	0.5	0.5	0.5	0.5	0.5
Other foreign	0.5	0.5	0.5	0.5	0.6	0.6	0.6	0.6	0.6	0.6	0.6	0.7
United States	10.1	8.3	7.8	7.8	7.9	7.9	7.9	8.2	8.2	8.2	8.2	8.2
Total exports	55.2	58.5	57.7	59.3	60.6	62.0	63.4	64.8	66.1	67.5	68.8	70.1
						Percent						
U.S. trade share	18.3	14.1	13.5	13.2	13.0	12.7	12.5	12.6	12.3	12.1	11.9	11.6

[1]/ Covers EU-27, excludes intra-EU trade.

[2]/ Covers FSU-12, includes intra-FSU trade.

The projections w ere completed in November 2010.

Table 12. Soybean Oil Trade Long-Term Projections

	2009/10	2010/11	2011/12	2012/13	2013/14	2014/15	2015/16	2016/17	2017/18	2018/19	2019/20	2020/21
Importers				**Imports, million metric tons**								
China	1.5	2.0	2.0	1.7	1.6	1.6	1.5	1.5	1.4	1.4	1.3	1.2
India	1.6	1.3	1.2	1.3	1.3	1.4	1.4	1.5	1.5	1.6	1.6	1.7
Other Asia	1.2	1.2	1.2	1.2	1.2	1.3	1.3	1.3	1.4	1.4	1.4	1.5
Latin America	1.6	1.7	1.7	1.8	1.9	1.9	2.0	2.0	2.1	2.2	2.2	2.3
North Africa & Middle East	1.6	1.7	1.7	1.8	1.8	1.9	1.9	2.0	2.0	2.1	2.1	2.2
European Union[1]	0.6	0.6	0.6	0.6	0.7	0.8	0.8	0.9	1.0	1.0	1.1	1.2
Other	1.0	1.1	0.9	0.9	0.9	0.9	0.9	1.0	1.0	1.0	1.0	1.0
Total imports	9.1	9.5	9.3	9.3	9.5	9.7	10.0	10.2	10.4	10.6	10.8	11.1
Exporters					*Exports, million metric tons*							
Argentina	4.4	5.3	5.4	5.4	5.6	5.8	5.9	6.0	6.1	6.3	6.3	6.4
Brazil	1.4	1.3	1.3	1.4	1.5	1.5	1.6	1.6	1.7	1.8	1.8	1.9
European Union[1]	0.4	0.3	0.3	0.3	0.3	0.3	0.3	0.3	0.3	0.3	0.3	0.3
Other foreign	1.3	1.3	1.4	1.5	1.5	1.5	1.5	1.5	1.6	1.6	1.6	1.7
United States	1.5	1.2	0.9	0.7	0.6	0.6	0.6	0.7	0.7	0.7	0.8	0.8
Total exports	9.1	9.5	9.3	9.3	9.5	9.7	10.0	10.2	10.4	10.6	10.8	11.1
					Percent							
U.S. trade share	16.9	13.0	9.5	7.4	6.2	6.1	6.4	6.7	6.9	6.9	7.0	7.0

[1]/ Covers EU-27, excludes intra-EU trade.

The projections w ere completed in November 2010.

Table 13. Rapeseed Trade Long-Term Projections

	2009/10	2010/11	2011/12	2012/13	2013/14	2014/15	2015/16	2016/17	2017/18	2018/19	2019/20	2020/21
Importers					**Imports, million metric tons**							
European Union[1]	2.2	2.1	2.6	3.1	3.4	3.7	4.0	4.2	4.6	4.8	5.1	5.3
Japan	2.3	2.2	2.2	2.2	2.2	2.2	2.2	2.2	2.2	2.2	2.2	2.2
Mexico	1.3	1.2	1.2	1.2	1.2	1.2	1.3	1.3	1.4	1.4	1.5	1.6
China	2.2	1.9	1.8	1.8	1.9	2.0	2.0	2.2	2.2	2.5	2.6	2.8
Bangladesh	0.2	0.2	0.2	0.2	0.2	0.2	0.2	0.2	0.2	0.2	0.2	0.2
Pakistan	0.8	0.7	0.7	0.8	0.8	0.8	0.8	0.8	0.9	0.9	0.9	0.9
Other foreign	1.4	1.0	0.8	0.8	0.9	0.9	0.9	0.9	1.0	1.0	1.1	1.2

	2009/10	2010/11	2011/12	2012/13	2013/14	2014/15	2015/16	2016/17	2017/18	2018/19	2019/20	2020/21
Importers					**Imports, million metric tons**							
United States	0.6	0.5	0.7	0.8	0.8	0.8	0.9	0.9	0.9	0.9	0.9	1.0
Total imports	10.9	9.7	10.2	10.8	11.3	11.7	12.2	12.7	13.3	13.9	14.5	15.1
Exporters					***Exports, million metric tons***							
Canada	7.2	6.4	6.6	6.7	6.8	7.0	7.1	7.4	7.7	8.0	8.3	8.6
Russia	0.1	0.0	0.1	0.1	0.2	0.2	0.2	0.2	0.3	0.3	0.3	0.4
Ukraine	1.8	1.3	1.8	2.2	2.5	2.8	3.0	3.2	3.4	3.6	3.8	4.0
Other Former Soviet Union	0.2	0.0	0.1	0.1	0.2	0.1	0.1	0.2	0.2	0.2	0.2	0.2
Australia	1.3	1.5	1.2	1.2	1.2	1.2	1.2	1.2	1.3	1.3	1.3	1.3
Other foreign	0.2	0.1	0.1	0.1	0.2	0.2	0.2	0.2	0.2	0.2	0.2	0.3
United States	0.2	0.3	0.3	0.3	0.3	0.3	0.3	0.3	0.3	0.3	0.4	0.4
Total exports	10.9	9.7	10.2	10.8	11.3	11.7	12.2	12.7	13.3	13.9	14.5	15.1
					Percent							
U.S. trade share	1.9	3.3	2.7	2.6	2.6	2.6	2.6	2.5	2.5	2.5	2.4	2.4

[1]/ Covers EU-27, excludes intra-EU trade.

The projections w ere completed in November 2010.

Table 14. All Cotton Trade Long-Term Projections

	2009/10	2010/11	2011/12	2012/13	2013/14	2014/15	2015/16	2016/17	2017/18	2018/19	2019/20	2020/21
				Imports, million bales								
Importers												
European Union[1]	1.0	0.9	1.1	1.0	1.0	1.0	0.9	0.7	0.6	0.5	0.4	0.3
Former Soviet Union[2]	0.7	0.7	0.7	0.7	0.7	0.7	0.7	0.7	0.7	0.7	0.7	0.6
Brazil	0.2	0.8	0.3	0.3	0.3	0.3	0.3	0.3	0.3	0.3	0.3	0.3
Mexico	1.4	1.3	1.3	1.3	1.4	1.4	1.4	1.4	1.4	1.4	1.4	1.4
Japan	0.3	0.3	0.3	0.3	0.3	0.3	0.3	0.3	0.3	0.3	0.3	0.3
South Korea	1.0	1.0	1.0	1.0	0.9	0.9	0.9	0.9	0.9	0.9	0.8	0.8
China	10.9	15.0	16.5	17.6	18.8	19.6	20.1	20.5	20.8	21.0	21.2	21.5
Indonesia	2.1	1.9	2.0	2.0	2.0	2.0	2.0	2.0	2.1	2.1	2.1	2.1
Thailand	1.8	1.6	1.7	1.8	1.8	1.8	1.9	1.9	1.9	2.0	2.0	1.0
Pakistan	1.4	1.7	1.9	2.0	2.2	2.1	2.2	2.3	2.3	2.3	2.4	2.4
India	0.6	0.5	0.5	0.6	0.6	0.6	0.7	0.7	0.7	0.7	0.7	0.7

Table 14. (Continued)

	2009/10	2010/11	2011/12	2012/13	2013/14	2014/15	2015/16	2016/17	2017/18	2018/19	2019/20	2020/21
				Imports, million bales								
Bangladesh	3.8	3.9	4.2	4.3	4.4	4.6	4.8	5.0	5.2	5.4	5.6	5.9
Taiw an	1.0	1.0	1.0	1.0	1.0	1.0	0.9	0.9	0.9	0.9	0.9	0.8
Other Asia & Oceania	2.7	2.5	2.7	2.8	2.9	3.0	3.1	3.2	3.3	3.4	3.4	3.5
Turkey	4.4	3.1	3.5	3.2	3.0	2.9	2.9	2.9	2.9	2.9	3.0	3.0
Other	2.4	2.6	1.8	1.8	1.9	2.0	2.1	2.1	2.1	2.2	2.2	3.3
Total imports	35.6	38.8	40.6	41.8	43.3	44.4	45.2	45.9	46.4	46.9	47.4	47.9
Exporters				Exports, million bales								
Former Soviet Union[2]	5.9	5.9	5.7	5.7	6.1	6.3	6.6	6.8	6.8	6.9	6.9	7.0
Australia	2.1	2.9	3.5	3.5	3.6	3.8	3.8	3.9	4.0	4.1	4.1	4.2
Argentina	0.1	0.3	0.5	0.4	0.4	0.4	0.4	0.4	0.5	0.5	0.5	0.5
Brazil	2.0	2.4	3.0	3.6	4.0	4.4	4.7	5.1	5.4	5.6	5.8	6.0
Other Latin America	0.1	0.2	0.2	0.2	0.2	0.2	0.2	0.2	0.2	0.2	0.3	0.3
Pakistan	0.7	0.3	0.3	0.2	0.2	0.2	0.2	0.2	0.2	0.2	0.2	0.2
India	6.6	4.8	5.7	6.0	6.1	6.1	5.9	5.5	5.3	5.2	5.0	5.0
Egypt	0.3	0.2	0.4	0.4	0.3	0.4	0.4	0.4	0.4	0.4	0.4	0.4
Sub-Saharan Africa[3]	3.8	4.0	4.0	4.4	4.9	5.3	5.6	5.8	6.0	6.1	6.3	6.4
				Exports, million bales								
Other foreign	2.0	2.1	1.7	1.7	1.7	1.7	1.7	1.7	1.7	1.7	1.7	1.7
United States	12.0	15.8	15.6	15.6	15.6	15.6	15.7	15.8	15.9	16.0	16.1	16.2
Total exports	35.6	38.8	40.6	41.8	43.3	44.4	45.2	45.9	46.4	46.9	47.4	47.9
						Percent						
U.S. trade share	33.8	40.5	38.3	37.2	36.0	35.1	34.7	34.4	34.3	34.1	34.0	33.9

[1]/ Covers EU-27, excludes intra-EU trade.

[2]/ Covers FSU-12, includes intra-FSU trade.

[3]/ Includes South Africa.

The projections w ere completed in November 2010.

Table 15. Beef Trade Long-Term Projections

	2009	2010	2011	2012	2013	2014	2015	2016	2017	2018	2019	2020
				Imports, thousand metric tons, carcass weight								
Importers												
Japan	697	695	704	679	662	673	675	682	691	707	713	724
South Korea	315	345	350	360	370	375	380	388	391	394	397	400
Taiwan	112	135	140	141	142	144	146	147	148	148	149	149
Philippines	123	150	160	166	171	180	187	192	197	201	209	215
European Union[1]	497	490	490	488	485	483	480	478	476	473	471	468
Russia	895	940	950	955	924	881	875	877	887	904	918	929
Other Europe	63	65	69	68	69	70	71	71	72	72	73	73
Egypt	180	190	210	217	221	226	229	231	233	235	238	240
Other N. Africa & M. East	690	846	878	874	898	922	948	973	996	1,016	1,036	1,057
Mexico	322	335	330	357	403	439	462	476	491	499	512	533
Canada	247	235	245	247	249	251	253	255	257	259	261	263
United States	1,191	1,119	1,152	1,252	1,270	1,300	1,329	1,359	1,388	1,417	1,447	1,476
Major importers	5,332	5,545	5,678	5,803	5,863	5,942	6,034	6,127	6,226	6,325	6,423	6,528
Exporters				**Exports, thousand metric tons, carcass weight**								
Australia	1,364	1,325	1,325	1,329	1,323	1,330	1,336	1,343	1,350	1,357	1,362	1,369
New Zealand	514	510	496	500	499	505	511	514	516	520	523	527
Other Asia	666	762	784	800	810	819	840	857	883	901	920	938
European Union[1]	148	160	160	159	161	160	156	158	161	163	166	166
Argentina	655	300	300	233	208	207	234	266	302	350	404	460
Brazil	1,596	1,675	1,810	1,846	1,903	1,934	1,960	1,986	2,013	2,038	2,064	2,090
Canada	480	525	530	512	499	508	524	535	542	547	548	553
United States	878	1,049	1,030	1,089	1,181	1,231	1,263	1,287	1,312	1,338	1,364	1,392
Major exporters	6,301	6,306	6,435	6,467	6,583	6,695	6,824	6,946	7,079	7,213	7,352	7,494

[1]/ Covers EU-27, excludes intra-EU trade.

The projections were completed in November 2010.

Table 16. Pork Trade Long-Term Projections

	2009	2010	2011	2012	2013	2014	2015	2016	2017	2018	2019	2020
				Imports, thousand metric tons, carcass weight								
Importers												
Japan	1,138	1,150	1,157	1,182	1,189	1,190	1,189	1,185	1,186	1,189	1,190	1,190
China	270	350	370	373	387	397	407	418	434	443	452	457
Hong Kong	369	370	380	392	398	405	414	422	430	439	447	456
South Korea	390	380	410	412	427	438	451	463	477	493	505	520
Russia	845	850	850	848	847	837	803	756	709	652	588	516
Mexico	678	685	690	724	772	803	837	881	919	960	1,002	1,047
Canada	180	200	230	232	234	235	236	237	238	238	238	238
United States	378	394	406	413	422	433	445	456	467	479	490	501
Major importers	4,248	4,379	4,493	4,574	4,675	4,738	4,781	4,817	4,860	4,894	4,911	4,924
Exporters				Exports, thousand metric tons, carcass weight								
Brazil	707	625	631	639	663	667	669	676	684	693	702	710
Canada	1,123	1,165	1,167	1,112	1,136	1,158	1,171	1,186	1,199	1,208	1,213	1,211
Mexico	70	80	85	86	87	88	90	91	91	92	93	94
European Union1	1,415	1,700	1,550	1,563	1,584	1,594	1,598	1,583	1,583	1,569	1,555	1,535
China	232	250	280	309	329	342	355	370	380	392	405	419
United States	1,857	1,981	2,121	2,170	2,215	2,268	2,325	2,370	2,409	2,448	2,488	2,530
Major exporters	5,404	5,801	5,834	5,880	6,014	6,118	6,207	6,275	6,346	6,402	6,455	6,499

[1]/ Covers EU-27, excludes intra-EU trade.

The projections w ere completed in November 2010.

Table 17. Poultry Trade Long-Term Projections[1]

	2009	2010	2011	2012	2013	2014	2015	2016	2017	2018	2019	2020
				Imports, thousand metric tons, ready to cook								
Importers												
Russia	954	500	610	543	300	200	187	176	166	157	149	143
European Union[2]	831	795	825	833	842	850	859	867	876	885	893	902
Other Europe	29	25	26	26	26	26	26	26	25	25	25	25
Canada	138	133	138	140	141	143	145	147	148	150	152	154
Mexico	636	670	700	740	785	810	845	880	915	960	1,005	1,050

	2009	2010	2011	2012	2013	2014	2015	2016	2017	2018	2019	2020
				Imports, thousand metric tons, ready to cook								
Central America/Caribbean	289	308	320	340	365	390	405	420	435	455	475	498
Japan	645	745	760	735	742	746	743	747	747	746	745	743
Importers												
Hong Kong	253	280	325	344	357	366	375	385	390	396	401	407
China	428	351	325	305	308	316	323	333	344	352	363	376
South Korea	71	90	90	88	88	90	90	92	94	97	101	104
Saudi Arabia	604	630	680	701	727	751	771	792	810	830	847	866
Other N. Africa & M. East	1,234	1,198	1,266	1,277	1,329	1,383	1,437	1,483	1,536	1,586	1,640	1,692
Sub-Saharan Africa	703	780	782	798	814	831	848	865	883	901	920	939
Major importers	6,815	6,505	6,847	6,869	6,824	6,902	7,053	7,211	7,370	7,539	7,716	7,897
Exporters				**Exports, thousand metric tons, ready to cook**								
European Union[2]	889	950	945	925	931	935	935	927	922	917	914	908
Brazi l	3,386	3,514	3,567	3,570	3,431	3,454	3,539	3,621	3,742	3,862	3,998	4,116
China	291	380	410	476	480	482	495	497	503	506	512	516
Thailand	379	410	440	484	497	503	512	525	541	555	567	579
United States	3,335	3,182	3,265	3,087	3,139	3,176	3,225	3,263	3,285	3,309	3,344	3,387
Major exporters	8,280	8,436	8,627	8,541	8,478	8,549	8,706	8,833	8,993	9,150	9,335	9,506

[1]/ Broilers and turkeys only.

[2]/ Covers EU-27, excludes intra-EU trade.

The projections w ere completed in November 2010.

Nonetheless, the large expansion in recent years keeps corn use for ethanol high. In combination, these factors support longer run increases in global consumption and trade. Prices fall from current high levels, but remain at historically high levels for many crops.

Projections for field crops reflect provisions of the Food, Conservation, and Energy Act of 2008 (2008 Farm Act), which are assumed to continue through the projection period. Acreage enrolled in the Conservation Reserve Program (CRP) has fallen from more than 36 million acres to about 31.4 million acres and is projected to remain close to 32 million acres throughout the projections. This reduction in CRP acreage provides some additional cropland for potential use in production.

The 45-cents-per-gallon tax credit available to blenders of ethanol and the 54-cents-per-gallon tariff on imported fuel ethanol are assumed to remain in effect through the end of the projection period. The tax credit for blending biodiesel that had expired at the end of 2009 was not assumed to be available because its reinstatement occurred after the projections were completed.

Current high prices lead to an increase in planted cropland in 2011, reaching 255 million acres for the 8 major field crops, up from 245 million in 2010 and above the recent high of 253 million in 2008. Although prices and plantings decline over the next several years, strong demand continues to keep prices historically high, providing economic incentives to hold projected plantings at 249- 250 million acres over the remainder of the projection period.

Continuing high levels of domestic corn-based ethanol production and gains in exports keep corn demand high. Strong producer returns keep corn acreage in a range of 90 to 92 million acres over the projection period compared to 88 million in 2010. Acreage changes for other feed grains are minimal.

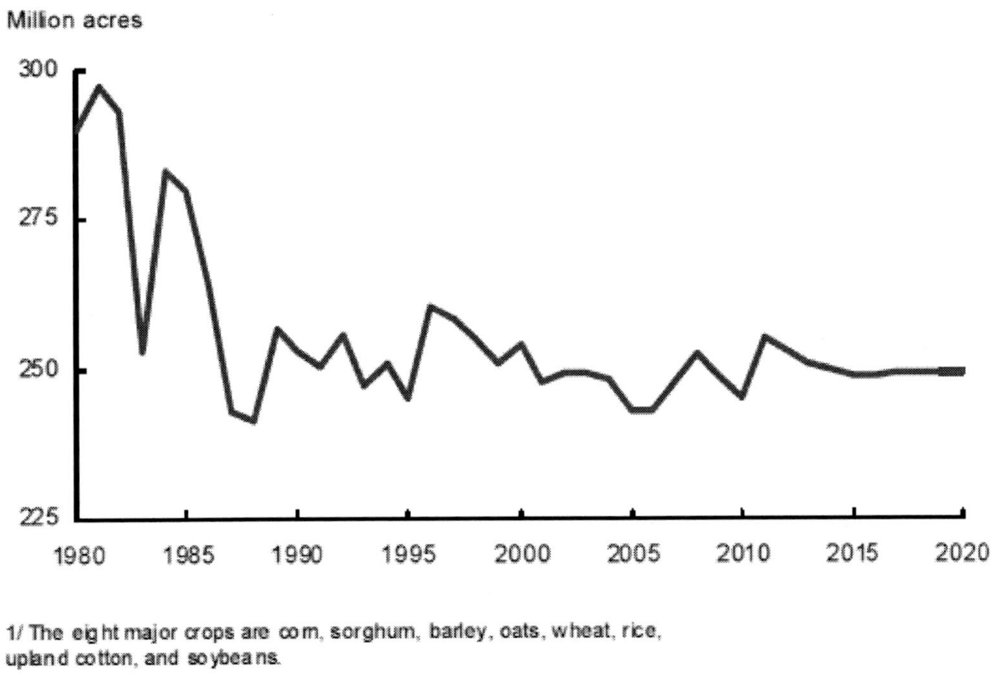

U.S. Planted Area: Eight Major Crops 1/.

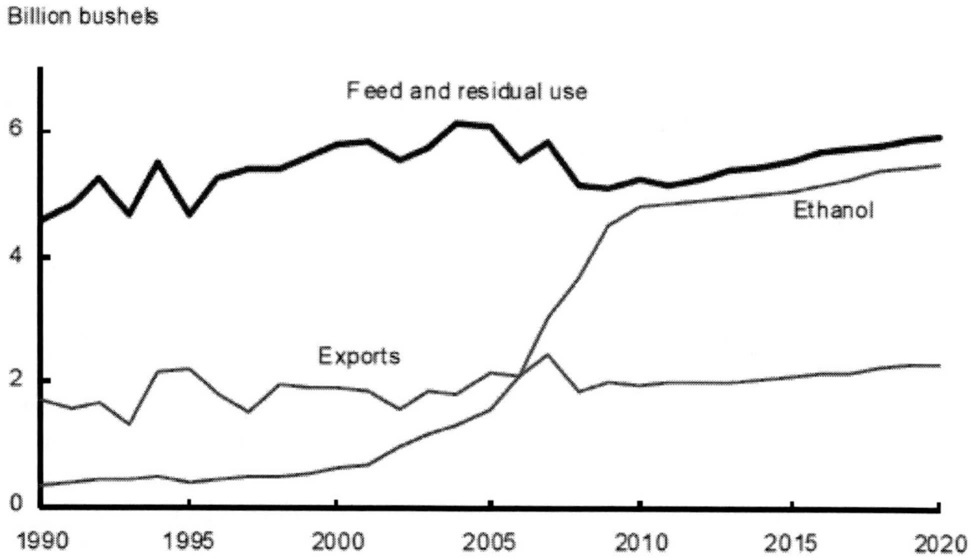

U.S. Corn: Feed and Residual Use, Ethanol, and Exports.

- Most ethanol production in the United States currently uses corn as the feedstock, with about 36 percent of total corn use expected to go to ethanol production over the projection period. Even with the U.S. Environmental Protection Agency's (EPA's) October 2010 announced approval for use of E15 in model year 2007 and newer passenger vehicles (including cars, sport utility vehicles, and light pickup trucks), smaller gains for corn-based ethanol are projected over the next 10 years than have occurred in recent years. This result reflects only moderate growth in overall gasoline consumption in the United States, limited potential for further market penetration of ethanol into the E10 (10-percent ethanol blend) market, constraints in the E15 market, and the small size of the E85 (85-percent ethanol blend) market. By the end of the projection period, corn-based ethanol production represents more than 10 percent of annual gasoline consumption.
- Feed and residual use of corn bottoms out in the initial years due to reduced meat production and increased feeding of distillers grains, a coproduct of dry mill ethanol production. Feed use rises through the rest of the projections as meat production picks up and growth in the availability of distillers grains slows with the reduced pace of corn-based ethanol expansion.
- Food and industrial use of corn (other than for ethanol production) is projected to rise over the next decade. Use of corn for high fructose corn syrup, glucose, and dextrose increases at less than half the rate of population gain, limited by consumer dietary concerns and other changes in tastes and preferences. Other food uses of corn are also projected to rise more slowly than the increase in population. Starch use of corn responds to industrial demand, rebounding as the U.S. economy recovers and rising faster than population throughout the projection period.
- U.S. corn exports rise in response to stronger global demand for feed grains to support growth in meat production. Although lower than has been typical in the past, the U.S. share of global corn trade remains above 50 percent in the projections.

Strong wheat prices and expected net returns boost wheat plantings for 2011. However, with relatively weak overall demand growth for wheat and continuing large stocks, producer returns fall in subsequent years, leading to a decline in wheat plantings to about 51 million acres by the end of the projection period.

- Domestic demand for wheat reflects a relatively mature market. Food use of wheat is projected to show moderate gains, generally in line with U.S. population increases.
- Feed use of wheat, a lower value market for the crop, increases moderately into 2011/12 reflecting favorable prices relative to corn in the summer. For later years, wheat feed use levels off at 175 million bushels per year as prices relative to corn allow some competition of feed wheat with feed grains.
- U.S. wheat exports are boosted in the near term due to relatively tight market conditions following the 2010 production shortfall in Russia and other countries of the former Soviet Union. In the longer run, U.S. wheat exports fall back to 900 million bushels annually and remain flat over the projection period. U.S. wheat trade is limited in early years by large exports from India to reduce their high stocks and later by renewed competition primarily from the Black Sea region. Notably, India's wheat exports reach as high as 3 million metric tons (a 2.2-percent share of global wheat trade) in 2013/14 before dropping off to negligible levels toward the end of the projections. Russia's wheat exports rebound from the drought-reduced low levels of 2010/11, rising to account for 15 percent of global trade by the end of the decade. The EU market share declines from 17 percent in 2010/11 to 14 percent in 2020/21. For the same time period, the U.S. market share declines from 27 percent to 16 percent.

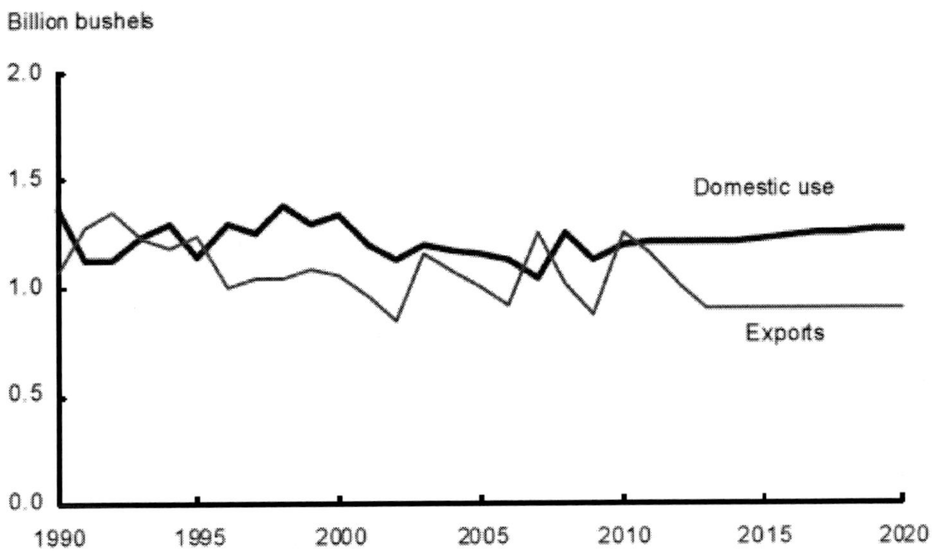

U.S. Wheat: Domestic Use and Exports.

U.S. soybean plantings rise over the projection period as growth in both domestic and export demand keep prices and producer returns favorable.

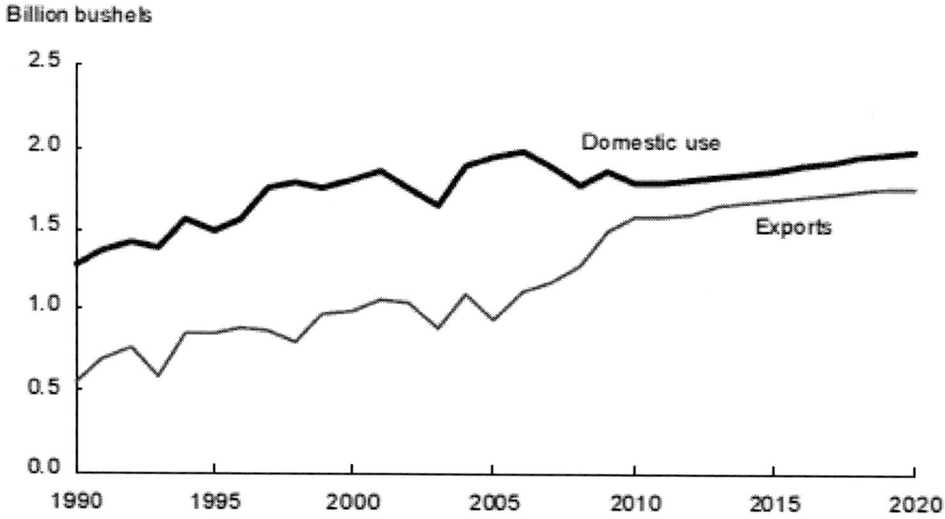

U.S. Soybeans: DomesticUse and Exports.

- Reductions in U.S. livestock production and increased availability of distillers grains have lowered demand for soybean meal for livestock feed in recent years, thereby reducing domestic soybean crush. However, as meat production gains resume, soybean crush will follow.
- Strong global demand for soybeans, particularly in China, supports increases in U.S. soybean exports. Despite rapid import growth, continued competition from South America, particularly Brazil, leads to a reduction in the U.S. share of global soybean trade from 44 percent in 2009/10 to about 37 percent toward the end of the projection period.
- Strengthening competition from Argentina and Brazil, combined with increasing use for the growing U.S. livestock sector, limit U.S. soybean meal exports in the projections. The U.S. export share in global soybean meal trade would decline from 14 percent in 2010/11 to below 12 percent by 2020/21. U.S. soybean oil exports similarly face increasing competition from South America. Argentina, in particular, is a competitive exporter of soybean oil because its graduated export taxes favor exports of soybean products over soybeans.
- Soybean oil used to produce methyl esters (biodiesel) grows to 3.6 billion pounds by the end of the projection period, representing about 17 percent of total use of soybean oil and supporting the production of close to 500 million gallons of biodiesel. Although some other first-use vegetable oils are also used to produce biodiesel, most of the remaining biodiesel production needed to reach the 1-billion-gallon use mandate of the 2007 Energy Act uses animal fats or recycled vegetable oil as the feedstock. Exports of biodiesel will continue to be constrained by the EU's anti-dumping and countervailing duties on U.S. shipments.

A number of short-term factors have led to high prices for grains and oilseeds in 2010/11, including reduced global wheat production (especially in Russia), a decline in U.S. corn yields, and strong global demand for soybeans.

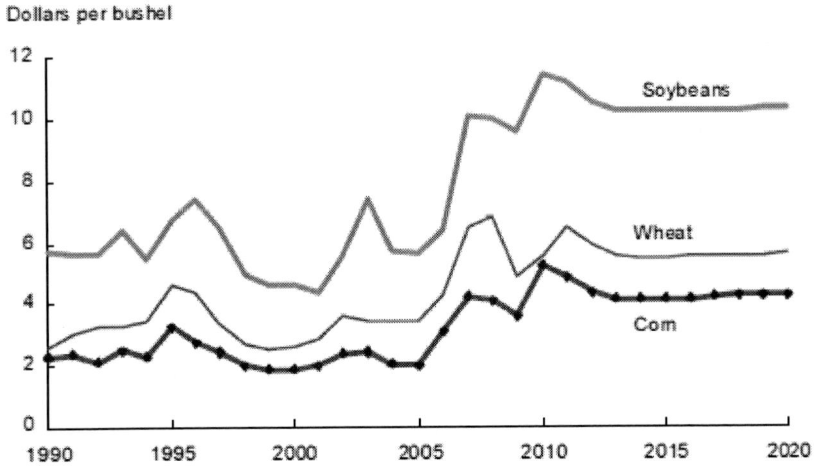

U.S. Farm-Level Prices: Corn, Wheat, and Soybeans.

Although market responses to these prices arc projected to reduce prices over the next several years, U.S. prices for corn, wheat, and soybeans are projected to remain historically high. The continuing influence of several factors, including global economic growth, a depreciating dollar, escalating costs for crude petroleum, and rising biofuel production, underlie these crop price projections over the long term.

- Although corn prices fall from their current high levels, they are projected to remain historically high due to continued demand for corn for ethanol production as well as growth in feed use and exports.
- Strengthening demand for soybeans and soybean products holds soybean prices high throughout the projections.
- Wheat prices decline from 2011/12 to 2015/16 and then are projected to rise moderately over the rest of the decade. Despite gains in wheat yields, declining acreage and increasing demand gradually reduce stocks.

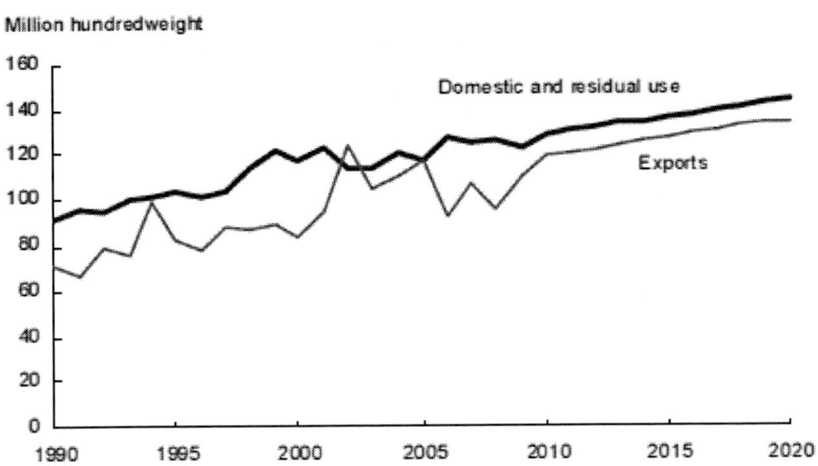

U.S. Rice: Domestic and Residual Use and Exports.

U.S. planted area to rice is projected to fall over the next couple of years from 2010's near-record in response to declining expected producer returns and increased competition for land from other crops. Plantings then increase marginally after 2012 as producer returns improve. Continued expansion in U.S. food use of rice is projected over the next decade. U.S. rice exports increase as well, but somewhat slower than overall growth in global rice trade.

- Domestic use of rice is projected to grow slightly faster than population growth. Imports of aromatic varieties of rice from Asia account for a growing share of domestic use in the projections.
- U.S. rice exports are projected to increase, reflecting a lower U.S. price difference over Asian competitors' price than in recent years. Nonetheless, export growth falls short of the pace of overall rice trade gains, so the U.S. market share declines. Rough rice exports to Latin America are expected to continue increasing, and account for most of the U.S. export expansion.
- Stocks of rice fall from initially large levels, reducing the stocks-to-use ratio to a more sustainable level of about 13 percent by the end of the projection period.
- Global rice prices have fallen from the highs of 2008/09 and are expected to continue dropping through 2013/14. Global prices then increase about 2 percent per year, reaching nearly $12 per hundredweight (rough basis) at the end of the projection period. These price increases largely reflect tightening global stocks of rice, which is due to slow yield growth and limited ability to expand area in most producing countries. This effect is partially offset by declining global per capita disappearance of rice, caused largely by dietary shifts away from staple foods in Asia as incomes rise.
- U.S. rice prices follow a pattern similar to global prices, continuing their fall from the record high in 2008/09 for the next couple of years, before rising in the latter years of the projections. By the end of the projection period, U.S. rice prices are approaching $14 per hundredweight.

High cotton prices lead to a large increase in cotton plantings in 2011, but plantings subsequently decline moderately as lower prices reduce returns. U.S. mill use of upland cotton continues to decline throughout the projections while cotton exports rise.

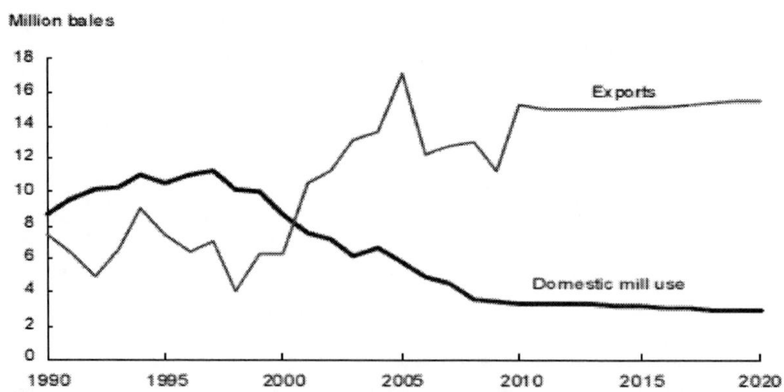

U.S. Upland Cotton: Domestic Mill Use and Exports.

- The decline in mill use of cotton is projected to continue over the next decade. At the end of the projection period, domestic mill use is projected to represent less than 16 percent of total use. Underlying this projection is an increase in apparel imports by the United States over the next 10 years, reducing domestic apparel production and lowering the apparel industry's demand for fabric and yarn produced in the United States.
- U.S. upland cotton exports rebounded in 2010/11 in response to strong global trade demand and facilitated by increased U.S. cotton plantings and production, boosting the U.S. trade share to over 40 percent. After falling back slightly during the first half of the projection period, continued strong global demand leads to moderate gains in U.S. cotton exports through the rest of the decade. Nonetheless, export gains are slower than global trade increases, so the U.S. share of world cotton trade falls to about 34 percent by 2020/21.

The two primary determinants of U.S. sugar supply and use over the long-term projection period are the implementation of the sugar and energy provisions of the 2008 Farm Act and reliance on sugar imports from Mexico to maintain balance in the U.S. sugar market. The projections assume that sugar tariff-rate quotas are not increased above initial levels and that U.S. policymakers aim for an ending year stocks-touse ratio of 13.5 percent. Mexico is assumed to export sugar to the United States to meet this level.

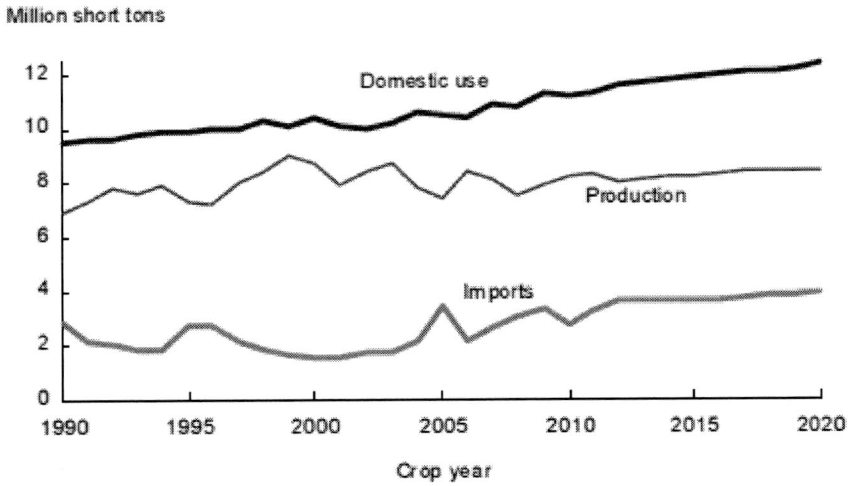

U.S. Sugar: Domestic Production, Use, and Imports.

- Sugar provisions of the North American Free Trade Agreement (NAFTA) removed all duties and quantitative restrictions on sweetener trade between Mexico and the United States as of January 1, 2008. Mexican exportable sugar supplies are expected to rise as a result of increased use of high fructose corn syrup (mostly imported from the United States) that displaces sugar in beverage and food manufacturing end uses in Mexico. As a consequence, Mexico's sugar exports to the higher-priced U.S. market grow over the decade and represent more than 15 percent of U.S. supplies at the end of the projection period, up from about 8 percent in 2010/11. The projections assume that Mexico will import sugar from the lower-priced world market when necessary to assure sufficient supplies to meet their domestic consumption requirements.

- Projected growth in U.S. beet and cane sugar production is low over the next decade. Beet sugar production averages 4.715 million short tons, raw value (STRV) over 2011/12 to 2020/21 and cane sugar production averages 3.567 million STRV. As a result, sugar production averages only 72 percent of domestic consumption, far below the 85-percent minimum allotment level.
- Deliveries of sugar for human use rebound in 2012/13 from the small changes in the prior 2 years. Gains over the remainder of the projections average 0.8 percent per year, slightly less than population growth.
- There are no sugar loan forfeitures in the projections nor any CCC purchases of sugar for ethanol for use in the Feedstock Flexibility Program. With an annual stocks-to-use ratio of 13.5 percent, raw cane and refined beet sugar prices are above the minimum prices to avoid forfeiture for the entire projection period. Sugar refining capacity is sufficient to keep refined sugar prices from rising. The long term equilibrium world raw sugar price is assumed to equal 16 cents per pound—historically high, but not high enough to exert upward pressure on U.S. raw and refined sugar prices.

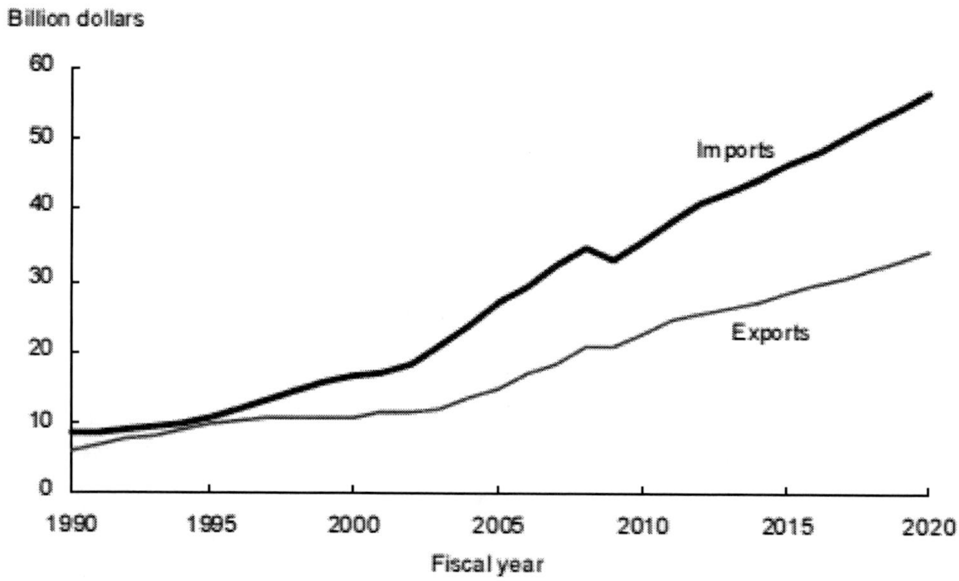

Value of U.S. Horticultural Trade.

Farm sales of horticultural crops are projected to grow by 1.5 percent annually over the next decade, reaching $67.4 billion in calendar year 2020, up from $58 billion in 2010.

- Vegetables and melons, which rank first in farm sales value at 38 percent of the total, are projected to grow at 1.7 percent annually. Fruits and tree nuts are expected to increase slightly faster at 1.8 percent per year, while greenhouse and nursery crops grow at 0.8 percent.

- The volume of farm production of horticultural crops is forecast to rise by 0.7 percent annually. Vegetables and melons lead production growth at 0.8 percent, reaching 150 billion pounds in 2020. Fruit and nut production expands by 0.6 percent per year to 66 billion pounds in 2020.
- Producer prices for vegetables are expected to rise at 0.9 percent per year. Producer prices for fruits rise by 1.3 percent per year due to somewhat slower production growth than vegetables.
- U.S. per capita use of fruits and tree nuts is forecast to increase from 267 pounds in 2010 to 279 pounds by 2020, an annual change of 0.4 percent. Per capita use of vegetables is anticipated to grow from 425 pounds in 2010 to 436 in 2020, up an average of 0.3 percent per year. The total supply of fruits and vegetables over the next decade, both domestic and imported, is projected to grow at an average rate of 1.2 percent per year.
- U.S. horticultural import value is projected to increase by 4.8 percent annually over the next decade after increasing by 8 percent on average in the past decade. Imports of fresh fruits and vegetables will largely drive this growth. The import value of vegetables is expected to expand faster than for fruits and nuts due to relatively greater import demand for vegetables.
- The U.S. trade deficit in horticultural crops and products expands from $13 billion in fiscal year 2010 to $22.6 billion in 2020. Of the $34 billion total U.S. exports of horticultural products in 2020, fruits and nuts contribute $15.9 billion and vegetables account for $7.1 billion. Total imports of about $56.9 billion in 2020 include $18.3 billion worth of fruits and nuts, and $14.6 billion of fresh and processed vegetables.
- Imports increasingly supplement the domestic supply of horticultural crops and products. In terms of farm weight, imports of fruits and nuts will account for 45 percent of domestic use by 2020, up from 42 percent in 2010. Imported vegetables are projected to represent 24 percent of domestic use in 2020, an increase from 20 percent in 2010.
- The export market also becomes increasingly important for U.S. horticulture products, although relative gains are smaller than for imports. Exports represent more than a quarter of fruits and nuts production in 2020 while about 16 percent of vegetable production will be sold abroad, each up about 1 percentage point from 2010.

U.S. LIVESTOCK

During the first several years of the projections, the livestock sector responds to high grain and soybean meal prices in 2011—with producer returns squeezed, production incentives are reduced, leading to declines in total U.S. red meat and poultry production in 2012 and only moderate increases in 2011 and 2013. Combined with strengthening exports, the result is declining domestic per capita consumption of red meat and poultry through 2013. As a consequence, prices in the sector rise, which improves net returns and provides economic incentives for expansion in the sector later in the projection period.

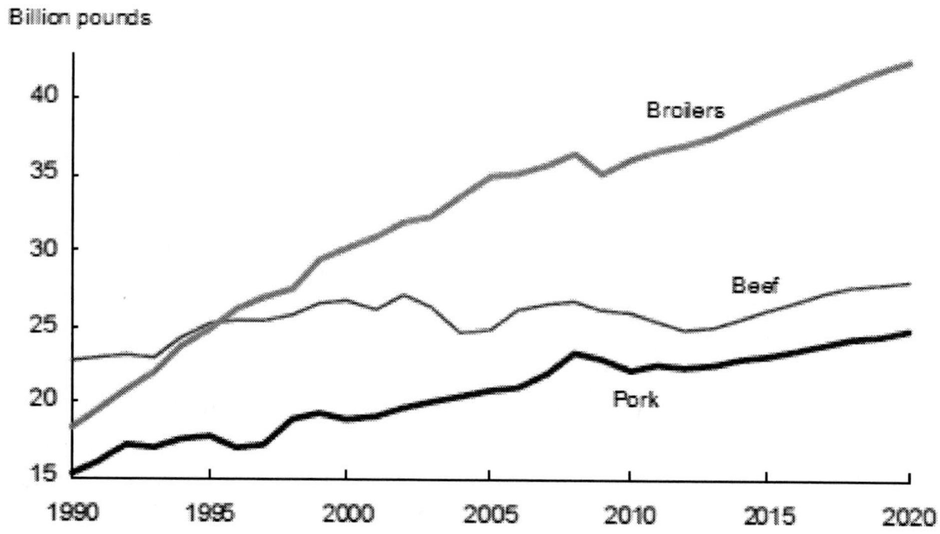

U.S. Red Meat and Poultry Production.

- Despite improved returns for cow-calf operators in 2010, strong demand for feeder cattle and cows for slaughter have limited producer interest in expanding beef cow inventories after several years of declines. Thus, reduced inventories and expected heifer retention during 2011 are expected to lead to reduced beef production through 2012. Beef production then rises in the remainder of the projection period as strengthening returns support herd rebuilding. Beef cow numbers rise from about 31 million head at the beginning of 2011 to over 34 million by 2020. The total cattle inventory drops below 92 million head before expanding to about 96.7 million at the end of the projection period. Rising slaughter weights also contribute to the longer term expansion of beef production. Although feed prices decline from current levels, continued historically-high feed costs result in stocker cattle remaining on pasture to heavier weights before entering feedlots.
- Pork production falls in 2012 in response to reduced returns in 2011, but as the projection period progresses, producers are expected to increase farrowings as higher hog prices and lower feed prices improve returns. Pork production increases will also be supported by gains in breeding herd productivity and increased slaughter weights albeit at slower rates of gain than in the past several years.
- Poultry production is projected to rise the most among the meats over the next decade, as poultry is the most efficient feed-to-meat converter. However growth in the sector will be slower than occurred in the 1980s and 1990s. Poultry prices are expected to improve with increased demand, although poultry will face competition from increased supplies of red meats. Additionally, despite declining from recent highs, feed prices are projected to remain relatively high. Poultry production growth is expected to come from both higher bird numbers and higher average weights. Both broiler production and turkey production expand over the projection period, with broilers increasing at a slightly faster rate.

Table 18. Acreage for Major Field Crops and Conservation Reserve Program (CRP) Assumptions, Long-Term Projections

	2009	2010	2011	2012	2013	2014	2015	2016	2017	2018	2019	2020
						Million acres						
Planted acreage, eight major crops												
Corn	86.5	88.2	92.0	91.5	91.0	90.5	90.5	90.5	91.0	91.5	92.0	92.0
Sorghum	6.6	5.4	6.0	6.0	6.0	6.0	6.0	6.0	6.0	6.0	6.0	6.0
Barley	3.6	2.9	3.2	3.2	3.2	3.2	3.2	3.2	3.2	3.2	3.2	3.2
Oats	3.4	3.1	3.0	3.0	3.0	3.0	3.0	3.0	3.0	3.0	3.0	3.0
Wheat	59.2	53.6	57.0	55.5	54.0	53.0	52.0	51.5	51.5	51.5	51.0	51.0
Rice	3.1	3.6	3.3	3.2	3.2	3.2	3.3	3.3	3.3	3.3	3.3	3.3
Upland cotton	9.0	10.8	12.8	12.5	12.2	12.0	11.9	11.8	11.8	11.7	11.7	11.6
Soybeans	77.5	77.7	78.0	78.3	78.5	79.0	79.0	79.5	79.5	79.5	79.5	79.5
Total	248.9	245.3	255.3	253.2	251.1	249.9	248.9	248.8	249.3	249.7	249.7	249.6
CRP acreage assumptions												
Total CRP	33.7	31.4	31.9	31.9	31.9	31.9	31.9	32.0	31.9	31.9	31.9	31.9
Total planted plus CRP	282.6	276.7	287.2	285.0	283.0	281.9	280.8	280.8	281.2	281.6	281.6	281.5
Harvested acreage, eight major crops												
Corn	79.6	81.3	84.9	84.4	83.9	83.4	83.4	83.4	83.9	84.4	84.9	84.9
Sorghum	5.5	4.7	5.2	5.2	5.2	5.2	5.2	5.2	5.2	5.2	5.2	5.2
Barley	3.1	2.5	2.8	2.8	2.8	2.8	2.8	2.8	2.8	2.8	2.8	2.8
Oats	1.4	1.3	1.2	1.2	1.2	1.2	1.2	1.2	1.2	1.2	1.2	1.2
Wheat	49.9	47.6	48.5	47.2	45.9	45.1	44.2	43. 8	43.8	43.8	43.4	43.4
Rice	3.1	3.6	3.3	3.2	3.2	3.2	3.3	3.3	3.3	3.3	3.3	3.3
Upland cotton	7.4	10.6	11.3	11.1	10.9	10.7	10.5	10.5	10.5	10.4	10.4	10.3
Soybeans	76.4	76.8	77.1	77.3	77.6	78.1	78.1	78.5	78.5	78.5	78.5	78.5
Total	226.4	228.4	234.3	232.4	230.7	229.7	228.7	228.7	229.2	229.6	229.7	229.6

Table 19. U.S. Corn Long-Term Projections

Item	2009/10	2010/11	2011/12	2012/13	2013/14	2014/15	2015/16	2016/17	2017/18	2018/19	2019/20	2020/21
Area (million acres):												
Planted acres	86.5	88.2	92.0	91.5	91.0	90.5	90.5	90.5	91.0	91.5	92.0	92.08
Harvested acres	79.6	81.3	84.9	84.4	83.9	83.4	83.4	83.4	83.9	84.4	84.9	4.9
Yields (bushels per acre):												
Yield/harvested acre	164.7	154.3	162.0	164.0	166.0	168.0	170.0	172.0	174.0	176.0	178.0	180.0
Supply and use (million bushels):												
Beginning stocks	1,673	1,708	827	1,127	1,332	1,437	1,447	1,442	1,342	1,262	1,227	1,242
Production	13,110	12,540	13,755	13,840	13,925	14,010	14,180	14,345	14,600	14,855	15,110	15,280
Imports	8	10	10	10	10	10	10	10	10	10	10	10
Supply	14,792	14,257	14,592	14,977	15,267	15,457	15,637	15,797	15,952	16,127	16,347	16,532
Feed & residual	5,159	5,300	5,200	5,300	5,400	5,500	5,600	5,700	5,750	5,800	5,875	5,950
Food, seed, & industrial	5,938	6,180	6,265	6,320	6,380	6,435	6,495	6,605	6,740	6,850	6,930	6,990
Ethanol for fuel	4,568	4,800	4,875	4,925	4,975	5,025	5,075	5,175	5,300	5,400	5,475	5,525
Domestic use	11,097	11,480	11,465	11,620	11,780	11,935	12,095	12,305	12,490	12,650	12,805	12,940
Exports	1,987	1,950	2,000	2,025	2,050	2,075	2,100	2,150	2,200	2,250	2,300	2,350
Total use	13,084	13,430	13,465	13,645	13,830	14,010	14,195	14,455	14,690	14,900	15,105	15,290
Ending stocks	1,708	827	1,127	1,332	1,437	1,447	1,442	1,342	1,262	1,227	1,242	1,242
Stocks/use ratio, percent	13.1	6.2	8.4	9.8	10.4	10.3	10.2	9.3	8.6	8.2	8.2	8.1
Price (dollars per bushel):												
Farm price	3.55	5.20	4.80	4.30	4.10	4.10	4.10	4.15	4.20	4.25	4.25	4.25
Variable costs of production (dollars):												
Per acre	299	287	304	310	314	318	323	329	335	341	347	353
Per bushel	1.82	1.86	1.87	1.89	1.89	1.90	1.90	1.91	1.93	1.94	1.95	1.96
Returns over variable costs (dollars per acre):												
Net returns	286	515	474	395	367	370	374	384	396	407	410	412

Note: Marketing year beginning September 1 for corn.

Table 20. U.S. Sorghum Long-Term Projections

Item	2009/10	2010/11	2011/12	2012/13	2013/14	2014/15	2015/16	2016/17	2017/18	2018/19	2019/20	2020/21
Area (million acres):												
Planted acres	6.6	5.4	6.0	6.0	6.0	6.0	6.0	6.0	6.0	6.0	6.0	6.0
Harvested acres	5.5	4.7	5.2	5.2	5.2	5.2	5.2	5.2	5.2	5.2	5.2	5.2
Yields (bushels per acre):												
Yield/harvested acre	69.4	72.5	65.3	65.3	65.3	65.3	65.3	65.3	65.3	65.3	65.3	65.3
Supply and use (million bushels):												
Beginning stocks	55	41	39	44	44	44	44	44	44	44	44	44
Production	383	338	340	340	340	340	340	340	340	340	340	340
Imports	0	0	0	0	0	0	0	0	0	0	0	0
Supply	438	379	379	384	384	384	384	384	384	384	384	384
Feed & residual	140	90	80	80	75	70	65	60	55	50	45	40
Food, seed, & industrial	90	90	90	90	90	90	90	90	90	90	90	90
Domestic use	230	180	170	170	165	160	155	150	145	140	135	130
Exports	166	160	165	170	175	180	185	190	195	200	205	210
Total use	396	340	335	340	340	340	340	340	340	340	340	340
Ending stocks	41	39	44	44	44	44	44	44	44	44	44	44
Stocks/use ratio, percent	10.4	11.5	13.1	12.9	12.9	12.9	12.9	12.9	12.9	12.9	12.9	12.9
Price (dollars per bushel):												
Farm price	3.22	5.30	4.35	3.95	3.80	3.80	3.80	3.85	3.90	3.95	3.95	3.95
Variable costs of production (dollars):												
Per acre	146	149	157	161	164	166	169	172	175	178	181	185
Per bushel	2.10	2.06	2.41	2.47	2.51	2.55	2.59	2.64	2.68	2.73	2.78	2.83
Returns over variable costs (dollars per acre):												
Net returns	78	235	127	97	84	82	79	79	80	80	77	73

Note: Marketing year beginning September 1 for sorghum.

Table 21. U.S. Barley Long-Term Projections

Item	2009/10	2010/11	2011/12	2012/13	2013/14	2014/15	2015/16	2016/17	2017/18	2018/19	2019/20	2020/21
Area (million acres):												
Planted acres	3.6	2.9	3.2	3.2	3.2	3.2	3.2	3.2	3.2	3.2	3.2	3.2
Harvested acres	3.1	2.5	2.8	2.8	2.8	2.8	2.8	2.8	2.8	2.8	2.8	2.8
Yields (bushels per acre):												
Yield/harvested acre	73.0	73.1	67.4	68.0	68.6	69.2	69.7	70.3	70.9	71.5	72.1	72.7
Supply and use (million bushels):												
Beginning stocks	89	115	86	80	80	82	81	81	82	80	79	80
Production	227	180	189	190	192	194	195	197	199	200	202	204
Imports	17	15	20	20	20	20	20	20	20	20	20	20
Supply	333	311	295	290	292	296	296	298	301	300	301	304
Feed & residual	48	50	40	35	35	40	40	40	45	45	45	45
Food, seed, & industrial	164	165	165	165	165	165	165	166	166	166	166	166
Domestic	212	215	205	200	200	205	205	206	211	211	211	211
Exports	6	10	10	10	10	10	10	10	10	10	10	10
Total use	217	225	215	210	210	215	215	216	221	221	221	221
Ending stocks	115	86	80	80	82	81	81	82	80	79	80	83
Stocks/use ratio, percent	53.0	38.2	37.2	38.1	39.0	37.7	37.7	38.0	36.2	35.7	36.2	37.6
Price (dollars per bushel):												
Farm price	4.66	4.00	4.70	4.95	4.75	4.70	4.75	4.80	4.85	4.90	4.90	4.90
Variable costs of production (dollars):												
Per acre	143	141	149	152	155	157	160	163	166	169	172	175
Per bushel	1.96	1.93	2.21	2.24	2.25	2.27	2.29	2.32	2.34	2.36	2.39	2.41
Returns over variable costs (dollars per acre):												
Net returns	197	151	168	184	171	168	171	175	178	181	181	181

Note: Marketing year beginning June 1 for barley.

Table 22. U.S. Oats Long-Term Projections

Item	2009/10	2010/11	2011/12	2012/13	2013/14	2014/15	2015/16	2016/17	2017/18	2018/19	2019/20	2020/21
Area (million acres):												
Planted acres	3.4	3.1	3.0	3.0	3.0	3.0	3.0	3.0	3.0	3.0	3.0	3.0
Harvested acres	1.4	1.3	1.2	1.2	1.2	1.2	1.2	1.2	1.2	1.2	1.2	1.2
Yields (bushels per acre):												
Yield/harvested acre	67.5	64.3	65.0	65.4	65.8	66.2	66.6	67.0	67.5	67.9	68.3	68.7
Supply and use (million bushels):												
Beginning stocks	84	80	48	47	46	45	44	44	43	43	43	43
Production	93	81	78	78	79	79	80	80	81	81	82	82
Imports	95	80	110	105	100	100	100	100	100	100	100	100
Supply	272	242	236	230	225	224	224	224	224	224	225	225
Feed & residual	115	115	110	105	100	100	100	100	100	100	100	100
Food, seed, & industrial	75	76	76	76	77	77	77	78	78	78	79	79
Domestic	190	191	186	181	177	177	177	178	178	178	179	179
Exports	2	3	3	3	3	3	3	3	3	3	3	3
Total use	192	194	189	184	180	180	180	181	181	181	182	182
Ending stocks	80	48	47	46	45	44	44	43	43	43	43	43
Stocks/use ratio, percent	41.7	24.7	24.9	25.0	25.0	24.4	24.4	23.8	23.8	23.8	23.6	23.6
Price (dollars per bushel):												
Farm price	2.02	2.35	2.75	2.55	2.50	2.50	2.50	2.50	2.55	2.55	2.55	2.55
Variable costs of production (dollars):												
Per acre	102	101	107	109	111	112	114	117	119	121	124	126
Per bushel	1.52	1.57	1.64	1.66	1.68	1.70	1.72	1.74	1.76	1.79	1.81	1.84
Returns over variable costs (dollars per acre):												
Net returns	34	50	72	58	54	53	52	51	53	52	50	4

Note: Marketing year beginning June 1 for oats.

Table 23. U.S. Wheat Long-Term Projections

Item	2009/10	2010/11	2011/12	2012/13	2013/14	2014/15	2015/16	2016/17	2017/18	2018/19	2019/20	2020/21
Area (million acres):												
Planted acres	59.2	53.6	57.0	55.5	54.0	53.0	52.0	51.5	51.5	51.5	51.0	51.0
Harvested acres	49.9	47.6	48.5	47.2	45.9	45.1	44.2	43.8	43.8	43.8	43.4	43.4
Yields (bushels per acre):												
Yield/harvested acre	44.5	46.4	43.8	44.2	44.5	44.8	45.2	45.5	45.8	46.1	46.5	46.8
Supply and use (million bushels):												
Beginning stocks	657	976	848	718	706	746	759	743	718	694	682	661
Production	2,218	2,208	2,125	2,085	2,045	2,020	2,000	1,995	2,005	2,020	2,020	2,030
Imports	119	110	110	110	110	115	115	120	120	125	125	130
Supply	2,993	3,294	3,083	2,913	2,861	2,881	2,874	2,858	2,843	2,839	2,827	2,821
Food	917	940	950	959	968	977	986	995	1,004	1,013	1,022	1,031
Seed	69	76	75	73	72	70	70	70	70	69	69	69
Feed & residual	150	180	190	175	175	175	175	175	175	175	175	175
Domestic	1,137	1,196	1,215	1,207	1,215	1,222	1,231	1,240	1,249	1,257	1,266	1,275
Exports	881	1,250	1,150	1,000	900	900	900	900	900	900	900	900
Total use	2,018	2,446	2,365	2,207	2,115	2,122	2,131	2,140	2,149	2,157	2,166	2,175
Ending stocks	976	848	718	706	746	759	743	718	694	682	661	646
Stocks/use ratio, percent	48.4	34.7	30.4	32.0	35.3	35.8	34.9	33.6	32.3	31.6	30.5	29.7
Price (dollars per bushel):												
Farm price	4.87	5.50	6.50	5.90	5.55	5.45	5.45	5.50	5.50	5.55	5.55	5.60
Variable costs of production (dollars):												
Per acre	129	125	133	136	138	140	142	145	148	151	154	157
Per bushel	2.89	2.70	3.03	3.07	3.09	3.12	3.15	3.19	3.23	3.27	3.30	3.35
Returns over variable costs (dollars per acre):												
Net returns	88	130	152	125	109	104	104	105	104	105	104	105

Note: Marketing year beginning June 1 for wheat.

Table 24. U.S. Soybeans and Products Long-Term Projections

Item	2009/10	2010/11	2011/12	2012/13	2013/14	2014/15	2015/16	2016/17	2017/18	2018/19	2019/20	2020/21
Soybeans												
Area (million acres):												
Planted	77.5	77.7	78.0	78.3	78.5	79.0	79.0	79.5	79.5	79.5	79.5	79.5
Harvested	76.4	76.8	77.1	77.3	77.6	78.1	78.1	78.5	78.5	78.5	78.5	78.5
Yield/harvested acre (bushels)	44.0	43.9	43.5	44.0	44.4	44.9	45.3	45.8	46.2	46.7	47.1	47.6
Supply (million bushels)												
Beginning stocks, September[1]	138	151	185	190	195	194	197	199	196	197	198	199
Production	3,359	3,375	3,355	3,395	3,445	3,505	3,540	3,590	3,625	3,660	3,695	3,735
Imports	15	10	10	10	10	10	10	10	10	10	10	10
Total supply	3,512	3,536	3,550	3,595	3,650	3,709	3,747	3,799	3,831	3,867	3,903	3,945
Disposition (million bushels)												
Crush	1,752	1,665	1,660	1,670	1,695	1,715	1,735	1,770	1,790	1,810	1,830	1,850
Seed and residual	108	117	125	125	126	127	128	128	129	129	129	130
Exports	1,501	1,570	1,575	1,605	1,635	1,670	1,685	1,705	1,715	1,730	1,745	1,765
Total disposition	3,361	3,351	3,360	3,400	3,456	3,512	3,548	3,603	3,634	3,669	3,704	3,745
Carryover stocks, August 31												
Total ending stocks	151	185	190	195	194	197	199	196	197	198	199	200
Stocks/use ratio, percent	4.5	5.5	5.7	5.7	5.6	5.6	5.6	5.4	5.4	5.4	5.4	5.3
Price (dollars per bushel)												
Soybean price, farm	9.59	11.45	11.20	10.55	10.25	10.20	10.25	10.25	10.30	10.30	10.35	10.35
Variable costs of production (dollars):												
Per acre	132	131	136	139	140	142	144	146	148	150	152	154
Per bushel	3.01	2.98	3.13	3.15	3.16	3.17	3.18	3.19	3.20	3.22	3.23	3.24
Returns over variable costs (dollars per acre):												
Net returns	290	372	351	325	315	315	320	323	328	330	335	338
Soybean oil (million pounds)												

Table 24. (Continued).

Item	2009/10	2010/11	2011/12	2012/13	2013/14	2014/15	2015/16	2016/17	2017/18	2018/19	2019/20	2020/21
Beginning stocks, October[1]	2,861	3,358	2,653	2,368	2,073	2,093	2,143	2,123	2,208	2,223	2,198	2,128
Production	19,615	18,980	18,940	19,070	19,375	19,620	19,865	20,285	20,530	20,780	21,025	21,275
Imports	105	115	125	135	145	155	165	175	185	195	205	215
Total supply	22,581	22,453	21,718	21,573	21,593	21,868	22,173	22,583	22,923	23,198	23,428	23,618
Domestic disappearance	15,822	17,100	17,400	18,000	18,200	18,425	18,650	18,875	19,125	19,375	19,625	19,875
For methyl ester[1]	1,682	2,900	3,100	3,500	3,500	3,500	3,500	3,500	3,525	3,550	3,575	3,600
Exports	3,400	2,700	1,950	1,500	1,300	1,300	1,400	1,500	1,575	1,625	1,675	1,700
Total demand	19,222	19,800	19,350	19,500	19,500	19,725	20,050	20,375	20,700	21,000	21,300	21,575
Ending stocks, September 30	3,358	2,653	2,368	2,073	2,093	2,143	2,123	2,208	2,223	2,198	2,128	2,043
Soybean oil price (dollars per lb)	0.357	0.445	0.455	0.455	0.455	0.460	0.460	0.460	0.463	0.465	0.468	0.470
Soybean meal (thousand short tons)												
Beginning stocks, October[1]	235	303	300	300	300	300	300	300	300	300	300	300
Production	41,702	39,532	39,435	39,685	40,235	40,685	41,235	41,985	42,485	42,985	43,485	43,985
Imports	150	165	165	165	165	165	165	165	165	165	165	165
Total supply	42,087	40,000	39,900	40,150	40,700	41,150	41,700	42,450	42,950	43,450	43,950	44,450
Domestic disappearance	30,634	30,600	31,000	31,250	31,700	32,150	32,650	33,150	33,650	34,150	34,650	35,150
Exports	11,150	9,100	8,600	8,600	8,700	8,700	8,750	9,000	9,000	9,000	9,000	9,000
Total demand	41,784	39,700	39,600	39,850	40,400	40,850	41,400	42,150	42,650	43,150	43,650	44,150
Ending stocks, September 30	303	300	300	300	300	300	300	300	300	300	300	300
Soybean meal price (dollars per ton)	311.27	330.00	312.50	286.00	275.00	271.00	273.50	273.50	275.00	274.00	275.00	275.00
Crushing yields (pounds per bushel)												
Soybean oil	11.20	11.40	11.41	11.42	11.43	11.44	11.45	11.46	11.47	11.48	11.49	11.50
Soybean meal	47.60	47.50	47.50	47.50	47.50	47.50	47.50	47.50	47.50	47.50	47.50	47.50
Crush margin (dollars per bushel)	1.81	1.46	1.41	1.44	1.48	1.50	1.51	1.52	1.54	1.55	1.55	1.59

Note: Marketing year beginning September 1 for soybeans; October 1 for soybean oil and soybean meal.

[1]/ Soybean oil used for methyl ester for production of biodiesel, history from the U.S. Department of Commerce.

Table 25. U.S. Rice Long-Term Projections, Rough Basis

Item	2009/10	2010/11	2011/12	2012/13	2013/14	2014/15	2015/16	2016/17	2017/18	2018/19	2019/20	2020/21
TOTAL												
Area (thousand acres):												
Planted	3,135	3,642	3,300	3,200	3,215	3,230	3,290	3,300	3,310	3,310	3,310	3,
Harvested	3,103	3,623	3,275	3,176	3,191	3,206	3,265	3,275	3,285	3,285	3,285	3,
Yields (pounds per acre):												
Yield/harvested acre	7,085	6,669	7,102	7,191	7,267	7,339	7,400	7,466	7,534	7,595	7,662	7,
Supply and use (million hundredweight):												
Beginning stocks	30.6	36.7	49.8	50.9	45.9	41.4	37.4	36.7	36.5	36.9	36.7	36.7
Production	219.9	241.6	232.6	228.4	231.9	235.3	241.6	244.5	247.5	249.5	251.7	253.8
Imports	19.0	19.5	20.0	20.6	21.1	21.7	22.3	22.8	23.4	24.0	24.7	25.3
Total supply	269.4	297.8	302.4	299.9	298.9	298.4	301.2	304.0	307.5	310.4	313.0	315.8
Domestic use and residual	122.6	129.0	130.5	132.0	133.5	135.0	136.5	138.0	139.6	141.2	142.8	144.4
Exports	110.2	119.0	121.0	122.0	124.0	126.0	128.0	129.5	131.0	132.5	133.5	134.5
Total use	232.7	248.0	251.5	254.0	257.5	261.0	264.5	267.5	270.6	273.7	276.3	278.9
Ending stocks	36.7	49.8	50.9	45.9	41.4	37.4	36.7	36.5	36.9	36.7	36.7	36.9
Stocks/use ratio, percent	15.8	20.1	20.2	18.1	16.1	14.3	13.9	13.7	13.6	13.4	13.3	13.2
Milling rate, percent	69.4	68.9	69.0	69.0	69.0	69.0	69.0	69.0	69.0	69.0	69.0	69.0
Prices (dollars per hundredweight): World price	11.24	11.15	11.00	10.30	10.30	10.51	10.72	10.93	11.15	11.37	11.60	11.83
Average farm price	14.00	12.60	12.50	12.10	12.20	12.51	12.72	12.93	13.15	13.37	13.60	13. 83
Variable costs of production (dollars):												
Per acre	472	480	502	513	520	528	536	544	553	562	571	580
Per hundredweight	6.71	7.19	7.07	7.13	7.16	7.19	7.24	7.29	7.34	7.39	7.45	7.51
Returns over variable costs (dollars per acre):												
Net returns	520	361	393	357	366	390	406	421	438	454	471	489
LONG GRAIN												
Area (thousand acres):												
Planted	2,290	2,836	2,500	2,400	2,400	2,400	2,450	2,450	2,450	2,450	2,450	2,450
Harvested	2,265	2,821	2,480	2,381	2,381	2,381	2,430	2,430	2,430	2,430	2,430	2, 430
Yields (lbs per acre):												
Yield/harvested acre	6,743	6,434	6,800	6,892	6,974	7,051	7,123	7,194	7,266	7,339	7,412	7, 486

Table 25. (Continued)

Item	2009/10	2010/11	2011/12	2012/13	2013/14	2014/15	2015/16	2016/17	2017/18	2018/19	2019/20	2020/21
Supply and use (million hundredweight):												
Beginning stocks	20.1	23.2	38.6	39.6	34.6	30.0	25.7	25.1	24.6	24.3	24.1	24.2
Production	152.7	181.5	168.6	164.1	166.1	167.9	173.1	174.8	176.6	178.3	180.1	181.9
Imports	16.5	17.0	17.4	17.9	18.3	18.8	19.3	19.7	20.2	20.7	21.3	21.8
Total supply	189.3	221.6	224.6	221.6	219.0	216.7	218.1	219.6	221.4	223.3	225.5	227.9
Domestic use & residual	90.8	99.0	100.0	101.0	102.0	103.0	104.0	105.0	106.1	107.2	108.3	109.4
Exports	75.4	84.0	85.0	86.0	87.0	88.0	89.0	90.0	91.0	92.0	93.0	94.0
Total use	166.2	183.0	185.0	187.0	189.0	191.0	193.0	195.0	197.1	199.2	201.3	203.4
Ending stocks	23.2	38.6	39.6	34.6	30.0	25.7	25.1	24.6	24.3	24.1	24.2	24.5
Stocks/use ratio, percent	13.9	21.1	21.4	18.5	15.9	13.5	13.0	12.6	12.3	12.1	12.0	12.0
Price (dollars per hundredweight):												
Average farm price	12.80	11.00	10.75	10.45	10.59	10.98	11.19	11.47	11.81	12.03	12.26	12. 47
MEDIUM & SHORT GRAIN												
Area (thousand acres):												
Planted	845	806	800	800	815	830	840	850	860	860	860	860
Harvested	838	802	795	795	810	825	835	845	855	855	855	855
Yields (lbs per acre):												
Yield/harvested acre	8,010	7,495	8,050	8,090	8,129	8,168	8,208	8,248	8,289	8,330	8,372	8, 414
Supply and use (million hundredweight):												
Beginning stocks	8.0	12.1	9.7	9.8	9.8	9.9	10.2	10.2	10.5	11.1	11.1	11.1
Production	67.1	60.1	64.0	64.3	65.8	67.4	68.5	69.7	70.9	71.2	71.6	71.9
Imports	2.5	2.5	2.6	2.7	2.8	2.9	3.0	3.1	3.2	3.3	3.4	3.5
Total supply	78.7	74.7	76.3	76.8	78.4	80.2	81.7	83.0	84.6	85.6	86.1	86.5
Domestic use & residual	31.8	30.0	30.5	31.0	31.5	32.0	32.5	33.0	33.5	34.0	34.5	35.0
Exports	34.8	35.0	36.0	36.0	37.0	38.0	39.0	39.5	40.0	40.5	40.5	40.5
Total use	66.6	65.0	66.5	67.0	68.5	70.0	71.5	72.5	73.5	74.5	75.0	75.5
Ending stocks	12.1	9.7	9.8	9.8	9.9	10.2	10.2	10.5	11.1	11.1	11.1	11.0
Stocks/use ratio, percent	18.1	14.9	14.7	14.6	14.4	14.6	14.3	14.5	15.1	14.9	14.8	14.6
Price (dollars per hundredweight):												
Average farm price	17.70	17.80	17.40	16.37	16.31	16.34	16.50	16.53	16.55	16.62	16.85	17.16

Note: Marketing year beginning August 1 for rice.

Table 26. U.S. Upland Cotton Long-Term Projections

Item	2009/10	2010/11	2011/12	2012/13	2013/14	2014/15	2015/16	2016/17	2017/18	2018/19	2019/20	2020/21
Area (million acres):												
Planted acres	9.0	10.8	12.8	12.5	12.2	12.0	11.9	11.8	11.8	11.7	11.7	11.6
Harvested acres	7.4	10.6	11.3	11.1	10.9	10.7	10.5	10.5	10.5	10.4	10.4	10.3
Yields (pounds per acre):												
Yield/harvested acre	766	814	820	825	830	835	840	845	850	855	850	865
Supply and use (thousand bales):												
Beginning stocks	6,032	2,929	2,179	3,100	3,870	4,390	4,760	4,880	5,050	5,270	5,340	5,460
Production	11,788	17,920	19,300	19,100	18,800	18,600	18,400	18,500	18,600	18,500	18,600	18,600
Imports	0	0	0	0	0	0	0	0	0	0	0	0
Supply	17,820	20,849	21,479	22,200	22,670	22,990	23,160	23,380	23,650	23,770	23,940	24,060
Domestic use	3,429	3,420	3,370	3,320	3,270	3,220	3,170	3,120	3,070	3,020	2,970	2,920
Exports	11,343	15,275	15,000	15,000	15,000	15,000	15,100	15,200	15,300	15,400	15,500	15,600
Total use	14,772	18,695	18,370	18,320	18,270	18,220	18,270	18,320	18,370	18,420	18,470	18,520
Ending stocks	2,929	2,179	3,100	3,870	4,390	4,760	4,880	5,050	5,270	5,340	5,460	5,530
Stocks/use ratio, percent	19.8	11.7	16.9	21.1	24.0	26.1	26.7	27.6	28.7	29.0	29.6	29.9
Price (dollars per pound):												
Farm price	0.629	0.800	0.850	0.750	0.700	0.705	0.710	0.715	0.720	0.725	0.730	0.735
Variable costs of production (dollars):												
Per acre	446	468	486	496	505	514	523	533	543	553	563	574
Per pound	0.58	0.58	0.59	0.60	0.61	0.62	0.62	0.63	0.64	0.65	0.65	0.66
Returns over variable costs (dollars per acre):												
Net returns	134	299	328	239	189	187	187	185	184	183	181	179

Note: Marketing year beginning August 1 for upland cotton.

Table 27. U.S. Sugar Long-Term Projections

Item	**Units**	**2009/10**	**2010/11**	**2011/12**	**2012/13**	**2013/14**	**2014/15**	**2015/16**	**2016/17**	**2017/18**	**2018/19**	**2019/20**	**2020/21**
Sugarbeets													
Planted area	1,000 acres	1,186	1,183	1,186	1,100	1,107	1,119	1,121	1,119	1,115	1,110	1,106	1,102
Harvested area	1,000 acres	1,149	1,154	1,138	1,055	1,062	1,073	1,075	1,073	1,069	1,065	1,060	1,057
Yield	Tons/acre	25.7	27.7	26.1	26.3	26.4	26.4	26.5	26.6	26.7	26.8	26.9	26.9
Production	Mil. s. tons	29.6	31.9	29.7	27.7	28.0	28.3	28.5	28.5	28.5	28.5	28.5	28.5

Table 27. (Continued)

Item	Units	2009/10	2010/11	2011/12	2012/13	2013/14	2014/15	2015/16	2016/17	2017/18	2018/19	2019/20	2020/21
Sugarcane													
Harvested area	1,000 acres	812	819	818	815	815	816	816	816	816	816	816	816
Yield	Tons/acre	34.8	33.6	34.1	34.2	34.4	34.6	34.8	34.9	35.1	35.3	35.5	35.7
Production	Mil. s. tons	28.3	27.5	27.8	27.9	28.0	28.2	28.4	28.5	28.7	28.8	29.0	29.1
Supply:													
Beginning stocks	1,000 s. tons	1,534	1,501	1,265	1,522	1,564	1,578	1,591	1,603	1,616	1,629	1,641	1,652
Production	1,000 s. tons	7,967	8,230	8,321	8,013	8,098	8,201	8,268	8,313	8,349	8,385	8,418	8,457
Beet sugar	1,000 s. tons	4,575	4,800	4,845	4,525	4,589	4,668	4,712	4,735	4,749	4,764	4,775	4,793
Cane sugar	1,000 s. tons	3,392	3,430	3,476	3,488	3,510	3,533	3,556	3,578	3,600	3,621	3,643	3,664
Total imports	1,000 s. tons	3,320	2,744	3,208	3,613	3,607	3,597	3,622	3,670	3,726	3,783	3,831	3,886
TRQ imports	1,000 s. tons	1,854	1,409	1,409	1,415	1,417	1,420	1,422	1,427	1,430	1,432	1,435	1,436
Mexico	1,000 s. tons	807	1,025	1,474	1,873	1,865	1,852	1,874	1,918	1,972	2,026	2,071	2,125
Other imports	1,000 s. tons	658	310	325	325	325	325	325	325	325	325	325	325
Total supply	1,000 s. tons	12,821	12,475	12,794	13,148	13,269	13,376	13,480	13,586	13,691	13,797	13,890	13,995
Use:													
Exports	1,000 s. tons	211	150	150	150	150	150	150	150	150	150	150	150
Domestic deliveries	1,000 s. tons	11,133	11,060	11,122	11,434	11,541	11,635	11,727	11,820	11,913	12,006	12,088	12,181
Miscellaneous	1,000 s. tons	-22	0	0	0	0	0	0	0	0	0	0	0
Total use	1,000 s. tons	11,321	11,210	11,272	11,584	11,691	11,785	11,877	11,970	12,063	12,156	12,238	12,331
CCC surplus disbursements[1]	1,000 s. tons	0	0	0	0	0	0	0	0	0	0	0	0
Ending stocks	1,000 s. tons	1,501	1,265	1,522	1,564	1,578	1,591	1,603	1,616	1,629	1,641	1,652	1,665
Raw sugar price:													
New York (No. 16)	Cents/lb.	35.36	23.99	22.92	22.92	22.92	22.92	22.92	22.92	22.92	22.92	22.92	22.92
Raw sugar loan rate	Cents/lb.	18.25	18.50	18.75	18.75	18.75	18.75	18.75	18.75	18.75	18.75	18.75	18.75
Beet sugar loan rate	Cents/lb.	23.45	23.77	24.09	24.09	24.09	24.09	24.09	24.09	24.09	24.09	24.09	24.09
Grower prices:													
Sugarbeets	Dol./ton	46.70	48.86	41.83	41.09	41.09	41.09	41.09	41.09	41.09	41.09	41.09	41.09
Sugarcane	Dol./ton	34.59	30.87	29.54	29.49	29.51	29.53	29.55	29.57	29.59	29.61	29.63	29.65

Table 28. Horticultural Crops Long-Term Supply and Use Projections, Calendar Years

Item	Unit	2009	2010	2011	2012	2013	2014	2015	2016	2017	2018	2019	2020
Production area[1] Fruit, nuts, and vegetables	1,000 acres	10,827	10,931	10,974	11,018	11,064	11,111	11,159	11,209	11,261	11,314	11,368	11,424
Fruit and tree nuts	1,000 acres	3,987	3,990	3,993	3,996	4,000	4,005	4,010	4,015	4,021	4,028	4,034	4,042
Vegetables and melons	1,000 acres	6,840	7,100	6,650	6,850	7,064	7,106	7,150	7,194	7,240	7,286	7,334	7,383
Supply													
Production, farm w eight Fruit and nuts	Mil. lbs.	63,954	62,502	64,523	64,666	64,816	64,972	65,134	65,303	65,479	65,661	65,850	66,045
Citrus	Mil. lbs.	23,678	21,856	23,502	23,267	23,034	22,804	22,576	22,350	22,127	21,905	21,686	21,469
Noncitrus	Mil. lbs.	36,258	35,548	36,840	37,135	37,432	37,732	38,034	38,338	38,645	38,954	39,265	39,579
Tree nuts	Mil. lbs.	4,018	4,098	4,180	4,264	4,349	4,436	4,525	4,615	4,708	4,802	4,898	4,996
Vegetables and melons[2]	Mil. lbs.	140,552	138,832	138,718	139,889	141,078	142,286	143,513	144,760	146,028	147,316	148,626	149,958
Fresh market	Mil. lbs.	58,662	56,850	59,602	60,261	60,934	61,622	62,325	63,043	63,777	64,527	65,293	66,077
Processing	Mil. lbs.	41,581	38,633	38,864	39,098	39,332	39,568	39,806	40,045	40,285	40,526	40,770	41,014
Potatoes	Mil. lbs.	35,349	33,000	35,108	35,284	35,460	35,638	35,816	35,995	36,175	36,356	36,537	36,720
Pulses	Mil. lbs.	4,959	5,475	5,143	5,246	5,351	5,458	5,567	5,678	5,792	5,908	6,026	6,146
Total fruit, nuts, vegetables	Mil. lbs.	204,506	201,334	203,241	204,555	205,893	207,258	208,648	210,064	211,507	212,977	214,476	216,003
Imports, farm w eight Fruit, nuts, and vegetables	Mil. lbs.	59,894	54,931	66,487	68,148	69,852	71,601	73,395	75,236	77,124	79,062	81,050	83,090
Fruit and tree nuts	Mil. lbs.	36,952	39,520	40,314	41,164	42,032	42,918	43,822	44,746	45,690	46,653	47,637	48,641
Vegetables & melons	Mil. lbs.	22,941	25,411	26,173	26,984	27,821	28,683	29,572	30,489	31,434	32,409	33,414	34,449
Use													
Exports, farm w eight Fruit, nuts, and vegetables	Mil. lbs.	33,409	34,899	35,323	35,753	36,189	36,633	37,083	37,540	38,004	38,476	38,955	39,441
Fruit and tree nuts	Mil. lbs.	13,577	14,325	14,440	14,557	14,675	14,796	14,918	15,043	15,170	15,299	15,430	15,564
Vegetables & melons	Mil. lbs.	19,833	20,574	20,883	21,196	21,514	21,837	22,164	22,497	22,834	23,177	23,525	23,877
Domestic use[3] Fruit, nuts, and vegetables	Mil. lbs.	222,423	222,827	226,045	228,480	230,973	233,527	236,143	238,821	241,565	244,375	247,253	250,201
Fruit and tree nuts	Mil. lbs.	94,300	94,697	97,612	98,558	99,529	100,524	101,544	102,589	103,661	104,758	105,882	107,033
Vegetables & melons	Mil. lbs.	128,123	128,130	128,433	129,921	131,444	133,003	134,599	136,232	137,905	139,617	141,371	143,168
Farm sales value[4] Fruit and nuts	$ Mil.	18,965	19,320	19,696	20,043	20,397	20,760	21,132	21,512	21,900	22,298	22,705	23,121

Table 28. (Continued)

Item	Unit	2009	2010	2011	2012	2013	2014	2015	2016	2017	2018	2019	2020
Citrus	$ Mil.	2,845	2,859	2,888	2,879	2,870	2,862	2,853	2,845	2,836	2,828	2,819	2,811
Noncitrus	$ Mil.	11,944	12,185	12,404	12,628	12,855	13,086	13,322	13,562	13,806	14,054	14,307	14,565
Tree nuts	$ Mil.	4,151	4,276	4,404	4,536	4,672	4,812	4,957	5,105	5,258	5,416	5,579	5,746
Vegetables and melons	$ Mil.	21,554	21,783	22,153	22,530	22,913	23,303	23,700	24,104	24,515	24,933	25,359	25,793
Fresh market	$ Mil.	13,394	13,518	13,709	13,903	14,099	14,298	14,500	14,704	14,912	15,122	15,335	15,551
Processing	$ Mil.	3,635	3,683	3,765	3,848	3,933	4,020	4,109	4,200	4,293	4,388	4,484	4,583
Potatoes	$ Mil.	3,396	3,430	3,496	3,562	3,630	3,699	3,769	3,840	3,913	3,988	4,064	4,141
Pulses	$ Mil.	1,129	1,151	1,184	1,217	1,251	1,286	1,322	1,359	1,397	1,436	1,476	1,518
Nursery and greenhouse[5]	$ Mil.	15,915	16,026	16,154	16,283	16,414	16,545	16,677	16,811	16,945	17,081	17,217	17,355
Other horticulture crops[6]	$ Mil.	859	875	899	925	950	977	1,004	1,033	1,061	1,091	1,122	1,153
Total horticulture crops	$ Mil.	57,294	58,003	58,902	59,780	60,674	61,585	62,513	63,459	64,422	65,403	66,403	67,422
Producer prices[7] Fresh fruits	1982=100	110.4	122.2	120.7	122.5	124.4	126.3	128.3	130.2	132.2	134.3	136.3	138.4
Citrus	1982=100	164.3	167.0	159.9	164.0	168.1	172.3	176.6	180.8	185.1	189.4	193.7	198.1
Noncitrus	1982=100	107.6	123.5	124.7	126.0	127.2	128.5	129.7	131.0	132.3	133.6	135.0	136.3
Tree nuts	1982=100	808.9	836.0	844.2	852.5	860.8	869.3	877.8	886.4	895.1	903.9	912.7	921.7
Vegetables	1982=100	162.2	181.7	184.9	186.5	188.1	189.7	191.2	192.8	194.4	196.0	197.6	199.2
Fresh vegetables	1982=100	169.4	195.0	183.3	186.9	190.4	193.9	197.5	201.0	204.5	207.9	211.4	214.8
Potatoes (fresh)	1982=100	155.7	137.0	137.2	139.1	141.1	143.0	145.0	147.0	149.1	151.2	153.3	155.4
Pulses (dried)	1982=100	156.6	145.0	158.7	175.0	176.4	177.8	179.2	180.6	182.0	183.4	184.8	186.3
Fruit, nuts, and vegetables	1982=100	146.7	162.3	163.7	165.5	167.2	169.0	170.8	172.6	174.5	176.3	178.2	180.0

[1]/ Bearing acreage for fruit and nuts; harvested area for vegetables.

[2]/ Utilized production is used for potatoes. Pulses include edible dry beans and peas, lentils, and other peas.

[3]/ In farm or fresh w eight units. Stock changes are accounted for.

[4]/ Farm cash receipts for fresh and processing vegetables are allocated based on their relative production value shares.

[5]/ Includes floral crops, greenhouse vegetables such as tomatoes, cucumbers, sweet and hot peppers, and fruit and vegetable transplants.

[6]/ Includes honey, maple syrup, hops, mint oils, taro, ginger root, and coffee from Haw aii and Puerto Rico.

[7]/ Not seasonally adjusted producer price indexes for farm commodities from U.S. Bureau of Labor Statistics. Prices for fresh fruits include melons.

Data sources: USDA, National Agricultural Statistics Service; Foreign Agricultural Service; Economic Research Service; U.S. Department of Labor, Bureau of Labor Statistics.

Table 29. Horticultural Crops Long-Term Export and Import Projections, Fiscal Years

Item	Unit	2009	2010	2011	2012	2013	2014	2015	2016	2017	2018	2019	2020
Exports													
Fruit and nuts Fresh fruits	$ Mil.	3,522	3,799	4,082	4,273	4,429	4,589	4,756	4,929	5,108	5,293	5,485	5,684
Citrus	$ Mil.	726	924	975	1,040	1,063	1,087	1,110	1,134	1,159	1,183	1,207	1,232
Noncitrus	$ Mil.	2,795	2,874	3,107	3,234	3,366	3,503	3,646	3,794	3,949	4,110	4,278	4,452
Processed fruits	$ Mil.	2,266	2,380	2,578	2,712	2,797	2,885	2,976	3,070	3,167	3,267	3,370	3,476
Fruit juices	$ Mil.	1,107	1,152	1,180	1,209	1,239	1,269	1,300	1,332	1,364	1,398	1,432	1,467
Tree nuts	$ Mil.	3,495	4,060	4,300	4,519	4,749	4,990	5,244	5,511	5,792	6,087	6,396	6,722
Total fruit and nuts	$ Mil.	9,283	10,239	10,960	11,504	11,974	12,465	12,977	13,510	14,066	14,646	15,251	15,882
Vegetables													
Fresh	$ Mil.	1,892	2,060	2,118	2,184	2,252	2,322	2,394	2,469	2,546	2,625	2,707	2,791
Processed[1]	$ Mil.	3,113	3,233	3,322	3,423	3,526	3,634	3,744	3,858	3,975	4,095	4,220	4,348
Total vegetables	$ Mil.	5,005	5,294	5,440	5,607	5,778	5,956	6,138	6,327	6,521	6,720	6,927	7,139
Other horticulture													
Nursery and greenhouse	$ Mil.	355	336	340	345	350	354	359	364	369	374	379	384
Essential oils	$ Mil.	1,234	1,367	1,424	1,484	1,546	1,611	1,679	1,750	1,823	1,900	1,980	2,063
Wine	$ Mil.	827	1,004	1,036	1,069	1,104	1,139	1,176	1,214	1,253	1,293	1,335	1,377
Beer	$ Mil.	296	296	304	313	321	330	340	349	359	369	379	390
Other[2]	$ Mil.	3,636	4,076	4,796	4,997	5,206	5,424	5,651	5,887	6,132	6,387	6,652	6,928
Total horticulture	$ Mil.	20,634	22,610	24,300	25,318	26,280	27,280	28,319	29,399	30,522	31,688	32,901	34,162
Fresh produce[3]	$ Mil.	5,414	5,859	6,200	6,457	6,681	6,912	7,150	7,398	7,654	7,918	8,192	8,475
Processed produce[3]	$ Mil.	5,379	5,613	5,900	6,134	6,324	6,519	6,720	6,928	7,142	7,362	7,589	7,824
Imports													
Fruit and nuts Fresh fruits	$ Mil.	6,074	6,803	7,500	7,938	8,287	8,650	9,029	9,425	9,838	10,270	10,720	11,190
Citrus	$ Mil.	442	464	500	527	549	571	594	618	644	670	697	725
Noncitrus	$ Mil.	5,632	6,339	7,000	7,411	7,738	8,079	8,435	8,807	9,195	9,600	10,023	10,465
Processed fruits	$ Mil.	3,375	3,276	3,500	3,682	3,826	3,976	4,131	4,293	4,461	4,635	4,816	5,004
Fruit juices	$ Mil.	1,414	1,279	1,400	1,447	1,483	1,521	1,559	1,598	1,638	1,679	1,722	1,765
Tree nuts	$ Mil.	1,151	1,332	1,500	1,559	1,619	1,683	1,748	1,817	1,888	1,961	2,038	2,118
Total fruit and nuts	$ Mil.	10,601	11,411	12,500	13,179	13,732	14,309	14,909	15,535	16,187	16,866	17,574	18,312
Vegetables													
Fresh	$ Mil.	4,237	5,180	5,800	6,172	6,468	6,779	7,105	7,446	7,804	8,179	8,573	8,985
Processed[1]	$ Mil.	3,483	3,574	3,800	4,104	4,270	4,442	4,621	4,807	5,001	5,203	5,412	5,630
Total vegetables	$ Mil.	7,720	8,754	9,600	10,276	10,738	11,221	11,726	12,254	12,805	13,382	13,985	14,615

Table 29. (Continued)

Item	Unit	2009	2010	2011	2012	2013	2014	2015	2016	2017	2018	2019	2020
Other horticulture													
Nursery and greenhouse	$ Mil.	1,357	1,441	1,600	1,617	1,635	1,653	1,671	1,689	1,707	1,726	1,744	1,763
Essential oils	$ Mil.	2,406	2,414	2,600	2,789	2,941	3,102	3,271	3,450	3,638	3,836	4,046	4,267
Wine	$ Mil.	4,084	4,258	4,500	4,792	4,999	5,215	5,441	5,676	5,922	6,178	6,445	6,724
Beer	$ Mil.	3,428	3,452	3,600	3,781	3,908	4,039	4,175	4,315	4,460	4,610	4,764	4,924
Other[2]	$ Mil.	3,421	3,820	4,100	4,407	4,604	4,809	5,023	5,247	5,481	5,725	5,981	6,247
Total horticulture	$ Mil.	33,017	35,549	38,500	40,843	42,558	44,348	46,216	48,165	50,200	52,323	54,539	56,852
Fresh produce[3]	$ Mil.	10,311	11,983	13,300	14,110	14,755	15,429	16,134	16,872	17,643	18,449	19,293	20,175
Processed produce[3]	$ Mil.	6,859	6,850	7,300	7,787	8,096	8,418	8,752	9,100	9,462	9,838	10,229	10,635

[1]/ Includes dry edible beans, peas, lentils, and potatoes.

[2]/ Includes hops, ginseng, sauces, condiments, mixed food, yeast, starches, and other products that contain horticulture ingredients.

[3]/ Includes fruits and vegetables only.

Exports are free alongside ship (FAS) value at U.S. port of exportation. Imports are customs value at U.S. port of entry.

Data source: U.S. Department of Commerce, Bureau of the Census.

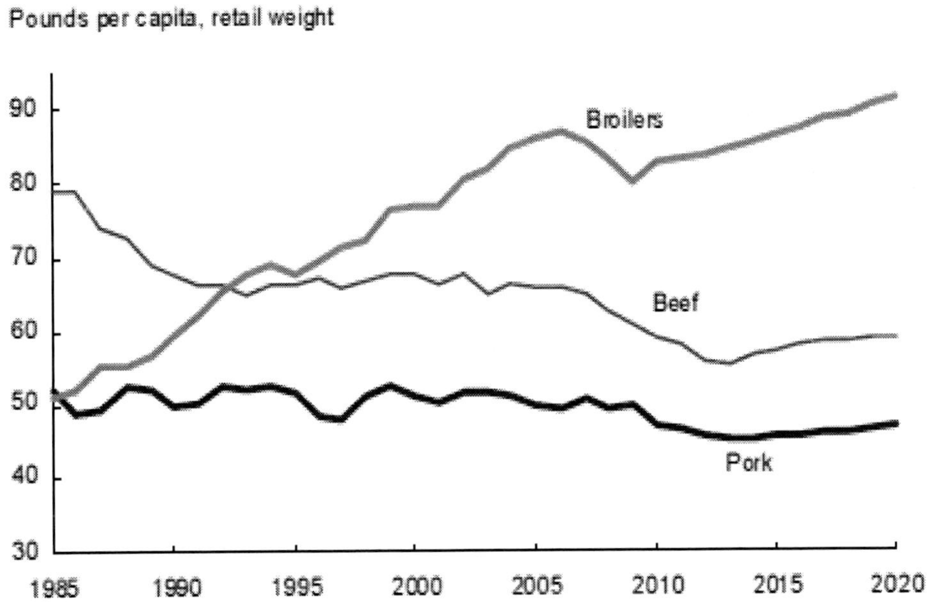

U.S. Per Capita Meat Consumption.

Moderate near-term changes in production in the livestock sector, along with projected gains in meat exports, result in higher consumer prices and lower per capita consumption. Annual average consumption of red meats and poultry falls from over 221 pounds per capita in 2004-07 to about 203 pounds in 2012 and 2013. As production increases over the remainder of the projection period, per capita consumption of red meats and poultry resumes growth, but only rises to about 216 pounds by 2020.

- Per capita beef consumption declines through 2013, before rising moderately over the remainder of the projection period. The initial decline reflects continuing reductions in beef production through 2012 coupled with expanding exports. However, as beef production increases in later years, per capita consumption grows.
- Gains in U.S. pork exports combine with moderate pork production changes to push per capita pork consumption down in 2010 through 2013. A gradual rebound in per capita pork consumption occurs over the remainder of the projection period as production gains strengthen.
- Due partly to higher feed conversion rates and a shorter production process, the poultry sector adjusts faster than the red meats sector to higher feed costs. As a result, poultry production is projected to grow throughout the decade. Per capita consumption rises through the end of the projection period and, in contrast to red meats, surpasses levels of the past decade. Further, poultry meat consumption exceeds red meat consumption toward the end of the projection period.

Prices in the livestock sector are projected to generally rise over the projection period, reflecting a moderate pace of expansion combined with improving domestic and export demands.

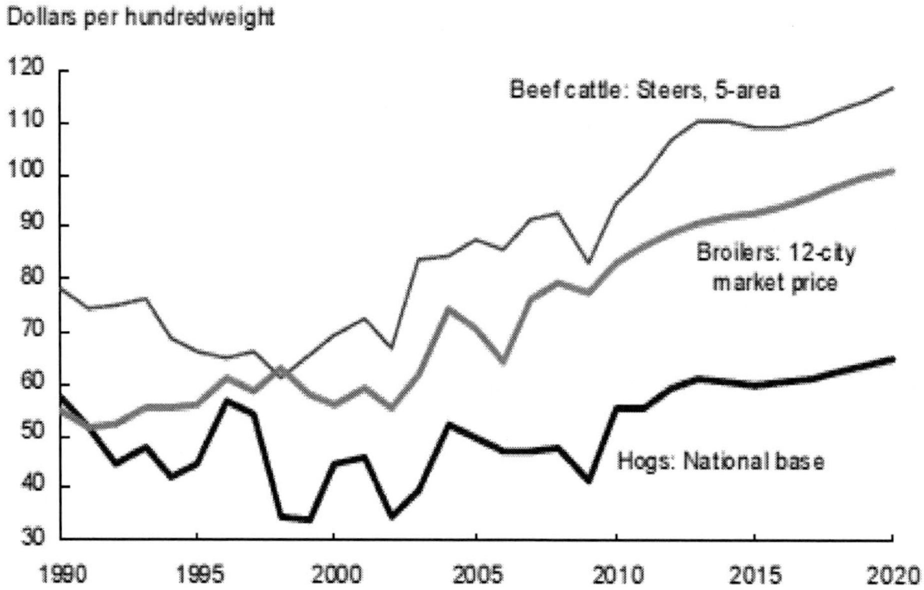

Nominal U.S. Livestock Prices.

The projected rise in U.S. meat and poultry exports over the next decade reflects the resumption of global economic growth, a depreciation of the U.S. dollar, and continued foreign demand for selected cuts and parts from the large U.S. market. As a result, exports account for a larger share of U.S. meat and poultry use, although the domestic market remains the dominant source of overall meat and poultry demand.

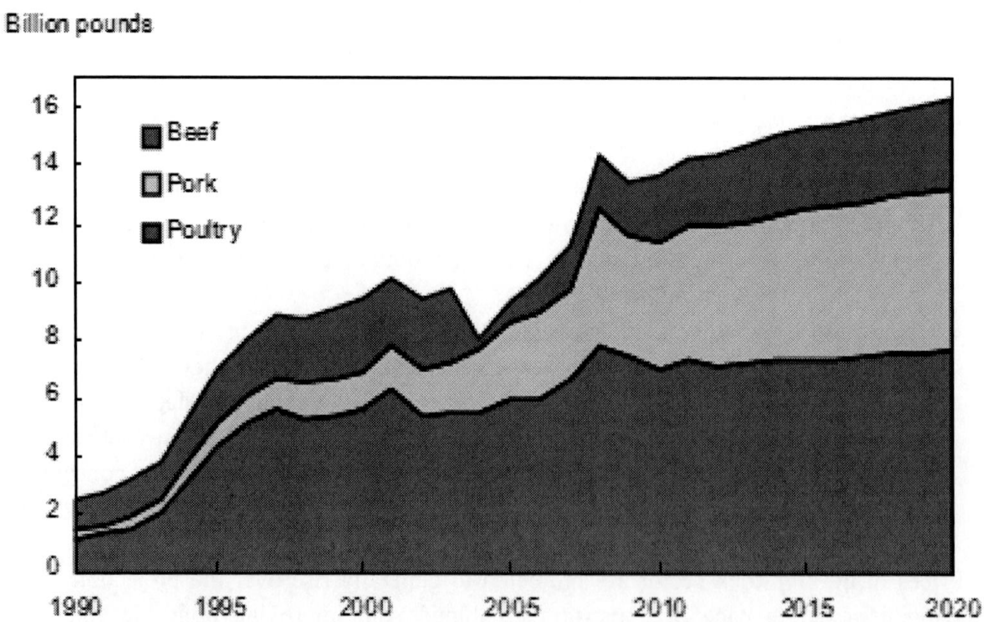

U.S. Meat Exports.

- Most U.S. beef exports are high-quality fed beef, typically going to Mexico, Canada, and Pacific Rim nations. A continuing recovery is assumed for U.S. beef exports to Japan and South Korea, export markets that were initially closed to the United States following the first U.S. case of bovine spongiform encephalopathy (BSE) in December 2003. Beef exports by competitor countries of Australia and Canada increase slowly as herds are rebuilt.
- U.S. imports of processing beef from Australia and New Zealand increase in the projection period. With more beef demand in East Asian markets being met by the U.S. grain-fed beef, exports of grass-fed beef from Australia and New Zealand to those markets are reduced, freeing more of that product for sale to the United States. Additionally, moderate beef cow inventories and beef cow slaughter in the United States raise import demand for processing beef.
- Production efficiency in the U.S. pork sector enhances the competitiveness of U.S. pork products in global trade. However, longer term U.S. pork export gains will be determined by costs of production and environmental regulations relative to competitors. Production costs tend to be lower in countries such as Brazil that have established or are developing integrated pork industries. However, Brazilian pork producers' ability to compete in some markets is limited because the projections assume that some countries do not recognize Brazil as free of foot-and-mouth disease (FMD). Thus, Pacific Rim nations and Mexico remain key markets for long-term growth of U.S. pork exports, while Brazil's pork exports expand to Argentina and Asian markets other than Japan and South Korea. Russia is projected to reduce pork imports to facilitate expansion of their domestic industry, with pork exports from the United States and Brazil affected the most.
- U.S. broiler exports rise from 2012 through the rest of the projection period. Major U.S. export markets include China and Mexico, but U.S. broiler exports also have been increasing to a number of other countries. Longer term gains in these markets reflect their economic growth and increasing consumer demand. International demand for poultry also remains strong because of its lower cost relative to beef and pork. U.S. producers continue to face strong competition from other major exporters, particularly Brazil. For most of the projection period, exports from avian influenza-affected countries are expected to be limited to fully cooked products. As with pork, Russia is projected to support their domestic poultry industry by limiting imports.

Milk production is projected to continue rising over the projection period, although at a slower pace than in the past several years.

An upward trend in output per cow continues, while milk cow numbers decrease in 2012-20.

- After a 4-year increase during 2005-08, milk cow numbers fell in 2009 and 2010 and are projected to continue on a more typical path of year-to-year declines in 2012-20. Cow numbers decline at lower rates toward the end of the projection period as the transition in most regions from smaller, diversified farms to larger, specialized dairy operations matures.

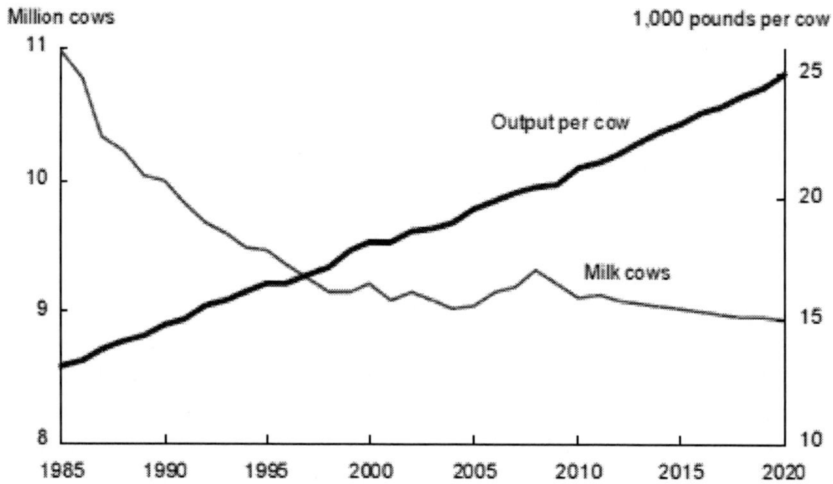

U.S. Dairy Herd and Milk Production Per Cow.

- Milk output per cow is projected to increase through the projection period, reflecting continued technological and genetic developments.
- Domestic commercial use of dairy products increases somewhat faster than the growth in U.S. population over most of the next decade. Cheese demand benefits from greater consumption of prepared foods and increased away-from-home eating.However, per capita consumption of fluid milk is expected to continue to decline slowly.
- Commercial U.S. dairy exports are forecast to increase steadilyover the next decade, reaching record levels on a fat and a skim-solids basis. Increased production among the major dairy exporting countries is expected to lag growth in global import demand. The United States is expected to be well positioned to expand exports of dairy products, with sales of cheese and nonfat dry milk growing strongly.
- Farm-level milk prices are projected to rise steadily over the projection period. However, increases are less than the overall rate of inflation largely because of efficiency gains in production resulting from technological improvements and consolidation in the sector.

U.S. Agricultural Sector Aggregate Indicators Farm Income, U.S. Trade Value, Food Prices, and Food Expenditures

High commodity prices underlie record projected levels of U.S. agricultural exports and U.S. net farm income in 2011. Although grain, oilseed, and cotton prices, export value, and farm income retreat somewhat in the next several years, a return to steady domestic and international economic growth supports demand for U.S. agricultural products over the next decade.

Table 30. Per Capita Meat Consumption, Rrtail Weight

Item	2009	2010	2011	2012	2013	2014	2015	2016	2017	2018	2019	2020
						Pounds						
Total beef	61.1	59.0	57.8	55.9	55.7	56.6	57.4	58.2	58.6	58.8	58.8	58.9
Total veal	0.5	0.5	0.4	0.4	0.4	0.4	0.4	0.4	0.4	0.4	0.4	0.4
Total pork	50.1	47.0	46.6	45.7	45.2	45.3	45.7	45.8	46.1	46.3	46.5	46.9
Lamb and mutton	1.0	0.9	0.9	0.9	0.9	0.9	0.9	0.8	0.8	0.8	0.8	0.8
Total red meat	112.7	107.4	105.8	103.0	102.2	103.2	104.4	105.2	105.9	106.3	106.5	106.9
Broilers	79.7	82.7	83.0	83.5	84.1	85.2	86.3	87.3	88.2	89.1	90.3	91.5
Other chicken	1.3	1.3	1.3	1.3	1.3	1.3	1.3	1.3	1.3	1.3	1.3	1.3
Turkeys	16.9	16.2	15.8	15.7	15.8	15.9	16.1	16.1	16.2	16.3	16.4	16.5
Total poultry	97.9	100.3	100.1	100.5	101.2	102.3	103.6	104.8	105.7	106.7	107.9	109.3
Red meat & poultry	210.6	207.7	205.9	203.5	203.4	205.5	208.0	210.0	211.6	212.9	214.5	216.2

Table 31. Beef Long-Term Projections

Item	Units	2009	2010	2011	2012	2013	2014	2015	2016	2017	2018	2019	2020
Beginning stocks	Mil. lbs.	642	565	535	515	515	515	515	515	515	515	515	515
Commercial production	Mil. lbs.	25,965	25,871	25,445	24,770	25,023	25,712	26,318	26,875	27,305	27,614	27,842	28,075
Change from previous year	Percent	-2.2	-0.4	-1.6	-2.7	1.0	2.8	2.4	2.1	1.6	1.1	0.8	0.8
Farm production	Mil. lbs.	102	102	102	102	102	102	102	102	102	102	102	102
Total production	Mil. lbs.	26,067	25,973	25,547	24,872	25,125	25,814	26,420	26,977	27,407	27,716	27,944	28,177
Imports	Mil. lbs.	2,626	2,468	2,540	2,760	2,800	2,865	2,930	2,995	3,060	3,125	3,190	3,255
Total supply	Mil. lbs.	29,335	29,006	28,622	28,147	28,440	29,194	29,865	30,487	30,982	31,355	31,649	31,947
Exports	Mil. lbs.	1,935	2,313	2,270	2,401	2,603	2,714	2,784	2,838	2,893	2,950	3,008	3,068
Ending stocks	Mil. lbs.	565	535	515	515	515	515	515	515	515	515	515	515
Total consumption	Mil. lbs.	26,835	26,158	25,837	25,231	25,322	25,965	26,566	27,134	27,574	27,891	28,126	28,364
Per capita, carcass weight	Pounds	87.3	84.3	82.6	79.9	79.5	80.9	82.0	83.1	83.8	84.0	84.1	84.1
Per capita, retail weight	Pounds	61.1	59.0	57.8	55.9	55.7	56.6	57.4	58.2	58.6	58.8	58.8	58.9
Change from previous year	Percent	-2.6	-3.4	-2.1	-3.2	-0.5	1.7	1.5	1.3	0.8	0.3	0.0	0.0
Prices:													
Beef cattle, farm	$/cw t	80.36	91.45	96.22	103.03	106.52	106.31	105.63	105.62	106.34	108.31	110.48	112.56
Calves, farm	$/cw t	106.42	118.78	119.82	132.61	137.04	135.10	132.75	131.61	131.65	133.98	136.65	139.67
Steers, 5-area	$/cw t	83.25	94.81	99.75	106.81	110.43	110.21	109.51	109.50	110.24	112.29	114.54	116.69

Table 31. (Continued)

Item	Units	2009	2010	2011	2012	2013	2014	2015	2016	2017	2018	2019	2020
Yearling steers, Oklahoma City	$/cw t	96.14	108.42	109.25	120.91	124.95	123.18	121.04	120.00	120.03	122.16	124.60	127.35
Costs and returns, cow-calf enterprise:													
Total cash expenses	$/cow	522.11	493.51	524.46	535.76	545.75	554.00	564.85	576.30	588.23	599.96	611.44	622.40
Returns above cash costs	$/cow	-30.11	72.69	54.97	112.80	133.66	125.69	112.99	105.64	104.03	114.84	128.25	144.48
Cattle inventory	1,000 head	94,521	93,701	92,550	91,951	92,271	93,661	94,849	95,496	95,799	95,991	96,219	96,696
Beef cow inventory	1,000 head	31,712	31,376	31,104	31,193	31,640	32,320	32,877	33,265	33,483	33,647	33,825	34,130
Total cow inventory	1,000 head	41,045	40,456	40,200	40,254	40,676	41,331	41,868	42,236	42,440	42,583	42,747	43,036

Table 32. Pork Long-Term Projections

Item	Units	2009	2010	2011	2012	2013	2014	2015	2016	2017	2018	2019	2020
Beginning stocks	Mil. lbs.	635	525	485	475	475	475	475	475	475	475	475	475
Commercial production	Mil. lbs.	22,999	2,234	2,560	2,446	2,474	2,757	3,178	3,486	3,798	4,105	4,445	24,827
Change from previous year	Percent	-1.5	-3.3	1.5	-0.5	0.1	1.3	1.9	1.3	1.3	1.3	1.4	1.6
Farm production	Mil. lbs.	21	21	21	21	21	21	21	21	21	21	21	21
Total production	Mil. lbs.	23,020	2,256	2,581	2,467	2,495	2,778	3,199	3,507	3,819	4,126	4,466	24,848
Imports	Mil. lbs.	834	868	895	910	930	955	980	1,005	1,030	1,055	1,080	1,105
Total supply	Mil. lbs.	24,489	3,649	3,961	3,852	3,900	4,208	24,654	4,987	5,324	5,656	6,021	26,428
Exports	Mil. lbs.	4,095	4,368	4,675	4,785	4,884	5,000	5,125	5,224	5,310	5,396	5,484	5,577
Ending stocks	Mil. lbs.	525	485	475	475	475	475	475	475	475	475	475	475
Total consumption	Mil. lbs.	19,869	8,796	8,811	8,592	8,541	8,733	9,054	9,288	9,539	9,785	0,062	20,376
Per capita, carcass w eight	Pounds	64.6	60.6	60.1	58.9	58.2	58.3	58.8	59.1	59.3	59.6	60.0	60.4
Per capita, retail w eight	Pounds	50.1	47.0	46.6	45.7	45.2	45.3	45.7	45.8	46.1	46.3	46.5	46.9
Change from previous year	Percent	1.5	-6.2	-0.8	-2.0	-1.1	0.2	0.9	0.4	0.5	0.4	0.6	0.8
Prices:													
Hogs, farm	$/cw t	41.98	54.97	55.43	58.55	60.34	60.17	59.57	60.16	60.99	62.15	63.27	64.28
National base, live equivalent	$/cw t	41.24	55.29	55.75	58.90	60.70	60.53	59.93	60.53	61.36	62.52	63.65	64.67
Costs and returns, farrow to finish:													
Total cash expenses	$/cw t	63.26	59.86	70.78	68.04	64.17	62.83	63.02	63.52	64.24	65.04	65.74	66.26
Returns above cash costs	$/cw t	-19.50	-1.20	-11.63	-5.54	0.23	1.40	0.57	0.70	0.87	1.30	1.80	2.36
Hog inventory,													
December 1, previous year	1,000 head	67,148	64,887	64,450	64,143	64,217	64,981	66,118	66,947	67,791	68,617	69,536	70,565

Table 33. Young Chicken Long-Term Projections

Item	Units	2009	2010	2011	2012	2013	2014	2015	2016	2017	2018	2019	2020
Beginning stocks	Mil. lbs.	745	616	695	660	660	660	660	660	660	660	660	660
Federally inspected slaughter	Mil. lbs.	35,511	36,612	37,150	37,490	38,056	38,760	39,502	40,243	40,899	41,580	42,383	43,208
Change from previous year	Percent	-3.8	3.1	1.5	0.9	1.5	1.8	1.9	1.9	1.6	1.7	1.9	1.9
Production	Mil. lbs.	35,131	36,220	36,752	37,088	37,649	38,345	39,079	39,812	40,461	41,135	41,929	42,746
Total supply	Mil. lbs.	35,961	36,919	37,543	37,838	38,399	39,095	39,829	40,562	41,211	41,885	42,679	43,496
Change from previous year	Percent	-3.6	2.7	1.7	0.8	1.5	1.8	1.9	1.8	1.6	1.6	1.9	1.9
Exports	Mil. lbs.	6,818	6,346	6,650	6,500	6,550	6,600	6,650	6,700	6,750	6,800	6,850	6,900
Ending stocks	Mil. lbs.	616	695	660	660	660	660	660	660	660	660	660	660
Consumption	Mil. lbs.	28,527	29,878	30,233	30,678	31,189	31,835	32,519	33,202	33,801	34,425	35,169	35,936
Per capita, carcass w eight	Pounds	92.8	96.3	96.6	97.2	98.0	99.1	100.4	101.7	102.7	103.7	105.1	106.5
Per capita, retail w eight	Pounds	79.7	82.7	83.0	83.5	84.1	85.2	86.3	87.3	88.2	89.1	90.3	91.5
Change from previous year	Percent	-4.5	3.8	0.3	0.6	0.8	1.2	1.3	1.3	1.0	1.0	1.3	1.4
Prices:													
Broilers, farm	Cents/lb.	45.2	48.5	50.0	51.5	52.6	53.3	53.8	54.4	55.4	56.6	57.6	58.6
12-city market price	Cents/lb.	77.6	83.4	86.0	88.8	90.7	91.9	92.8	93.8	95.6	97.6	99.4	101.0
Costs and returns:													
Total costs	Cents/lb.	79.65	77.50	85.09	83.80	82.07	82.14	83.27	84.71	86.26	87.93	89.50	91.03
Net returns	Cents/lb.	-2.04	5.90	0.91	4.98	8.67	9.75	9.52	9.12	9.33	9.70	9.86	9.95

Table 34. Turkey Long-Term Projections

Item	Units	2009	2010	2011	2012	2013	2014	2015	2016	2017	2018	2019	2020
Beginning stocks	Mil. lbs.	396	262	210	225	250	275	300	300	300	300	300	300
Federally inspected slaughter	Mil. lbs.	5,663	5,587	5,560	5,598	5,685	5,776	5,859	5,934	6,010	6,089	6,175	6,268
Change from previous year	Percent	-9.3	-1.3	-0.5	0.7	1.5	1.6	1.4	1.3	1.3	1.3	1.4	1.5
Production	Mil. lbs.	5,588	5,514	5,487	5,525	5,611	5,700	5,783	5,857	5,932	6,010	6,094	6,186
Total supply	Mil. lbs.	5,997	5,788	5,709	5,762	5,873	5,987	6,095	6,169	6,244	6,322	6,406	6,498
Change from previous year	Percent	-6.8	-3.5	-1.4	0.9	1.9	2.0	1.8	1.2	1.2	1.3	1.3	1.4
Exports	Mil. lbs.	534	555	550	560	570	580	590	600	610	620	630	640
Ending stocks	Mil. lbs.	262	210	225	250	275	300	300	300	300	300	300	300
Consumption	Mil. lbs.	5,201	5,023	4,934	4,952	5,028	5,107	5,205	5,269	5,334	5,402	5,476	5,558
Per capita	Pounds	16.9	16.2	15.8	15.7	15.8	15.9	16.1	16.1	16.2	16.3	16.4	16.5

Table 34. (Continued)

Item	Units	2009	2010	2011	2012	2013	2014	2015	2016	2017	2018	2019	2020
Change from previous year	Percent	-3.8	-4.3	-2.6	-0.5	0.7	0.7	1.0	0.4	0.4	0.5	0.6	0.7
Prices:													
Turkey, farm	Cents/lb.	49.9	60.0	60.0	61.7	62.3	61.4	60.6	60.4	60.7	61.4	62.2	63.0
Hen turkeys, National	Cents/lb.	76.5	90.0	90.0	92.6	93.5	92.2	90.9	90.6	91.1	92.2	93.4	94.6
Costs and returns:													
Total costs	Cents/lb.	77.49	74.94	84.23	82.21	79.17	78.32	78.74	79.52	80.37	81.29	82.07	82.73
Net returns	Cents/lb.	-0.99	15.05	5.77	10.40	14.29	13.85	12.16	11.08	10.74	10.87	11.29	11.83

Table 35. Egg long-term projections

Item	Units	2009	2010	2011	2012	2013	2014	2015	2016	2017	2018	2019	2020
Beginning stocks	Mil. doz.	17	18	18	18	18	18	18	18	18	18	18	18
Production	Mil. doz.	7,534	7,607	7,635	7,597	7,574	7,574	7,612	7,688	7,765	7,843	7,913	7,984
Change from previous year	Percent	0.4	1.0	0.4	-0.5	-0.3	0.0	0.5	1.0	1.0	1.0	0.9	0.9
Imports	Mil. doz.	11	12	12	12	12	12	12	12	12	12	12	12
Total supply	Mil. doz.	7,562	7,637	7,665	7,627	7,604	7,604	7,642	7,718	7,795	7,873	7,943	8,014
Change from previous year	Percent	0.5	1.0	0.4	-0.5	-0.3	0.0	0.5	1.0	1.0	1.0	0.9	0.9
Hatching use	Mil. doz.	955	982	1,010	1,018	1,028	1,041	1,055	1,069	1,082	1,095	1,110	1,125
Exports	Mil. doz.	242	244	237	240	243	246	249	252	255	258	261	264
Ending stocks	Mil. doz.	18	18	18	18	18	18	18	18	18	18	18	18
Consumption	Mil. doz.	6,347	6,393	6,400	6,351	6,315	6,300	6,320	6,379	6,440	6,501	6,555	6,607
Per capita	Number	247.7	247.3	245.4	241.4	238.0	235.4	234.2	234.4	234.7	235.0	235.1	235.1
Change from previous year	Percent	-0.2	-0.2	-0.8	-1.6	-1.4	-1.1	-0.5	0.1	0.1	0.1	0.0	0.0
Prices:													
Eggs, farm	Cents/doz.	82.1	82.8	79.7	86.4	93.6	98.4	103.2	105.6	106.4	107.2	108.0	109.2
New York, Grade A large	Cents/doz.	103.0	103.0	99.3	108.0	117.0	123.0	129.0	132.0	133.0	134.0	135.0	136.5
Costs and returns:													
Total costs	Cents/doz.	115.40	109.58	133.24	127.84	120.10	117.72	118.54	120.05	121.97	124.06	125.93	127.41
Net returns	Cents/doz.	-12.40	-6.58	-33.94	-19.84	-3.10	5.28	10.46	11.95	11.03	9.94	9.07	9.09

Table 36. Dairy long-term projections

Item	Units	2009	2010	2011	2012	2013	2014	2015	2016	2017	2018	2019	2020
Milk production and marketings:													
Number of cow s	1,000	9,201	9,115	9,130	9,095	9,070	9,045	9,025	9,005	8,990	8,970	8,955	8,940
Milk per cow	Pounds	20,576	21,160	21,425	21,780	22,180	22,600	22,990	23,425	23,735	24,105	24,480	24,950
Milk production	Bil. lbs.	189.3	192.8	195.6	198.1	201.2	204.4	207.5	210.9	213.4	216.2	219.2	223.1
Farm use	Bil. lbs.	1.0	1.0	1.0	1.0	1.0	0.9	0.9	0.9	0.9	0.8	0.8	0.8
Marketings	Bil. lbs.	188.3	191.9	194.6	197.1	200.2	203.5	206.6	210.0	212.5	215.4	218.4	222.3
Supply and use, milkfat basis:													
Beginning commercial stocks	Bil. lbs.	10.1	11.3	10.1	10.6	10.9	11.1	11.1	10.9	10.5	10.0	9.6	9.3
Marketings	Bil. lbs.	188.3	191.9	194.6	197.1	200.2	203.5	206.6	210.0	212.5	215.4	218.4	222.3
Imports	Bil. lbs.	5.6	4.6	4.1	4.3	4.4	4.5	4.6	4.7	4.8	4.9	5.1	5.2
Commercial supply	Bil. lbs.	204.0	207.8	208.9	212.0	215.5	219.1	222.3	225.6	227.8	230.3	233.1	236.8
Domestic commercial use1	Bil. lbs.	187.3	189.7	192.1	194.9	197.6	200.4	203.3	206.6	208.8	211.1	213.7	216.9
Commercial exports	Bil. lbs.	4.5	7.7	6.2	6.2	6.8	7.6	8.1	8.5	9.0	9.6	10.1	10.8
Ending commercial stocks	Bil. lbs.	11.3	10.1	10.6	10.9	11.1	11.1	10.9	10.5	10.0	9.6	9.3	9.1
Total utilization	Bil. lbs.	203.1	207.5	208.9	212.0	215.5	219.1	222.3	225.6	227.8	230.3	233.1	236.8
CCC net removals2	Bil. lbs.	0.7	0.2	0.0	0.0	0.0	0.0	0.0	0.0	0.0	0.0	0.0	0.0
Supply and use, skim solids basis:													
Beginning commercial stocks	Bil. lbs.	10.9	11.3	11.8	11.5	11.1	10.9	10.7	10.6	10.5	10.5	10.5	10.6
Marketings	Bil. lbs.	188.3	191.9	194.6	197.1	200.2	203.5	206.6	210.0	212.5	215.4	218.4	222.3
Imports	Bil. lbs.	5.5	5.1	4.9	5.1	5.3	5.5	5.7	5.9	6.1	6.4	6.6	6.9
Commercial supply	Bil. lbs.	204.7	208.2	211.3	213.7	216.6	219.9	223.0	226.5	229.1	232.3	235.5	239.8
Domestic commercial use1	Bil. lbs.	168.6	167.0	170.3	172.5	174.8	177.5	180.3	183.3	185.5	188.0	190.5	193.8
Commercial exports	Bil. lbs.	22.4	29.8	29.5	30.1	30.9	31.7	32.1	32.7	33.1	33.8	34.4	35.3
Ending commercial stocks	Bil. lbs.	11.3	11.8	11.5	11.1	10.9	10.7	10.6	10.5	10.5	10.5	10.6	10.7
Total utilization	Bil. lbs.	202.3	208.6	211.3	213.7	216.6	219.9	223.0	226.5	229.1	232.3	235.5	239.8
CCC net removals2	Bil. lbs.	2.9	0.0	0.0	0.0	0.0	0.0	0.0	0.0	0.0	0.0	0.0	0.0
Prices:													
All milk	$/cw t	12.83	16.35	16.40	16.95	17.10	17.30	17.45	17.70	17.90	18.20	18.50	18.70

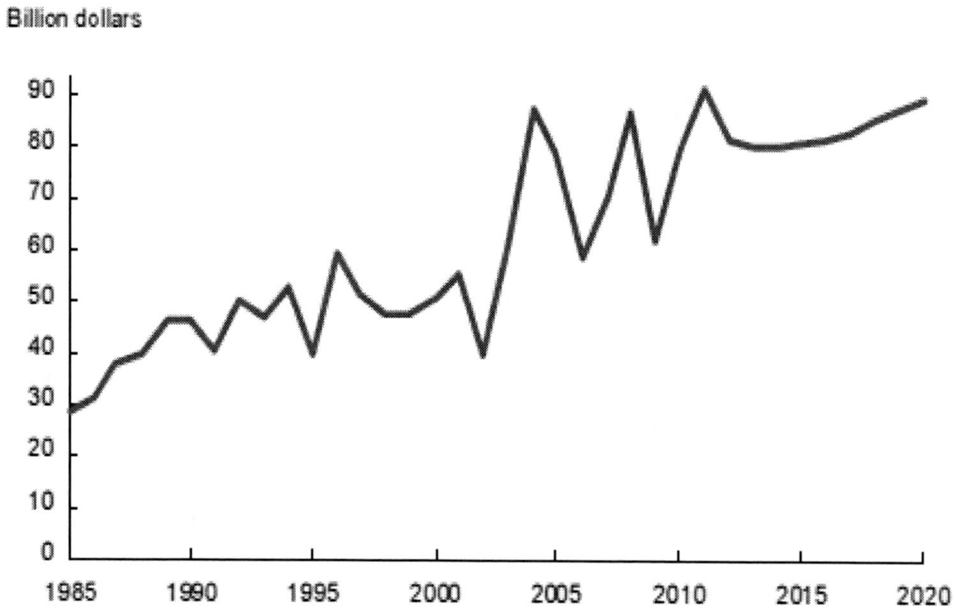

U.S. Net Farm Income.

In addition, rising global demand for agricultural commodities for the production of biofuels continues. Thus, after the near-term declines, the value of U.S. agricultural exports and net farm income each rise through the rest of the decade.

U.S. retail food prices increase faster than the overall rate of inflation in 2011 and 2012, reflecting higher food commodity prices and energy costs and improved demand as the economic recovery continues.

Net farm income rises to record levels in 2011, largely reflecting the recent runup in prices for many agricultural commodities. While income declines in 2012-14, it grows over the rest of the decade and remains well above the average of the previous decade (2001-10) throughout the projection period.

- Strengthening global food demand and sustained biofuel demand provide a major impetus for projections of rising cash receipts.
- Lower Government payments and rising farm production expenses offset some of the gains in cash receipts and other sources of farm income.

Direct Government payments to farmers fall to about $8.5 billion for the latter half of the next decade. Price-dependent program benefits have become less important. Ad hoc and emergency payments are projected to fall from recent levels, in part because the supplemental agricultural disaster assistance programs authorized under the 2008 Farm Act only cover qualifying losses that occur before October 2011.

As a result, the Conservation Reserve Program (CRP) and fixed direct payments represent about 88 percent of direct Government payments toward the end of the projection period.

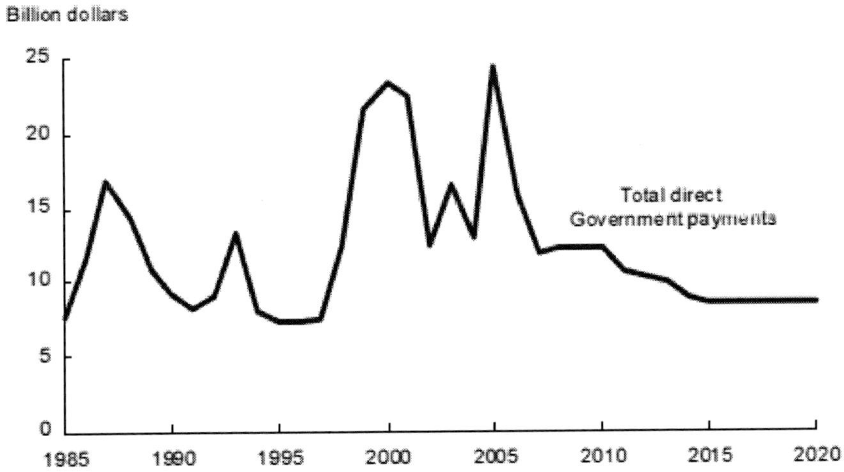

Direct Government Payments.

- Improving domestic and international demand holds prices for most crops above levels that would result in marketing loan benefits or counter-cyclical payments, so projected benefits for these programs are negligible over the next decade. Similarly, with relatively low enrollment and projected long-run stability in commodity prices, projections of payments under the Average Crop Revenue Election (ACRE) program average less than $100 million over 2012-20.
- High crop prices make the use of land for production more valuable, so rental rates for land in the CRP rise. Even with reduced CRP acreage enrollment due to the 2008 Farm Act's lowering of the maximum acreage permitted in the program, CRP payments rise from about $1.9 billion in 2010 to $2.4 billion in 2020.
- With high prices, Government payments have a smaller role in the agricultural sector's income. Government payments, which represented more than 8 percent of gross cash income in 2005, fall to about 2 percent by the end of the projection period. Conversely, the sector relies on the market for more of its income.

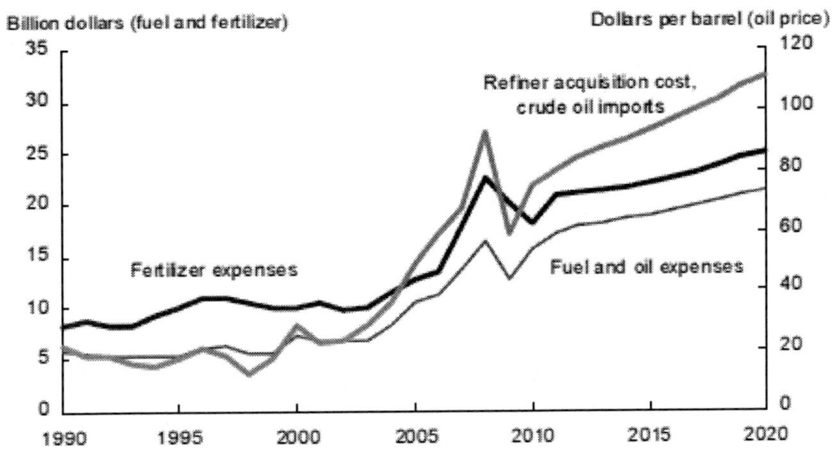

Selected Energy-Related Production Expenses and Crude Oil Prices.

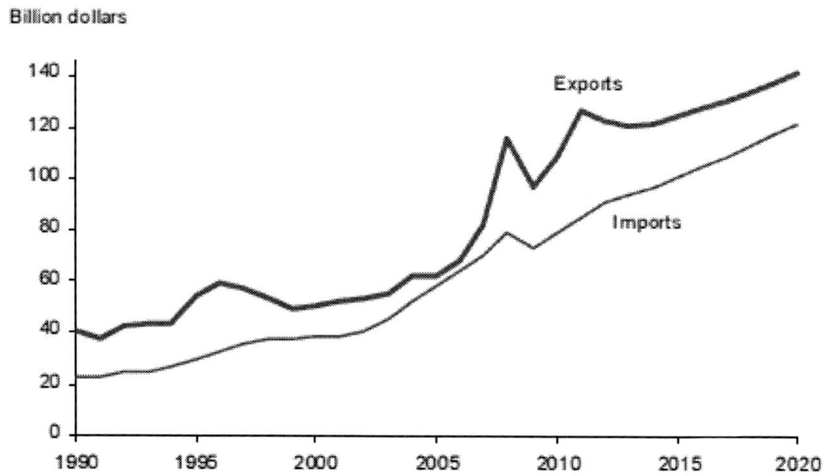

U.S. Agricultural Trade Value.

Total farm production expenses are projected to rise somewhat less rapidly than the overall rate of inflation over 2011-2020. While interest expenses and some energy-related costs rise faster than the general inflation rate, expenses for farm-origin inputs (seed, feed, and livestock) and most other nonfarm-origin expenses are up less than the general inflation rate.

- Projected increases in interest costs rise faster than the general inflation rate, due to rising interest rates from the low rates of recent years as well as increased debt.
- Energy-related production expenses for fertilizer and for fuel and oil also rise faster than the general inflation rate over the projection period, largely reflecting increases in crude oil prices.

The value of U.S. agricultural exports initially falls from the record levels projected for fiscal year 2011 as prices for major field crops decline from current high levels. Agricultural exports then rise through the remainder of the projections because of increased global economic growth and agricultural demand and a weaker U.S. dollar. Domestic economic growth boosts demand for U.S. agricultural imports. (Fiscal years are October 1 through September 30 and are named after the second calendar year that they span.)

- The value of U.S. agricultural exports is projected to reach a new record exceeding $126 billion in 2011 largely reflecting high commodity prices. With declining prices projected for major crops over the next several years, export values fall through fiscal 2013. Agricultural export values are then projected to grow over the next decade and surpass the 2011 record. A resumption of world economic growth, particularly in developing countries, provides a foundation for increases in global food demand, trade, and U.S. agricultural exports. Continued global biofuel demand also contributes to high commodity prices and gains in export values. Furthermore, a depreciation of the U.S. dollar is an important factor underlying projected gains in U.S. exports.

- The share of U.S. agricultural exports represented by high-value products (HVP) falls in 2011 as high commodity prices boost bulk commodity exports. However, for the remainder of the projection period, HVP exports grow in importance and reach nearly two-thirds of the value of U.S. exports. Much of the growth in HVP exports is for animal products and horticultural products.
- U.S. agricultural import values rise to $122 billion in 2020, boosted by gains in consumer income and demand for a large variety of foods. Strong growth in horticultural imports is assumed to continue, contributing about half of the overall agricultural import increase over the projection period.
- The agricultural trade balance declines from the record surplus of $41 billion projected for 2011, but remains a surplus of about $19 billion at the end of the projection period.

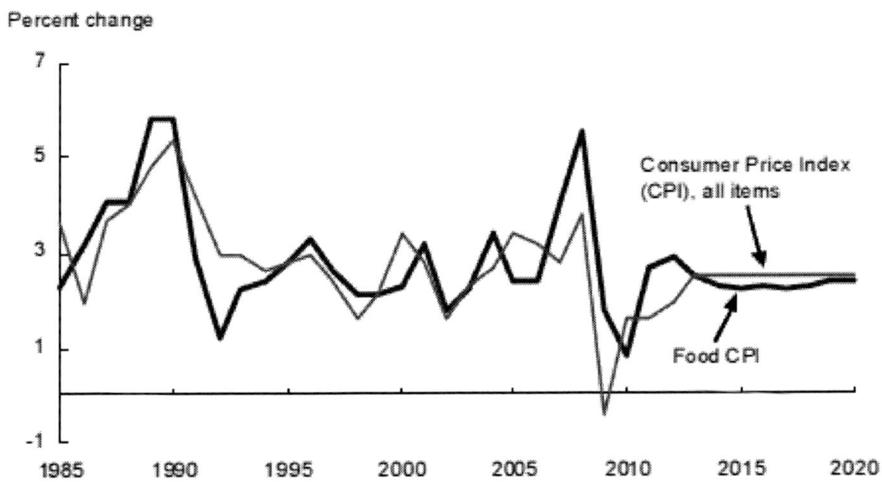

U.S. Food Inflation.

U.S. consumer food prices in 2010 had the smallest annual increase since the 1960s. In particular, the 1.3 percent rise in prices for away-from-home meals was the smallest increase since 1955, partly reflecting promotions to augment otherwise weak demand following the recession.

- Higher food commodity and energy prices will exert pressure on retail food prices into 2011. Additionally, as the economy recovers, retail food prices are projected to rise faster than overall inflation in 2011 and 2012. Over the remainder of the projection period, consumer food prices in the United States rise less than the general inflation rate. This moderation largely reflects production increases in the livestock sector which facilitate gains in per capita meat consumption and limit meat price increases.
- Higher commodity prices for food grains and oil-bearing crops push projected retail prices for cereals and bakery products and for fats and oils up more than the overall inflation rate in the near term. However, in the longer run, prices for these highly

processed foods tend to reflect processing and marketing costs, thus keeping their increases near the general rate of inflation.

- Retail price increases for food away from home slowed in 2009 and 2010 as demand weakened due to the recession and the away-from-home food industry used promotions in response. As the economy rebounds, income gains will support growth in food consumption away from home. This factor, along with some linkage to price increases for meat and poultry, suggests that retail prices for food consumed away from home are likely to rise more than the overall rate of inflation over the next several years.
- In the longer run, prices for food away from home largely reflect the overall rate of inflation. Competition in the fast-food and foodservice industries tends to moderate awayfrom-home price increases, keeping their gains close to the general inflation rate over the rest of the projection period.

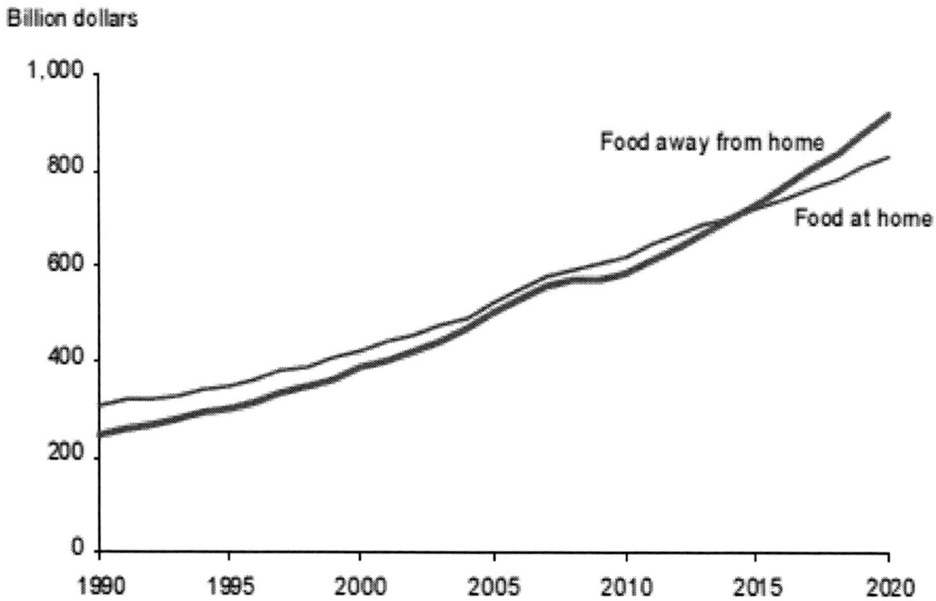

U.S. Food Expenditures.

The U.S. economic recession reduced consumer sales for meals eaten away from home in 2009. In response, the away-from-home food industry relied heavily on promotions in 2010 to partly offset otherwise continued weak demand.

- As the domestic economy rebounds, food expenditures resume stronger growth. As consumer demand strengthens, expenditures for meals away from home rise faster than expenditures for food at home and account for a growing share of total food spending.

Table 37. Farm Receipts, Expenses, and Income, Long-Term Projections

	2009	2010	2011	2012	2013	2014	2015	2016	2017	2018	2019	2020
						Billion dollars						
Cash receipts:												
Crops	163.7	171.4	192.8	187.8	182.6	182.3	184.3	186.8	189.9	193.1	195.9	198.5
Livestock and products	119.8	140.6	143.0	149.0	153.6	156.3	158.6	161.5	164.5	168.5	172.6	176.6
All commodities	283.4	312.1	335.8	336.9	336.2	338.5	342.8	348.4	354.4	361.6	368.5	375.2
Farm-related income	22.0	21.0	21.1	21.4	21.9	22.4	22.9	23.5	24.0	24.5	25.1	25.6
Government payments	12.3	12.2	10.6	10.3	9.9	8.8	8.4	8.4	8.4	8.5	8.4	8.4
Gross cash income	317.6	345.2	367.6	368.6	368.0	369.8	374.2	380.2	386.8	394.6	402.0	409.2
Cash expenses	248.5	254.4	271.7	276.1	278.1	281.1	284.9	289.6	295.0	300.6	305.9	311.0
Net cash income	69.1	90.8	95.8	92.6	89.9	88.6	89.3	90.6	91.8	94.0	95.1	98.2
Value of inventory change	4.5	-0.2	5.6	-0.1	0.9	2.2	2.0	1.7	1.6	1.4	1.5	1.6
Non-money income	21.1	21.7	23.1	23.6	24.1	24.6	25.0	25.5	26.0	26.5	27.1	27.6
Gross farm income	343.2	366.7	396.3	392.2	393.1	396.5	401.2	407.4	414.4	422.6	430.6	438.4
Noncash expenses	20.8	21.2	21.5	21.9	22.4	22.7	23.0	23.2	23.5	23.7	24.0	24.2
Operator dw elling expenses	11.7	11.8	12.1	12.3	12.4	12.6	12.7	12.9	13.0	13.1	13.3	13.5
Total production expenses	281.0	287.5	305.4	310.2	312.9	316.4	320.6	325.7	331.5	337.5	343.2	348.7
Net farm income	62.2	79.3	90.9	81.9	80.2	80.0	80.6	81.8	82.9	85.1	37.4	89.7

The projections were completed in December 2010.

Table 38. Summary Of U.S. Agricultural Trade Long-Term Projections, Fiscal Years

	2009	2010	2011	2012	2013	2014	2015	2016	2017	2018	2019	2020
				Billion dollars								
Agricultural exports (value):												
Livestock, dairy, and poultry	18.6	21.5	23.0	22.8	24.2	25.5	26.2	26.8	27.3	28.0	28.9	29.7
Livestock, poultry, and products	16.4	18.2	19.8	19.5	20.7	21.8	22.4	22.8	23.2	23.7	24.4	25.1
Dairy products	2.3	3.4	3.2	3.3	3.5	3.7	3.8	4.0	4.1	4.3	4.5	4.7
Grain and feeds	26.3	27.3	35.4	32.4	29.3	28.2	28.7	29.3	30.2	31.2	32.1	32.8
Coarse grains	10.0	9.8	13.3	12.6	11.5	11.1	11.3	11.4	11.8	12.2	12.7	13.0
Oilseeds and products	20.9	25.4	28.3	27.5	26.3	26.0	26.3	26.7	27.1	27.4	27.6	27.9
Soybeans and products	17.6	22.1	24.8	23.7	22.5	22.1	22.4	22.8	23.1	23.4	23.6	23.9
				Billion dollars								
Horticultural products	20.6	22.6	24.3	25.3	26.3	27.3	28.3	29.4	30.5	31.7	32.9	34.2
Fruits and vegetables, fresh	5.4	5.9	6.2	6.5	6.7	6.9	7.2	7.4	7.7	7.9	8.2	8.5
Fruits and vegetables, processed	5.4	5.6	5.9	6.1	6.3	6.5	6.7	6.9	7.1	7.4	7.6	7.8
Cotton	3.5	4.8	8.0	6.9	6.3	5.9	6.0	6.0	6.1	6.2	6.3	6.3
Other exports	6.3	7.0	7.5	7.5	7.8	8.1	8.4	8.8	9.1	9.3	9.6	10.0
Total agricultural exports	96.3	108.7	126.5	122.4	120.1	121.1	124.0	127.0	130.3	133.8	137.4	140.9
Bulk commodity exports	36.8	41.0	55.0	50.7	46.2	44.3	44.7	45.2	46.1	46.8	47.7	48.4
High-value product exports	59.5	67.6	71.5	71.6	73.9	76.8	79.3	81.7	84.2	86.9	89.7	92.6
High-value product share	61.8%	62.3%	56.5%	58.5%	61.5%	63.4%	63.9%	64.4%	64.6%	65.0%	65.3%	65.7%
					Million metric tons							
Agricultural exports (volume):												
Bulk commodity exports	115.2	128.9	139.5	137.9	135.6	135.1	136.9	138.2	140.5	142.6	144.8	146.9
					Billion dollars							
Agricultural imports (value):												
Livestock, dairy, and poultry	10.7	10.8	11.5	12.4	12.8	13.2	13.5	13.8	14.2	14.7	15.2	15.7
Livestock and meats	7.6	7.9	8.5	9.3	9.6	9.8	10.0	10.2	10.5	10.8	11.2	11.5
Dairy products	2.7	2.4	2.5	2.6	2.7	2.8	2.9	3.0	3.1	3.2	3.3	3.4
Grain and feeds	7.4	7.5	8.2	8.4	8.7	9.1	9.5	9.9	10.3	10.8	11.3	11.8
Grain products	4.5	4.9	5.4	5.7	6.0	6.3	6.6	6.9	7.2	7.6	8.0	8.4
Oilseeds and products	5.4	5.3	5.6	5.9	6.2	6.5	6.8	7.2	7.5	7.9	8.3	8.8
Vegetable oils	3.7	3.8	4.0	4.2	4.5	4.7	5.0	5.2	5.5	5.8	6.1	6.5

	2009	2010	2011	2012	2013	2014	2015	2016	2017	2018	2019	2020
Horticultural products	33.0	35.5	38.5	40.8	42.6	44.3	46.2	48.2	50.2	52.3	54.5	56.9
Fruits and vegetables, fresh	10.3	12.0	13.3	14.1	14.8	15.4	16.1	16.9	17.6	18.4	19.3	20.2
Fruits and vegetables, processed	6.9	6.8	7.3	7.8	8.1	8.4	8.8	9.1	9.5	9.8	10.2	10.6
Wine and beer	7.5	7.7	8.1	8.6	8.9	9.3	9.6	10.0	10.4	10.8	11.2	11.6
Sugar and tropical products	15.3	18.3	20.3	21.3	21.9	22.6	23.3	24.1	24.8	25.7	26.5	27.4
Sugar and related products	3.3	4.1	4.6	5.1	5.1	5.2	5.3	5.4	5.6	5.7	5.9	6.0
Cocoa, coffee, and products	7.4	8.6	9.5	9.9	10.2	10.6	11.0	11.4	11.8	12.3	12.8	13.2
Other imports	1.6	1.6	1.6	1.7	1.7	1.7	1.7	1.7	1.8	1.8	1.8	1.8
Total agricultural imports	73.4	79.0	85.5	90.5	93.9	97.4	101.0	104.9	108.9	113.2	117.6	122.3
Net agricultural trade balance	22.9	29.7	41.0	31.9	26.2	23.7	23.0	22.1	21.4	20.6	19.8	18.6

Sources: U.S. Department of Agriculture and Bureau of Census, U.S. Department of Commerce.

U.S. trade value projections were completed in November 2010. For updates of the nearby year forecasts, see USDA's Outlook for U.S. Agricultural Trade report, published in February, May, August, and November.

Notes: Other exports includes tobacco, seeds, sugar and tropical products, and beverages. Bulk commodity exports covers wheat, rice, feed grains, soybeans, cotton, and tobacco. High-value product (HVP) exports is calculated as total exports less bulk commodities. HVP's include semiprocessed and processed grains and oilseeds, animals and animal products, horticultural products, and sugar and tropical products. Other imports include cotton, tobacco, and planting seeds.

Table 39. Prices Received By Farmers, Selected Food Commodities, Long-Term Projections

CPI category	2009	2010	2011	2012	2013	2014	2015	2016	2017	2018	2019	2020
Price indexes:						*1990-92=100*						
Food commodities[1]	128.0	144.0	146.8	151.4	153.4	153.9	154.4	155.3	156.7	158.8	161.0	163.0
Food grains	186.0	177.0	207.3	198.0	188.6	186.8	187.4	189.4	190.0	192.0	192.7	194.8
Oil-bearing crops	177.0	173.0	192.0	188.8	183.4	182.6	183.4	183.4	184.3	184.3	185.2	185.2
Fruit and nuts	135.0	150.0	148.6	150.9	153.2	155.6	158.0	160.4	162.9	165.4	167.9	170.5
Vegetables[2]	158.4	164.4	165.2	167.6	169.0	170.4	171.8	173.3	174.7	176.1	177.5	179.0
Meat animals	105.0	124.0	128.4	137.6	142.5	142.1	140.9	140.9	141.8	144.3	147.1	149.9
Dairy products	98.0	125.0	125.0	129.2	130.4	131.9	133.0	134.9	136.5	138.7	141.0	142.6
Poultry and eggs	139.0	151.0	151.4	158.0	163.8	166.9	169.7	171.7	174.0	176.5	178.9	181.4

Changes in price indexes:						Percent						
Food commodities[1]	6.5	12.5	1.9	3.1	1.3	0.3	0.3	0.6	0.9	1.3	1.4	1.2
Food grains	39.2	-4.8	17.1	-4.5	-4.7	-1.0	0.3	1.1	0.3	1.1	0.4	1.1
Oil-bearing crops	47.4	-2.3	11.0	-1.7	-2.9	-0.4	0.4	0.0	0.5	0.0	0.5	0.0
Fruit and nuts	-6.3	11.1	-0.9	1.5	1.5	1.6	1.5	1.5	1.6	1.5	1.5	1.5
Vegetables[2]	1.5	3.8	1.1	0.8	0.8	0.8	0.8	0.9	0.8	0.8	0.8	0.8
Meat animals	-0.8	18.1	3.5	7.2	3.6	-0.3	-0.8	0.0	0.6	1.8	1.9	1.9
CPI category	2009	2010	2011	2012	2013	2014	2015	2016	2017	2018	2019	2020
Price indexes:						1990-92=100						
Dairy products	-4.1	27.6	0.0	3.4	0.9	1.2	0.8	1.4	1.2	1.6	1.7	1.1
Poultry and eggs	7.9	8.6	0.3	4.4	3.7	1.9	1.7	1.2	1.3	1.4	1.4	1.4

[1]/ The aggregate price index for food commodities is a weighted average using NASS relative weights, which are based on average shares of farm cash receipts from 1990 to 1992.

[2]/ The price index for vegetables is a weighted average of the index for commercial vegetables and the index for potatoes and dry beans.

Sources: USDA, National Agricultural Statistics Service (NASS), Agricultural Prices; Economic Research Service.

Table 40. Consumer Food Price Indexes And Food Expenditures, Long-Term Projections

CPI category	**2009**	**2010**	**2011**	**2012**	**2013**	**2014**	**2015**	**2016**	**2017**	**2018**	**2019**	**2020**
Consumer price indices						***1982-84=100***						
All food	217.955	219.625	225.5	232.0	237.9	243.3	248.7	254.4	260.1	266.2	272.5	279.0
Food away from home	223.272	226.114	231.1	237.6	244.3	250.7	257.2	263.9	270.8	277.8	285.0	292.4
Food at home	215.124	215.836	222.3	228.8	234.2	239.1	243.9	248.9	254.0	259.6	265.4	271.3
Meats	200.545	206.232	212.4	222.5	227.9	230.1	231.5	233.4	235.8	239.5	243.4	247.4
Beef and veal	218.273	224.511	231.3	243.3	248.5	250.0	250.8	252.1	254.4	258.7	263.6	268.6
Pork	181.366	189.957	196.6	207.0	213.4	216.0	217.1	219.1	221.3	224.0	226.7	229.4
Other meats	194.901	194.787	198.5	203.7	207.9	211.4	214.8	218.0	221.3	224.6	228.0	231.4
Poultry	204.220	203.978	209.3	217.3	221.5	223.5	225.1	226.9	229.4	232.6	235.6	238.4
Fish and seafood	240.556	243.229	250.5	258.0	265.7	273.7	281.9	290.4	299.1	308.1	317.3	326.8
Eggs	190.024	192.833	198.6	207.0	217.8	227.0	236.3	242.4	246.3	250.2	254.2	258.9
Dairy products	197.013	199.245	209.0	214.5	218.5	223.0	227.5	232.5	237.0	242.0	247.5	252.5

CPI category	2009	2010	2011	2012	2013	2014	2015	2016	2017	2018	2019	2020
Fats and oils	201.224	200.587	208.1	212.7	217.8	223.2	228.7	234.4	240.1	246.1	252.3	258.5
Fruits and vegetables	272.945	273.458	281.8	287.9	294.9	302.1	309.3	316.7	324.2	331.8	339.6	347.4
Sugar and sweets	196.933	201.242	206.0	210.4	215.1	220.0	225.0	230.0	235.2	240.5	245.9	251.5
Cereals and bakery products	252.567	250.449	257.0	263.4	269.1	275.2	281.9	289.0	296.4	304.0	311.6	319.6
Nonalcoholic beverages	163.034	161.602	164.0	167.3	171.5	175.8	180.2	184.7	189.3	194.0	198.9	203.9
Other foods	205.497	204.553	208.3	212.5	217.6	222.9	228.2	233.6	239.2	245.0	250.9	256.9
Food expenditures:						***Billion dollars***						
All food	1,182.0	1,213.6	1,257.2	1,307.0	1,356.7	1,406.2	1,457.2	1,511.2	1,567.7	1,627.2	1,689.2	1,753.6
Food at home	607.4	622.0	643.7	665.8	684.9	703.3	722.1	742.2	763.2	785.8	809.2	833.2
Food away from home	574.5	591.6	613.5	641.2	671.8	702.9	735.1	769.0	804.5	841.4	880.0	920.4
Changes in consumer food prices:						***Percent***						
All food	1.8	0.8	2.7	2.9	2.5	2.3	2.2	2.3	2.2	2.3	2.4	2.4
Food aw ay from home	3.5	1.3	2.2	2.8	2.8	2.6	2.6	2.6	2.6	2.6	2.6	2.6
Food at home	0.5	0.3	3.0	2.9	2.4	2.1	2.0	2.1	2.0	2.2	2.2	2.2
Meats	-0.6	2.8	3.0	4.8	2.4	1.0	0.6	0.8	1.0	1.6	1.6	1.6
Beef and veal	-1.0	2.9	3.0	5.2	2.1	0.6	0.3	0.5	0.9	1.7	1.9	1.9
Pork	-2.0	4.7	3.5	5.3	3.1	1.2	0.5	0.9	1.0	1.2	1.2	1.2
Other meats	2.3	-0.1	1.9	2.6	2.1	1.7	1.6	1.5	1.5	1.5	1.5	1.5
Poultry	1.7	-0.1	2.6	3.8	1.9	0.9	0.7	0.8	1.1	1.4	1.3	1.2
Fish and seafood	3.6	1.1	3.0	3.0	3.0	3.0	3.0	3.0	3.0	3.0	3.0	3.0
Eggs	-14.7	1.5	3.0	4.2	5.2	4.2	4.1	2.6	1.6	1.6	1.6	1.8
Dairy products	-6.4	1.1	4.9	2.6	1.9	2.1	2.0	2.2	1.9	2.1	2.3	2.0
Fats and oils	2.3	-0.3	3.7	2.2	2.4	2.5	2.5	2.5	2.4	2.5	2.5	2.5
Fruits and vegetables	-2.1	0.2	3.1	2.2	2.4	2.4	2.4	2.4	2.4	2.3	2.4	2.3
Sugar and sweets	5.6	2.2	2.4	2.1	2.2	2.3	2.3	2.2	2.3	2.3	2.2	2.3
Cereals and bakery products	3.2	-0.8	2.6	2.5	2.2	2.3	2.4	2.5	2.6	2.6	2.5	2.6
Nonalcoholic beverages	1.9	-0.9	1.5	2.0	2.5	2.5	2.5	2.5	2.5	2.5	2.5	2.5
Other foods	3.7	-0.5	1.8	2.0	2.4	2.4	2.4	2.4	2.4	2.4	2.4	2.4

In: Global Agriculture:
Editors: Christopher R. Fisher and Wade P. Ellis
ISBN: 978-1-61942-859-1

Chapter 2

U.S. AGRICULTURAL TRADE: TRENDS, COMPOSITION, DIRECTION, AND POLICY*

Charles E. Hanrahan,
Carol Canada, and Beverly A. Banks

U.S. agricultural exports, imports, and the agricultural trade surplus are expected by the U.S. Department of Agriculture (USDA) to reach record levels in FY2011. FY2011 U.S. farm exports are forecast by the U.S. Department of Agriculture to reach $137 billion, while agricultural imports are expected to reach $93 billion. The agricultural trade surplus is projected to be $44 billion. Exports of high-value products (e.g., fruits, vegetables, meats, wine and beer) have increased since the early 1990s and now account for 60% of total U.S. agricultural exports. Exports of bulk commodities (e.g., soybeans, wheat, and feed grains) remain significant.

Leading markets for U.S. agricultural exports are China, Canada, Mexico, Japan, the European Union (EU), South Korea, and Taiwan. The United States in 2011 is forecast to be the world's leading exporter of corn, wheat, soybeans, and cotton. The U.S. share of world beef exports, which declined after the 2003 discovery of a case of "mad cow disease" in the United States, is recovering as more countries have re-opened their markets to U.S. product. The United States, European Union, Australia, and New Zealand are dominant suppliers of dairy products in global agricultural trade. New Zealand and the United States are the main suppliers of nonfat dry milk to world markets, while the EU is the leading supplier of cheeses.

China has been among the fastest-growing markets for U.S. agricultural exports. Agricultural exports to Canada and Mexico, both partners of the United States in the North American Free Trade Agreement (NAFTA), have also grown rapidly.

Most U.S. agricultural imports are high-value products, including fruits, nuts, vegetables, wine, and beer. The biggest import suppliers are NAFTA partners Canada and Mexico, and the EU. Together these three are forecast to provide more than 50% of total U.S. agricultural imports in FY2011. Brazil, Australia, Indonesia, New Zealand, and Colombia are also important suppliers of agricultural imports to the United States.

---

* This is an edited, reformatted and augmented version of a Congressional Research Service publication, CRS Report for Congress 98-253, from www.crs.gov, Prepared for Members and Committees of Congress, dated July 29, 2011.

According to estimates by the Organization for Economic Cooperation and Development (OECD), the United States provides the third-lowest amount of government policy-generated support to its agricultural sector among OECD countries. The United States' average applied tariff for agricultural products is estimated by the World Trade Organization to be 8.9%, a little more than twice the average applied tariff for non-agricultural products. Export subsidies, export credit guarantees, and market development programs are among the programs used by the United States to promote U.S. agricultural exports. The United States also provides U.S. agricultural commodities to developing countries as food aid for emergency relief or use in nonemergency development activities.

U.S. Agricultural Exports, Imports, and Trade Balance

- According to USDA, FY2011 agricultural exports are forecast to reach $137 billion, well above the fiscal 2008 record level of $115 billion. Increased demand for commodities as the global economy recovers from recession is a major reason for the increase in FY2011 exports.
- U.S. agricultural imports are forecast to reach $93 billion—a new record high—in FY2011, a $14 billion increase over FY2010 agricultural imports.
- The expected $44 billion U.S. agricultural trade surplus for FY2011 is well above FY2008's all-time high of $36 billion.

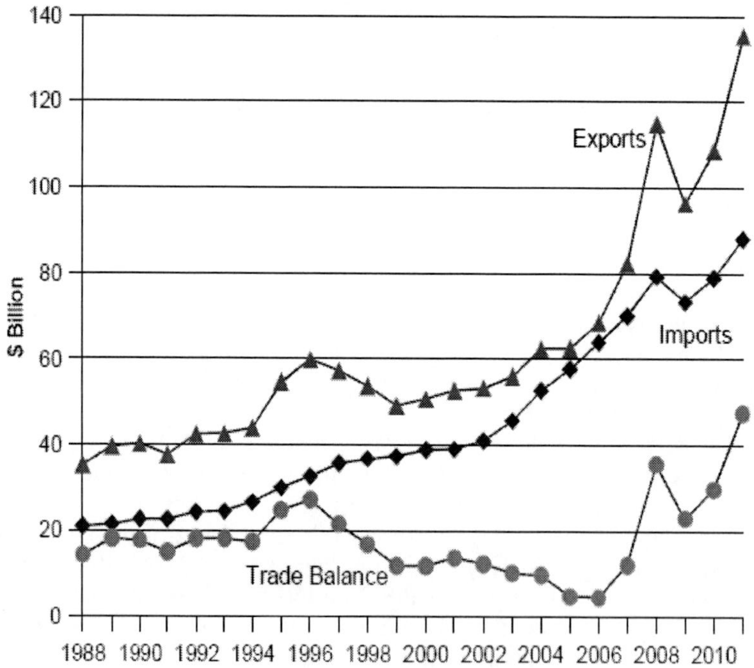

Source: U.S. Department of Agriculture. Economic Research Service.
F = Forecast.

Figure 1. U.S. Agricultural Exports, Imports, and the Trade Balance, FY1998-FY2011F.

Table 1. U.S. Agricultural Exports and Imports, FY1988-FY2011F ($ billion)

Year	Exports	Imports	Balance
1988	35.3	21.0	14.3
1989	39.6	21.5	18.1
1990	40.2	22.6	17.7
1991	37.6	22.6	15.0
1992	42.4	24.3	18.1
1993	42.6	24.4	18.1
1994	43.9	26.6	17.3
1995	54.6	29.9	24.7
1996	59.8	32.6	27.2
1997	57.3	35.8	21.5
1998	53.6	36.8	16.8
1999	49.1	37.3	11.8
2000	50.7	38.9	11.9
2001	52.7	39.0	13.7
2002	53.3	41.0	12.3
2003	56.0	45.7	10.3
2004	62.4	52.7	9.7
2005	62.5	57.7	4.8
2006	68.6	64.0	4.6
2007	82.2	70.1	12.1
2008	114.9	79.3	35.6
2009	96.3	73.4	22.9
2010	108.7	79.0	29.7
2011F	137.0	93.0	44.0

Source: U.S. Department of Agriculture. Economic Research Service, Outlook for U.S. Agricultural Trade, AES70, May 26, 2011, available at http://usda.mannlib. cornell.edu/usda/ers/AES//2010s/2011/AES-05-26-2011.pdf.

Note: F= Forecast.

SHARES OF U.S. CROP PRODUCTION EXPORTED: SELECTED COMMODITIES

- In 2010/2011, a forecast 58.2% of the U.S. wheat crop will be exported, while 15.8% of the U.S. corn crop will move into world markets.
- The export share of soybeans is forecast to be 47.8% in 2010/2011. Tight world stocks of oilseeds and strong foreign demand have pushed soybean exports up.
- Cotton's export share in 2010/2011 is forecast to be 86%. Cotton is the United States' most export-dependent field crop.

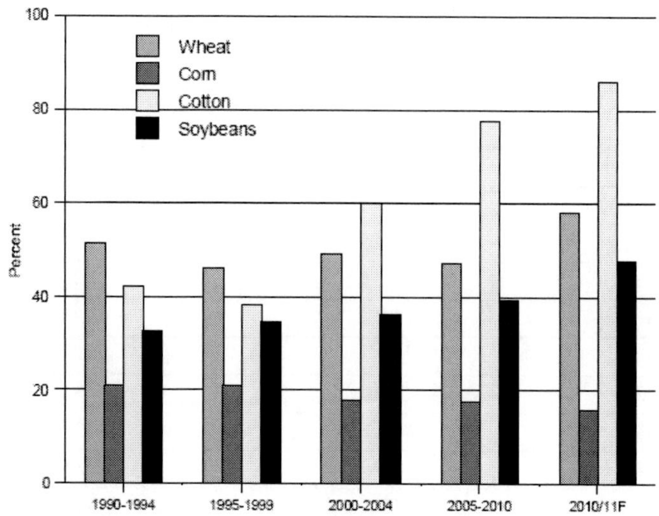

Source: U.S. Department of Agriculture. Economic Research Service.

Figure 2. U.S. Agricultural Exports: Share of U.S. Production Exported, 1990/1991-2010/2011F.

Table 2. U.S. Agricultural Exports: Shares of U.S. Crop Production Exported, 1990/1991-2010/2011F (percent)

Year	Wheat	Corn	Cotton	Soybeans
1990/91	38.4	22.1	50.3	28.9
1991/92	65.5	21.4	37.7	34.4
1992/93	55.5	17.7	32.1	35.2
1993/94	50.8	20.6	42.5	31.5
1994/95	51.5	23.0	47.8	33.4
1995/96	56.9	28.1	42.9	39.1
1996/97	44.0	19.9	36.2	37.2
1997/98	41.9	16.2	39.9	32.5
1998/99	41.8	21.0	30.9	29.4
1999/00	47.1	20.7	39.8	36.7
2000/01	46.2	19.2	39.2	36.1
2001/02	49.6	19.6	54.2	36.8
2002/03	51.7	18.0	69.1	37.9
2003/04	50.3	19.0	75.4	36.1
2004/05	48.4	15.1	62.1	35.1
2005/06	47.3	19.9	74.0	30.6
2006/07	50.5	20.3	60.0	34.9
2007/08	61.4	18.3	71.0	43.3
2008/09	39.8	15.5	103.5	43.1
2009/10	40.0	15.0	98.8	44.7
2010/11F	58.2	15.8	86.0	47.8

Source: Calculated by CRS using data from the U.S. Department of Agriculture's Foreign Agricultural Service Production, Supply and Distribution Online database, http://www.fas.usda.gov/psdonline/psdHome.aspx.

Note: F = Forecast.

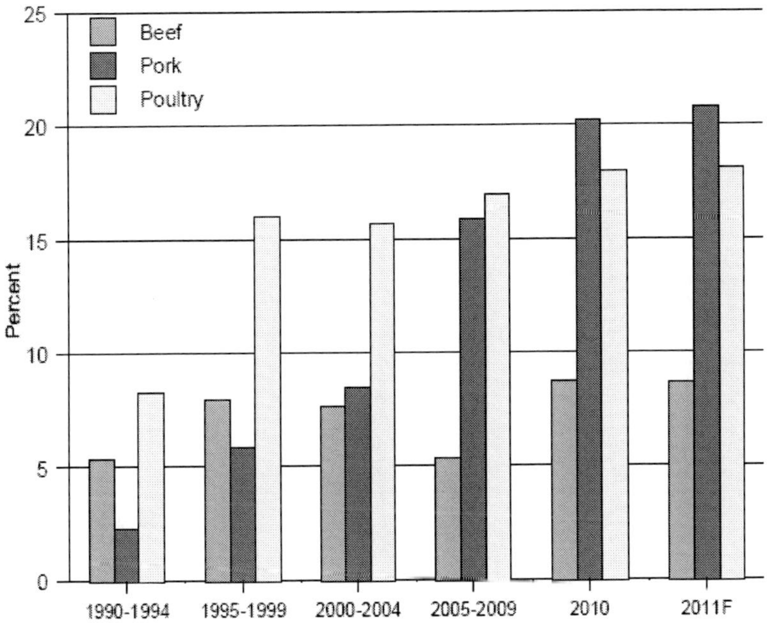

Source: U.S. Department of Agriculture. Economic Research Service.

Figure 3. U.S. Agricultural Exports: Shares of U.S. Livestock Products Exported, 1990-2011F.

SHARES OF U.S. LIVESTOCK PRODUCTS EXPORTED: SELECTED COMMODITIES

- U.S. livestock products are much less export-dependent than crops.
- Beef exports, which grew from around 4% of production in 1990 to almost 10% by 2003, have slowly recovered from export bans on U.S. beef following the 2003 discovery of a BSE-infected cow in the United States. The beef export share of production in 2011 is forecast to be 8.7%.
- Pork exports as a share of production have grown substantially, from 1.6% in 1990 to a forecast 20.8% in 2011.
- Poultry's export share of production has almost tripled since 1990, from 6.2% to a forecast 18.1% in 2011.

COMPOSITION OF U.S. AGRICULTURAL EXPORTS: MAJOR COMMODITY COMPONENTS

- The United States exports a wide range of agricultural products, including horticultural products, field crops, livestock products, and poultry.
- Oilseeds (mainly soybeans) and oilseed products (mainly meal and oil)—with a forecast value of $30.2 billion in FY2011—are the largest commodity component of U.S. agricultural exports.

Table 3. USAgricultural Exports: Shares of U.S. Production of Livestock Exported, 1990-2011F

Year	Beef	Pork	Poultry
1990	4.4	1.6	6.2
1991	5.1	1.8	6.4
1992	5.7	2.4	7.1
1993	5.5	2.6	8.9
1994	6.5	3.1	12.1
1995	7.1	4.4	15.7
1996	7.2	5.7	16.9
1997	8.3	6.0	16.3
1998	8.3	6.5	15.8
1999	9.0	6.6	15.6
2000	9.1	6.8	16.3
2001	8.6	8.0	18.0
2002	8.9	8.2	15.1
2003	9.5	8.6	15.2
2004	1.9	10.6	14.2
2005	2.8	12.9	14.9
2006	4.3	14.2	14.8
2007	5.4	14.3	16.5
2008	7.0	20.0	19.1
2009	7.4	17.8	19.4
2010	8.8	20.2	18.0
2011F	8.7	20.8	18.1

Source: Calculated by CRS using data from the U.S. Department of Agriculture's Foreign Agricultural Service Production, Supply and Distribution Online database, http://www.fas.usda.gov/psdonline/psdHome.aspx.

Note: F = Forecast.

- Horticultural product exports (fruits, vegetables, tree nuts, and their preparations)—forecast to be $25 billion in FY2011—comprise the second-largest commodity category of U.S. agricultural exports in FY2011.
- Livestock and poultry products together would amount to more than $21 billion in FY2011.
- Field crop exports (including feed grains, wheat, cotton, and tobacco) are forecast to account for almost $37 billion of U.S. agricultural exports in FY2011.

Composition of U.S. Agricultural Exports: Bulk, Consumer-Ready, and Intermediate Product Exports

- *Bulk agricultural export*s include products like wheat, coarse grains, cotton, and soybeans.
- *Intermediate product*s have been processed to some extent and include products like wheat flour, soybean oil, and feeds.

- *Consumer-ready products* include both processed products such as breakfast cereals and products such as fresh fruits and vegetables, meat and dairy products, and wine and beer.
- Until 1990, bulk agricultural exports were the mainstay of U.S. farm export trade. The total of high-value (intermediate plus consumer-ready) products has exceeded the value of bulk agricultural exports in every fiscal year since FY1991.
- In FY2010, high-value exports accounted for 60.5% of total U.S. agricultural exports and bulk exports for 39.5%.

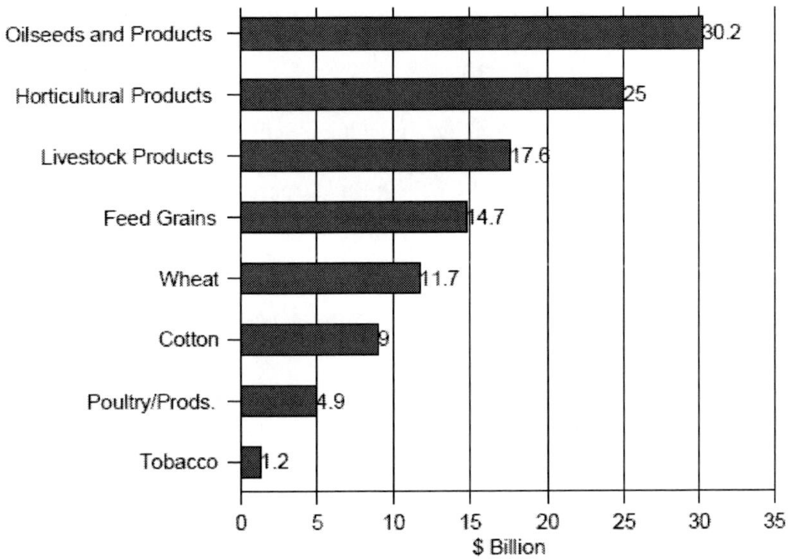

Source: U.S. Department of Agriculture. Economic Research Service. F = Forecast.

Figure 4. U.S. Agricultural Exports of Major Commodities, FY2011F.

Table 4. U.S. Agricultural Exports of Major Commodities, FY2011F ($ billions)

Commodity	FY2011F Exports
Oilseeds and Products	30.2
Horticultural Products	25.0
Livestock Products	17.6
Feed Grains	14.7
Wheat	11.7
Cotton	9.0
Poultry/Prods.	4.9
Tobacco	1.2

Source: U.S. Department of Agriculture. Economic Research Service, Outlook for U.S. Agricultural Trade AES70, May 26, 2011, available at http://usda.mannlib. cornell.edu/usda/ers/AES// 2010s/ 2011/AES-05-26-2011.pdf.

Note: F = Forecast.

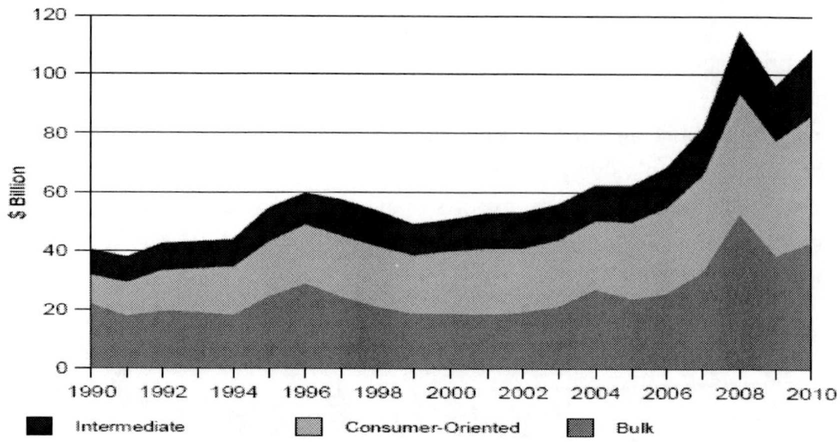

Source: U.S. Department of Agriculture. Foreign Agricultural Service.

Figure 5. U.S. Agricultural Exports, FY1990-FY2010: Bulk, Consumer-Oriented, and Intermediate Product Exports.

Major Country Markets for U.S. Agricultural Exports

- *China* is now forecast to be the top market for U.S. agricultural exports in FY2011, with exports valued at $21 billion, surpassing *Canada* with $18.5 billion.
- *Mexico*, with Canada a U.S. partner in the North American Free Trade Agreement (NAFTA), is the third-largest market for U.S. agricultural exports, with exports valued at $17 billion. Total U.S. agricultural exports to its NAFTA partners are forecast at $37 billion for FY2011.
- *Japan* ($13 billion forecast for FY2010), which was the number-one U.S. destination for agricultural products for many years, is forecast to be the fourth-largest export destination. It is followed by the *EU-27*, the fifth-largest U.S. farm export market, with forecast agricultural exports of $10 billion.
- Other Asian markets—*South Korea, Taiwan, Hong Kong*—also are major markets for U.S. agricultural exports, with forecast values in FY2011 of $6.5 billion, $3.5 billion, and $3.3 billion, respectively.

World Export Market Shares: Crops

- *Wheat*: The United States is the major supplier of wheat and wheat products to the world market, with a forecast export market share of 28.2% in marketing year 2010/2011. The EU (16.9%), Canada (14.1%), and Australia (12.1%) are major competitors in this market (see *Figure 7* and *Table 7*).
- *Rice:* Thailand (33.1% export market share forecast for 2010/2011) is the world's major rice exporter; but Vietnam (19.9%) has emerged as a major competitor. Both Pakistan's and India's export market shares in 2010/2011 are forecast to be 8%. The United States would be the world's third-largest rice exporter with a forecast share in 2010/2011 of 11.4% (see *Figure 8* and *Table 8*).

Table 5. U.S. Agricultural Exports, FY1990-FY2010: Total, Bulk, Consumer-Ready, and Intermediate Product Exports ($ thousands)

Year	Total	Bulk	% of Total	Consumer-Oriented	% of Total	Intermediate	% of Total
1990	40,347,960	21,793,461	54.0	9,891,735	24.5	8,662,764	21.5
1991	37,864,207	17,701,487	46.7	11,574,646	30.6	8,588,074	22.7
1992	42,554,780	19,523,240	45.9	13,689,029	32.2	9,342,511	22.0
1993	43,057,753	19,084,550	44.3	14,889,726	34.6	9,083,477	21.1
1994	43,893,020	17,940,578	40.9	16,460,463	37.5	9,491,979	21.6
1995	54,613,152	24,446,611	44.8	18,847,340	34.5	11,319,201	20.7
1996	59,785,653	28,781,235	48.1	20,167,462	33.7	10,836,956	18.1
1997	57,305,347	24,250,805	42.3	20,878,010	36.4	12,176,532	21.2
1998	53,661,663	20,925,957	39.0	20,641,538	38.5	12,094,168	22.5
1999	49,118,260	18,596,897	37.9	19,898,512	40.5	10,622,851	21.6
2000	50,761,767	18,580,955	36.6	21,481,221	42.3	10,699,591	21.1
2001	52,716,911	18,436,458	35.0	22,541,751	42.8	11,738,702	22.3
2002	53,319,318	19,122,275	35.9	21,708,519	40.7	12,488,524	23.4
2003	56,013,986	21,224,523	37.9	22,723,487	40.6	12,065,977	21.5
2004	62,400,350	26,903,911	43.1	23,353,486	37.4	12,142,954	19.5
2005	62,516,299	23,613,456	37.8	26,287,920	42.0	12,614,923	20.2
2006	68,592,956	25,619,902	37.4	29,363,783	42.8	13,609,271	19.8
2007	82,216,762	32,883,623	40.0	33,191,509	40.4	16,141,630	19.6
2008	114,909,725	52,375,640	45.6	41,387,674	36.0	21,146,412	18.4
2009	96,295,144	38,438,804	39.9	39,406,888	40.9	18,449,452	19.2
2010	108,663,682	42,882,719	39.5	43,277,761	39.8	22,503,203	20.7

Source: Data in this table are compiled from U.S. Department of Agriculture, Foreign Agricultural Service databases, available at http://www.fas.usda.gov/ gats/default. aspx.

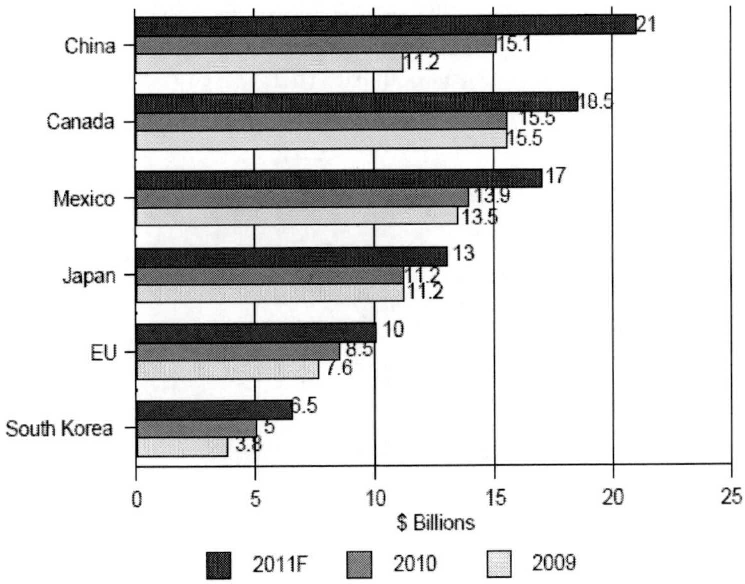

Source: U.S. Department of Agriculture. Economic Research Service. F = Forecast.

Figure 6. Major Country Markets for U.S. Exports, FY2009-FY2011F.

Table 6. Major Country Markets for USAgricultural Exports, FY2009-FY2011F ($ billion)

Country	2009	2010	2011F
China	11.2	15.1	21.0
Canada	15.5	16.6	18.5
Mexico	13.5	13.9	17.0
Japan	11.2	11.2	13.0
EU-27	7.6	8.5	10.0
South Korea	3.8	5.0	6.5
Taiwan	2.9	3.2	3.5
Hong Kong	1.8	2.5	3.3
Turkey	1.4	2.0	2.9
Russia	1.4	1.0	1.4

Source: U.S. Department of Agriculture. Economic Research Service, Outlook for U.S. Agricultural Trade, AES70, May 26, 2011, available at http://usda.mannlib. cornell.edu/usda/rs/AES// 2010s/2011/AES-05-26-2011.pdf.

Note: F = Forecast.

- *Corn:* The United States has the world's largest export market for corn with a 2010/2011 forecast export share of 54.3% (see *Figure 9* and *Table 9*). Since the mid-1990s, Brazil has increased its share of world corn exports, while China, an exporter of corn during most of the last 16 years, has lost export market share.
- *Soybeans:* The United States is forecast to be the world's main supplier of soybeans to the world market in 2010/2011 with a share of 44%, down from 73% in 1995/1996. Over that same period, Brazil's export market share has grown from 10.9% to 33.1%. (see *Figure 10* and *Table 10*).
- *Cotton:* U.S. cotton exports are estimated to be 40.8% of the world total in 2010/2011. U.S. competitors include India (12.4%), Uzbekistan (9.1%), Australia (7.8%) and West/Central African countries (6.3%) (see *Figure 11* and *Table 11*).

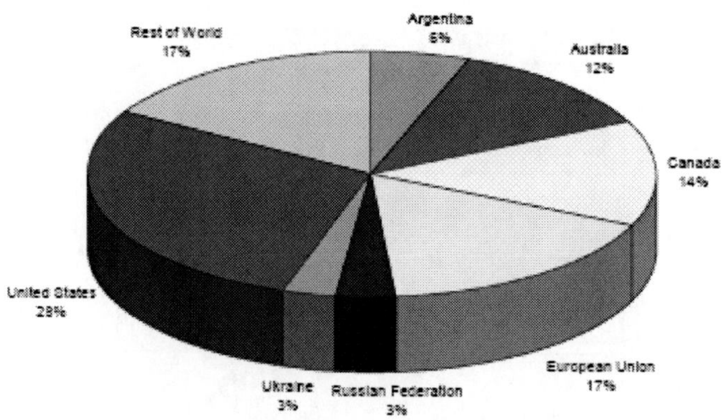

Source: U.S. Department of Agriculture, Foreign Agricultural Service.

Notes: F = Forecast.

Figure 7. Shares of World Exports of Wheat and Wheat Products, 2010/2011F.

Table 7. Shares of World Exports of Wheat and Wheat Products, 1995/1996-2010/2011F (percent)

Country	*1995/96*	*1996/97*	*1997/98*	*1998/99*	*1999/00*	*2000/01*	*2001/02*
Argentina	4.5	9.7	9.4	9.0	9.9	11.2	10.8
Australia	12.2	17.5	14.7	15.8	15.3	16.3	15.3
Canada	17.2	17.4	20.4	14.1	17.3	16.9	15.5
European Union[a]	13.3	17.1	13.6	14.3	18.2	15.3	11.8
Russian Federation	0.2	0.7	1.1	1.6	0.5	0.7	4.0
Ukraine	1.4	1.2	1.3	4.6	1.7	0.1	5.1
United States	34.1	26.2	27.1	28.4	26.3	27.4	24.3
Rest of World	17.2	10.1	12.4	12.1	10.8	12.1	13.1
Country	*2002/03*	*2003/04*	*2004/05*	*2005/06*	*2006/07*	*2007/08*	*2008/09*
Argentina	5.9	7.1	11.9	7.3	10.6	8.8	6.0
Australia	10.2	14.6	13.9	13.3	9.7	6.4	9.4
Canada	8.8	15.0	13.3	13.7	16.7	14.2	13.0
European Union[a]	17.0	9.5	12.9	13.8	11.9	10.5	17.7
Russian Federation	11.8	3.0	7.4	9.3	9.3	10.5	12.8
Ukraine	6.2	0.1	3.9	5.7	2.9	1.1	9.1
United States	21.2	31.0	25.0	23.7	21.5	29.4	18.9
Rest of World	18.9	19.7	11.7	13.1	17.3	19.1	13.0
Country	*2009/2010E*	*2010/2011F*					
Argentina	3.9	5.6					
Australia	10.2	12.1					
Canada	14.1	14.1					
European Union[a]	16.5	16.9					
Russian Federation	13.8	3.2					
Ukraine	7.0	3.2					
United States	18.0	28.2					
Rest of World	16.5	16.7					

Source: U.S. Department of Agriculture, Foreign Agricultural Service Production, Supply and Distribution Online database, http://www.fas.usda.gov/ psdonline/ psdHome.aspx.

Notes: July-June marketing year. E = Estimate. F = Forecast.

[a].1995/1996-1998/1999 data are EU-15 and 1990/2000 to present are EU-27.

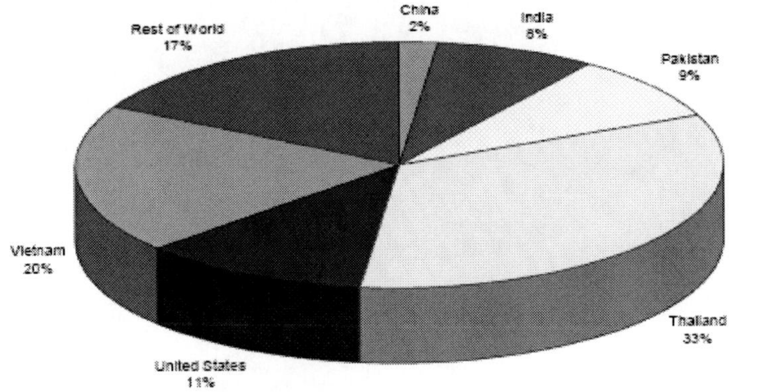

Source: U.S. Department of Agriculture, Foreign Agricultural.

Figure 8. Shares of World Exports of Rice, 2010/2011F.

Table 8. Shares of World Exports of Rice, 1994/1995-2010/2011F (percent)

Country	*1994/95*	*1995/96*	*1996/97*	*1997/98*	*1998/99*	*1999/00*	*2000/01*
China	0.2	1.3	5.0	13.5	10.9	13.0	7.6
India	20.0	18.6	11.1	16.9	11.1	6.4	7.9
Pakistan	8.5	8.5	9.4	7.2	7.4	8.9	9.9
Thailand	28.6	26.8	27.7	23.0	26.9	28.7	30.8
United States	14.6	13.3	12.2	11.5	10.7	12.5	10.2
Vietnam	11.1	15.4	17.6	13.7	18.4	14.8	14.5
Rest of World	17.1	16.1	17.0	14.2	14.7	15.8	19.0
Country	*2001/02*	*2002/03*	*2003/04*	*2004/05*	*2005/06*	*2006/07*	*2007/08*
China	7.1	9.4	3.2	2.3	4.2	4.2	3.3
India	23.9	16.1	11.7	16.2	15.6	19.8	11.4
Pakistan	5.8	7.1	7.3	10.5	12.3	8.5	10.3
Thailand	26.1	27.4	37.2	25.1	25.4	30.0	33.7
United States	11.6	13.8	11.2	13.3	11.2	9.4	10.8
Vietnam	11.7	13.8	15.8	17.9	16.2	14.2	15.6
Country	*2008/09*	*2009/10E*	*2010/11F*				
Rest of World	13.9	12.5	13.6	14.8	15.0	14.0	14.9
China	2.7	2.0	2.0				
India	7.3	6.3	8.0				
Country	*2008/09*	*2009/10E*	*2010/11F*				
Pakistan	10.9	12.8	8.8				
Thailand	29.3	28.9	33.1				
United States	10.2	12.3	11.4				
Vietnam	20.3	21.6	19.9				
Rest of World	19.3	16.1	16.9				

Source: U.S. Department of Agriculture, Foreign Agricultural Service Production, Supply and Distribution Online database, http://www.fas.usda.gov/psdonline/ psdHome.aspx.

Notes: July-June marketing year.

E = Estimate.

F = Forecast.

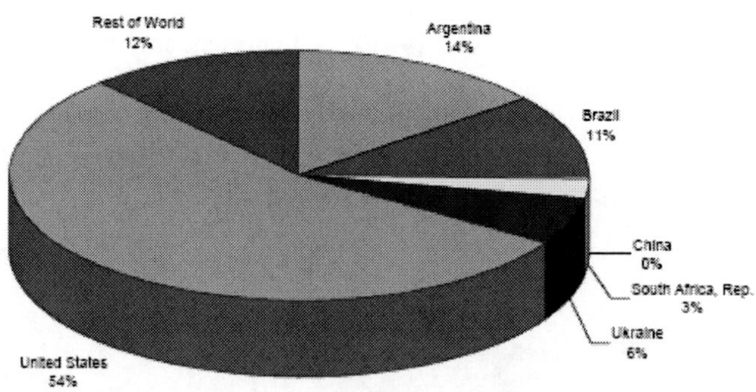

Source: U.S. Department of Agriculture, Foreign Agricultural Service.

Note: F = Forecast.

Figure 9. Shares of World Exports of Corn, 2010/2011F.

Table 9. Shares of World Exports of Corn, 1995/1996-2010/2011F (percent)

Country	*1995/96*	*1996/97*	*1997/98*	*1998/99*	*1999/00*	*2000/01*	*2001/02*
Argentina	10.7	15.3	20.2	11.4	12.3	16.1	11.8
Brazil	0.3	0.7	0.0	0.0	0.1	4.9	5.3
China	0.2	5.8	9.8	4.9	13.7	9.6	11.8
South Africa, Rep.	2.7	2.4	1.7	1.2	1.2	1.9	1.6
Ukraine	0.1	0.0	0.9	0.5	0.1	0.5	0.5
United States	81.4	70.0	59.9	75.7	68.4	63.7	64.9
Rest of World	4.5	5.7	7.5	6.3	4.3	3.3	4.1
Country	***2002/03***	***2003/04***	***2004/05***	***2005/06***	***2006/07***	***2007/08***	***2008/09***
Argentina	16.0	13.2	18.1	12.9	17.2	16.0	10.1
Brazil	4.1	7.4	1.9	3.4	8.8	8.0	8.6
China	19.8	9.6	10.0	4.5	5.8	0.6	0.2
South Africa, Rep.	1.5	1.0	2.0	1.7	0.5	1.1	2.5
Ukraine	1.1	1.6	3.1	3.0	1.1	2.1	6.5
United States	53.2	61.7	59.6	67.8	59.3	61.7	56.9
Rest of World	4.3	5.6	5.3	6.7	7.4	10.5	15.2
Country	***2009/10E***	***2010/11F***					
Argentina	18.2	14.1					
Brazil	9.3	10.9					
China	0.2	0.2					
South Africa, Rep.	1.7	2.7					
Ukraine	5.4	6.0					
United States	53.5	54.3					
Rest of World	11.7	11.8					

Source: U.S. Department of Agriculture, Foreign Agricultural Service Production, Supply and Distribution Online database, http://www.fas.usda.gov/psdonline/ psdHome.aspx.

Notes: October-September marketing year.

E = Estimate.

F = Forecast.

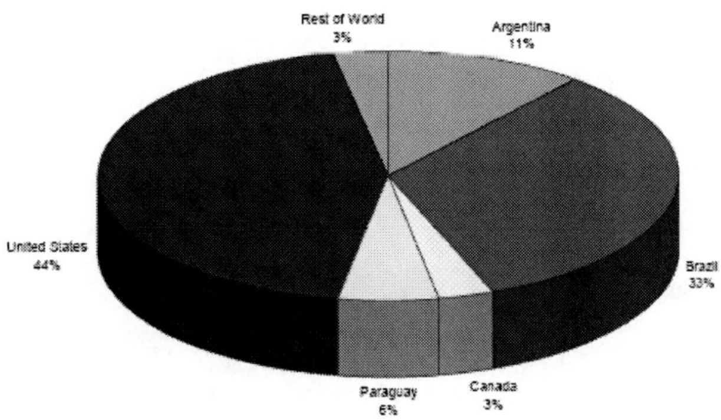

Source: U.S. Department of Agriculture, Foreign Agricultural Service.

Note: F = Forecast.

Figure 10. Shares of World Exports of Soybeans, 2010/2011F.

Table 10. Shares of World Exports of Soybeans, 1995/1996-2010/2011F (percent)

Country	*1995/96*	*1996/97*	*1997/98*	*1998/99*	*1999/2000*	*2000/01*	*2001/02*
Argentina	6.6	2.1	7.2	8.1	9.0	13.6	11.3
Brazil	10.9	22.9	22.3	23.5	24.3	28.8	27.4
Canada	1.9	1.3	2.0	2.3	2.1	1.4	0.9
Paraguay	5.0	5.8	5.8	6.1	4.4	4.4	4.3
United States	73.0	65.6	60.5	57.7	58.2	50.5	54.7
Rest of World	2.5	2.3	2.2	2.3	2.0	1.3	1.3
Country	***2002/03***	***2003/04***	***2004/05***	***2005/06***	***2006/07***	***2007/08***	***2008/09***
Argentina	14.1	12.0	14.8	11.4	13.5	17.6	7.3
Brazil	32.1	36.4	31.1	40.8	33.1	32.2	39.0
Canada	1.2	1.6	1.7	2.1	2.4	2.2	2.6
Paraguay	5.0	4.8	4.6	3.2	5.5	5.8	2.9
United States	46.4	43.1	46.1	40.3	42.9	40.0	45.3
Rest of World	1.3	2.1	1.8	2.1	2.6	2.2	2.9
Argentina	14.1	11.2					
Brazil	30.8	33.1					
Canada	2.4	2.9					
Paraguay	5.8	5.7					
United States	44.0	44.0					
Rest of World	2.8	3.1					

Source: U.S. Department of Agriculture, Foreign Agricultural Service Production, Supply and Distribution Online database, http://www.fas.usda.gov/psdonline/ psdHome.aspx.

Notes: Marketing year.

E = Estimate.

F = Forecast.

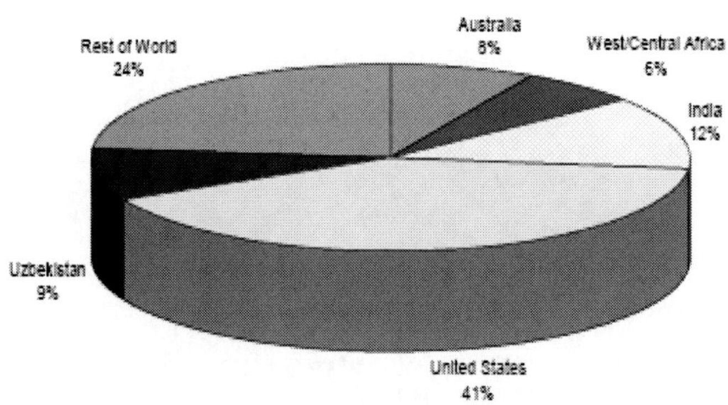

Source: U.S. Department of Agriculture, Foreign Agricultural Service.

Notes: West/Central Africa includes Benin, Burkina Faso, Cameroon, Central African Republic, Chad, Cote

d'Ivoire, Mali, Niger, Senegal, and Togo.

F = Forecast.

Figure 11. Shares of World Exports of Cotton, 2010/2011F.

Table 11. Shares of World Exports of Cotton, 1995/1996-2010/2011F

Country	*1995/96*	*1996/97*	*1997/98*	*1998/99*	*1999/00*	*2000/01*	*2001/02*
Australia	5.3	8.9	10.1	12.9	11.8	14.9	10.7
West/Central Africa[a]	10.2	12.3	13.5	15.3	13.8	12.4	12.2
India	2.1	4.4	1.2	0.8	0.3	0.4	0.2
United States	28.1	25.6	28.1	18.3	24.8	25.7	37.7
Uzbekistan	16.5	17.0	17.1	16.2	15.5	13.2	12.0
Rest of World	37.8	31.8	30.0	36.5	33.9	33.4	27.1
Country	***2002/03***	***2003/04***	***2004/05***	***2005/06***	***2006/07***	***2007/08***	***2008/09***
Australia	8.7	6.5	5.7	6.4	5.7	3.1	4.0
West/Central Africa[a]	12.4	13.4	11.8	9.9	10.3	6.8	7.1
India	0.2	2.1	1.9	8.2	13.0	19.2	7.8
United States	39.1	41.4	41.2	39.4	34.6	35.0	44.1
Uzbekistan	11.2	9.3	11.3	10.7	12.0	10.8	10.0
Rest of World	28.4	27.3	28.1	25.4	24.4	25.1	26.9
Country	***2009/10E***	***2010/11F***					
Australia	5.9	7.8					
West/Central Africa[a]	6.4	6.3					
India	18.4	12.4					
United States	33.9	40.8					
Uzbekistan	10.7	9.1					
Rest of World	24.7	23.6					

Source: U.S. Department of Agriculture, Foreign Agricultural Service Production, Supply and Distribution Online database, http://www.fas.usda.gov/psdonline/ psdHome.aspx.

Notes: Marketing year. E = Estimate. F = Forecast.

[a] Includes Benin, Burkina Faso, Cameroon, Central African Republic, Chad, Cote d'Ivoire, Mali, Niger, Senegal, and Togo.

World Market Shares: Livestock and Dairy

- *Beef:* Brazil, with 24.4% (forecast) of world exports in 2011, is the largest supplier of beef to world markets. The U.S. share of world beef exports is forecast to be 13.5% in 2010. Lingering effects of mad cow disease continue to affect demand for U.S. beef in world markets; the U.S. share of world beef exports had reached 18.9% in 2000. (See *Figure 12* and *Table 12.)*
- *Pork***:** The United States is forecast to have the largest export market share for pork (35%) in 2011. Main competitors for pork export market shares include the EU (25.5%) and Canada (19.4%). (See *Figure 13* and *Table 13*.)
- *Poultry:* Brazil is the world's leading supplier of poultry meat to the world market (37.1% forecast export market share for 2011). The United States, with 33.3% of world poultry meat exports, and the EU with 10.5% have lost market share to Brazil over the past decade. (See *Figure 14* and *Table 14.)*
- *Dairy Products:* For 2011, New Zealand (29.4%) and the United States (27.4%) are forecast to be the leading suppliers of nonfat dry milk to world markets (see *Figure 15* and *Table 15*). The EU (42.4%) is the leading supplier of cheese to world markets (see *Figure 16* and *Table 16*), while New Zealand (58.5%) is the world's largest exporter of butter (see *Figure 17* and *Table 17*).

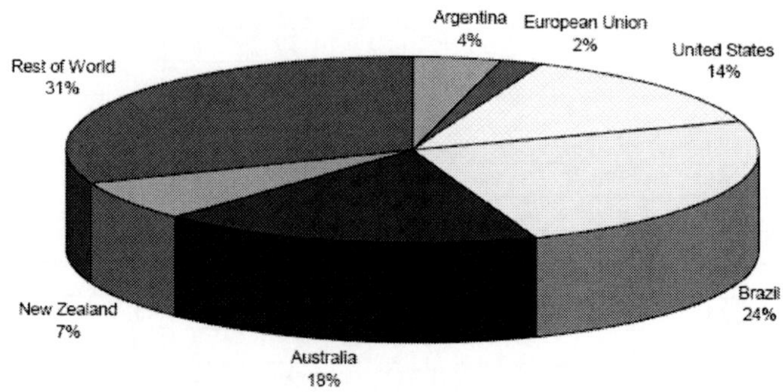

Source: U.S. Department of Agriculture, Foreign Agricultural Service.
Note: F = Forecast.

Figure 12. Shares of World Exports of Beef and Veal, 2011F.

Table 12. Shares of World Exports of Beef and Veal, 1995-2011F

Country	*1995*	*1996*	*1997*	*1998*	*1999*	*2000*	*2001*
Argentina	9.8	9.5	7.8	5.5	6.0	6.0	2.9
European Union[a]	22.0	21.1	18.8	14.2	17.3	11.2	10.4
United States	15.1	16.3	16.7	18.0	18.6	18.9	17.6
Brazil	4.2	4.3	4.0	5.5	7.8	8.2	12.7
Australia	20.3	19.7	20.1	22.7	21.3	22.2	23.5
New Zealand	9.1	9.6	8.6	8.7	7.4	8.0	8.3
Rest of World	19.5	19.5	24.0	25.3	21.5	25.5	24.7
Country	*2002*	*2003*	*2004*	*2005*	*2006*	*2007*	*2008*
Argentina	5.4	5.9	9.3	10.3	7.4	7.1	5.6
European Union[a]	9.0	6.7	5.5	3.5	2.9	1.8	2.7
United States	17.3	17.6	3.1	4.3	6.9	8.6	11.4
Brazil	13.6	17.9	24.2	25.2	27.8	28.9	24.0
Australia	20.9	19.1	20.6	19.0	19.1	18.5	18.8
New Zealand	7.4	8.4	8.9	7.9	7.1	6.6	7.1
Rest of World	26.6	24.4	28.5	29.8	28.9	28.5	30.3
Country	*2009*	*2010P*	*2011F*				
Argentina	8.9	4.1	4.0				
European Union[a]	2.0	2.2	2.2				
United States	12.0	14.3	13.5				
Brazil	21.8	23.1	24.4				
Australia	18.6	18.3	17.9				
New Zealand	7.0	7.0	6.7				
Rest of World	29.6	31.0	31.3				

Source: U.S. Department of Agriculture, Foreign Agricultural Service Production, Supply and Distribution Online database, http://www.fas.usda.gov/psdonline/ psdHome.aspx.

Notes:

P = Preliminary.

F = Forecast.

[a] 1995-1998 data are EU-15 and 1999 to present are EU-27.

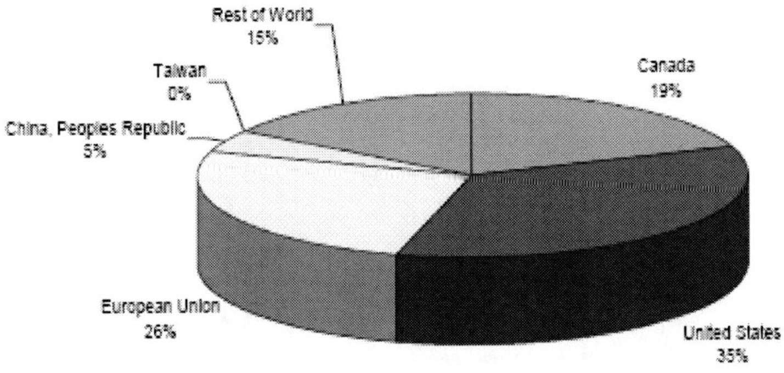

Source: U.S. Department of Agriculture, Foreign Agricultural Service.
Note: F = Forecast.

Figure 13. Shares of World Pork Exports, 2011F.

Table 13. Shares of World Pork Exports, 1994-2011F (percent)

Country	*1995*	*1996*	*1997*	*1998*	*1999*	*2000*	*2001*
Canada	15.5	13.6	14.4	14.7	17.0	21.4	22.7
United States	15.1	15.6	16.2	19.0	17.9	18.9	21.8
European Union[a]	32.6	30.5	32.6	35.1	49.0	43.3	30.2
China	4.4	4.8	6.9	6.9	4.4	4.7	7.0
Taiwan	16.1	13.7	2.2	0.1	0.0	0.0	0.1
Rest of World	16.3	21.8	27.6	24.3	11.8	11.7	18.3
Country	*2002*	*2003*	*2004*	*2005*	*2006*	*2007*	*2008*
Canada	23.1	23.3	20.6	21.7	20.7	20.0	18.4
United States	19.6	18.7	21.0	24.2	26.0	27.6	34.4
European Union[a]	26.6	27.3	27.6	22.8	24.6	24.9	28.1
China	8.2	9.5	11.4	10.0	10.4	6.8	3.6
Country	*2002*	*2003*	*2004*	*2005*	*2006*	*2007*	*2008*
Taiwan	0.1	0.0	0.0	0.0	0.0	0.0	0.0
Rest of World	22.5	21.1	19.4	21.3	18.3	20.7	15.4
Country	*2009*	*2010P*	*2011F*				
Canada	19.9	19.2	19.4				
United States	32.9	33.5	35.0				
European Union[a]	25.1	28.1	25.5				
China	4.1	4.1	4.6				
Taiwan	0.0	0.0	0.0				
Rest of World	17.9	15.0	15.5				

Source: U.S. Department of Agriculture, Foreign Agricultural Service Production, Supply and Distribution Online database, http://www.fas.usda.gov/psdonline/ psdHome.aspx.
Notes: F = Forecast.
[a] 1995-1998 data are EU-15 and 1999 to present are EU-27.

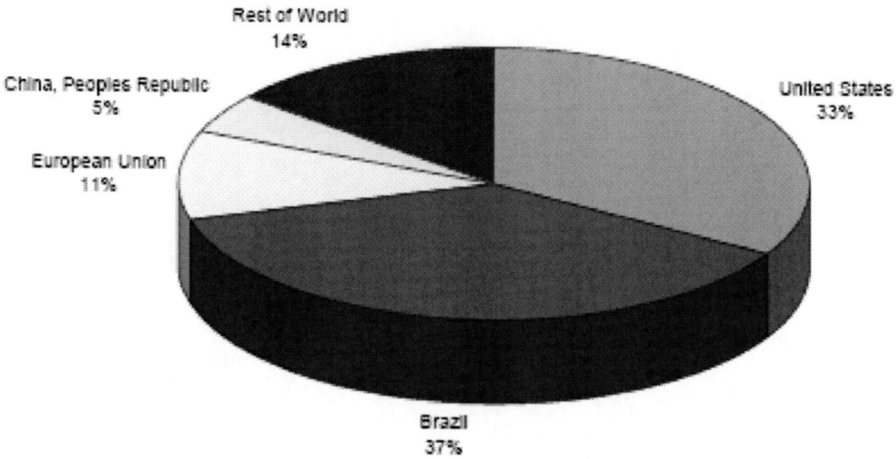

Source: U.S. Department of Agriculture, Foreign Agricultural Service.
Note: F = Forecast.

Figure 14. Shares of World Poultry Meat Exports, 2011F.

Table 14. Shares of World Total Poultry Meat Exports, 1994-2011F (percent)

Country	***1995***	***1996***	***1997***	***1998***	***1999***	***2000***	***2001***
United States	41.3	41.9	48.8	46.7	47.3	46.7	45.9
Brazil	10.0	11.7	15.1	13.8	16.7	18.2	22.3
European Union[a]	NA	NA	17.8	19.0	17.6	15.2	11.8
China (PRC)	6.2	6.6	8.1	7.6	8.5	9.7	8.9
Rest of World	42.5	39.8	10.3	12.9	9.9	10.1	11.1
Country	*2002*	*2003*	*2004*	*2005*	*2006*	*2007*	*2008*
United States	38.7	37.0	35.8	34.6	36.0	36.3	37.5
Brazil	28.0	31.6	39.9	40.1	38.2	39.6	38.5
European Union[a]	13.6	12.0	12.0	10.2	10.5	8.6	8.8
China (PRC)	7.8	6.4	4.0	4.9	4.9	4.9	3.4
Rest of World	12.1	12.9	8.3	10.3	10.3	10.7	11.7
Country	*2009*	*2010F*	*2011P*				
United States	37.7	34.9	33.3				
Brazil	36.4	36.2	37.1				
European Union[a]	9.5	11.3	10.5				
China (PRC)	3.5	4.3	4.9				
Rest of World	12.8	13.3	14.0				

Source: U.S. Department of Agriculture, Foreign Agricultural Service Production, Supply and Distribution Online database, http://www.fas.usda.gov/psdonline/ psdHome.aspx. Notes: NA = Not Available. P = Preliminary. F = Forecast.

[a] 1997-1998 data are EU-15 and 1999 to present are EU-27.

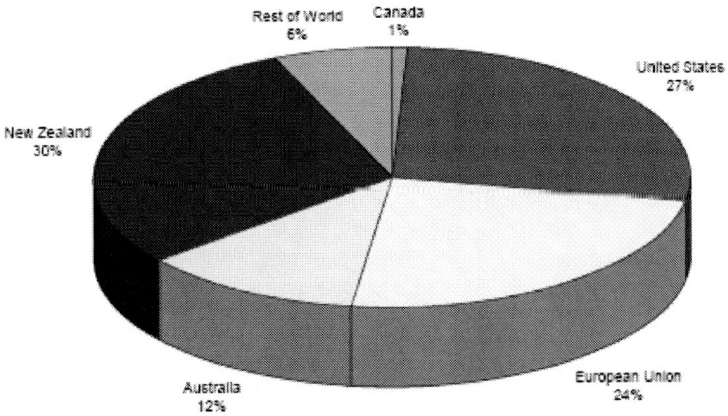

Source: U.S. Department of Agriculture, Foreign Agricultural Service.
Note: F = Forecast.

Figure 15. Shares of World Nonfat Dry Milk Exports, 2011F.

Table 15. Shares of World Nonfat Dry Milk Exports, 1995-2011F (percent)

Country	***1995***	***1996***	***1997***	***1998***	***1999***	***2000***	***2001***
Canada	2.5	2.5	2.9	3.8	2.7	1.9	3.7
United States	9.5	2.4	11.3	11.5	14.4	8.5	7.7
European Union[a]	NA	NA	27.3	19.4	24.4	27.1	22.3
Australia	10.9	12.8	19.8	22.1	15.9	15.2	17.5
New Zealand	9.7	11.5	20.7	21.8	13.6	10.5	15.6
Rest of World	67.4	70.8	18.0	21.4	29.1	36.7	33.3
Country	*2002*	*2003*	*2004*	*2005*	*2006*	*2007*	*2008*
Canada	3.7	2.4	1.1	0.5	1.2	1.1	1.0
United States	9.6	9.3	15.9	23.0	26.1	20.8	35.4
European Union[a]	19.9	22.3	19.1	15.8	8.0	16.3	16.2
Australia	17.6	12.8	12.9	11.7	17.2	14.1	10.9
New Zealand	18.9	20.8	21.0	18.4	22.1	26.3	22.8
Rest of World	30.3	32.4	30.0	30.5	25.5	21.4	13.7
Country	*2009*	*2010P*	*2011F*				
Canada	0.9	0.8	0.7				
United States	22.1	28.5	27.4				
European Union[a]	20.1	27.2	24.3				
Australia	14.5	9.7	11.8				
New Zealand	35.4	27.6	29.4				
Rest of World	7.0	6.2	6.5				

Source: U.S. Department of Agriculture, Foreign Agricultural Service Production, Supply and Distribution Online database, http://www.fas.usda.gov/psdonline/ psdHome.aspx.
Notes: NA = Not Available. P = Preliminary. F = Forecast.
[a] 1997-1998 data are EU-15 and 1999 to present are EU-27.

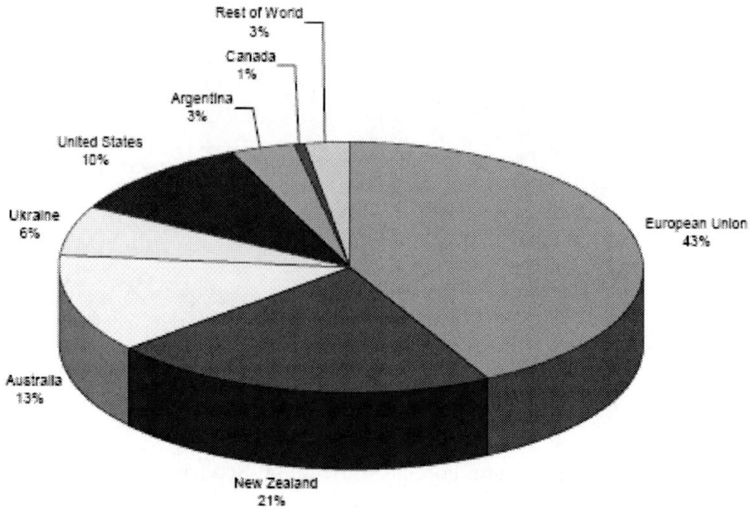

Source: U.S. Department of Agriculture, Foreign Agricultural Service.
Note: F = Forecast.

Figure 16. Shares of World Cheese Exports, 2011F.

Table 16. Shares of World Cheese Exports, 1994-2011F

Country	***1994***		***1995***		***1996***		***1997***	***1998***	***1999***	***2000***	***2001***
European Union[a]	NA		NA		NA		51.0	46.2	45.2	31.1	30.8
New Zealand[b]		5.9		6.9		6.7	25.0	25.6	26.1	16.3	16.0
Australia[c]		4.1		4.5		4.3	13.3	16.6	18.7	14.4	13.9
Ukraine		0.2		0.2		0.1	0.2	0.4	0.7	0.8	2.0
United States		1.1		1.1		1.2	4.0	4.1	4.1	3.0	3.4
Argentina		0.6		0.5		0.4	2.0	1.9	2.2	1.4	1.1
Canada		0.3		0.6		0.6	2.4	3.0	2.7	1.2	1.2
Rest of World		87.8		86.2		86.6	2.0	2.2	0.3	31.8	31.5
Country	***2002***		***2003***		***2004***		***2005***	***2006***	***2007***	***2008***	***2009***
European Union[a]		30.3		31.3		29.7	28.7	31.7	28.8	38.8	41.3
New Zealand[b]		16.7		16.9		16.4	15.2	15.1	16.7	22.4	23.5
Australia[c]		13.1		12.0		12.0	13.1	11.4	11.4	16.0	13.1
Ukraine		2.2		3.5		5.3	6.7	2.8	3.3	6.1	6.2
United States		3.3		3.0		3.5	3.3	4.0	5.4	10.4	8.7
Argentina		1.6		1.3		1.8	2.6	3.3	2.4	2.9	3.9
Canada		1.0		0.6		0.6	0.5	0.5	0.5	0.8	0.7
Rest of World		31.8		31.2		30.8	29.9	31.2	31.5	2.6	2.6
Country	***2010P***		***2011F***								
European Union[a]		42.5		42.4							
New Zealand[b]		20.9		21.2							
Australia[c]		12.1		12.9							
Ukraine		6.2		6.5							
United States		12.0		10.5							
Argentina		3.3		3.4							
Canada		0.7		0.6							

Country	*1994*	*1995*	*1996*	*1997*	*1998*	*1999*	*2000*	*2001*
Rest of World	2.3	2.5						

Source: U.S. Department of Agriculture, Foreign Agricultural Service Production, Supply and Distribution Online database, http://www.fas.usda.gov/psdonline/ psdHome.aspx.

Notes: NA = Not Available. P = Preliminary. F = Forecast.

[a] 1997-1998 data are EU-15 and 1999 to present are EU-27.

[b] Year ending May 31 of the year shown.

[c] Year ending June 30 of the year shown.

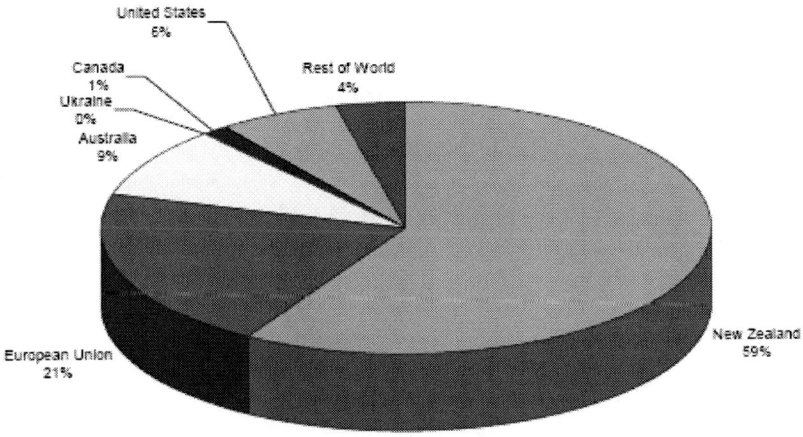

Source: U.S. Department of Agriculture, Foreign Agricultural Service.

Note: F = Forecast.

Figure 17. Shares of World Butter Exports, 2011F.

Table 17. Shares of World Butter Exports, 1994-2011F (percent)

Country	*1994*	*1995*	*1996*	*1997*	*1998*	*1999*	*2000*	*2001*
New Zealand[a]	20.2	19.3	21.0	42.1	50.2	34.1	37.0	36.3
European Union[b]	NA	NA	NA	29.2	26.8	24.5	21.4	21.7
Australia[c]	7.1	6.9	6.6	14.8	16.7	14.3	15.2	12.9
Ukraine	1.7	5.6	8.4	7.9	1.6	1.0	3.4	5.5
Canada	0.2	0.5	1.1	1.6	1.9	1.3	1.1	1.7
United States	7.1	5.2	1.7	2.4	0.5	0.2	0.4	0.0
Rest of World	63.7	62.5	61.1	2.0	2.2	24.5	21.5	21.9
Country	*2002*	*2003*	*2004*	*2005*	*2006*	*2007*	*2008*	*2009*
New Zealand[a]	35.9	33.5	31.6	27.8	35.7	40.2	50.9	60.1
European Union[b]	23.4	27.0	27.9	29.9	24.2	19.8	21.1	20.8
Australia[c]	12.7	9.2	5.9	6.2	8.0	7.3	8.0	10.2
Ukraine	1.5	1.5	3.3	2.1	1.8	0.4	0.8	0.1
Canada	1.7	1.0	1.3	1.8	1.8	1.2	0.1	0.4
United States	0.3	1.0	0.7	0.5	1.1	3.7	12.3	2.2
Rest of World	24.3	26.7	29.2	31.8	27.4	27.5	6.8	6.3
Country	*2010P*	*2011F*						
New Zealand[a]	55.9	58.5						
European Union[b]	24.8	20.9						
Australia[c]	8.2	9.1						

Ukraine	0.1	0.1							
Canada	1.2	1.3							
United States	7.0	6.3							
Rest of World	2.7	3.7							

Source: U.S. Department of Agriculture, Foreign Agricultural Service Production, Supply and Distribution Online database, http://www.fas.usda.gov/psdonline/ psdHome.aspx.

Notes: NA = Not Available. P = Preliminary. F = Forecast.

[a] Year ending May 31 of the year shown.

[b] 1997-1998 data are EU-15 and 1999 to present are EU-27.

[c] Year ending June 30 of the year shown.

World Market Shares: Sugar

- Brazil is the world's leading exporter of sugar with an export market share forecast to be 51.8% for 2010/2011.
- Australia, with 7.2% of global sugar exports, is the world's second-largest exporter of sugar.
- The United States is a sugar importer with negligible sugar exports (forecast to be 0.3% for 2010/2011).

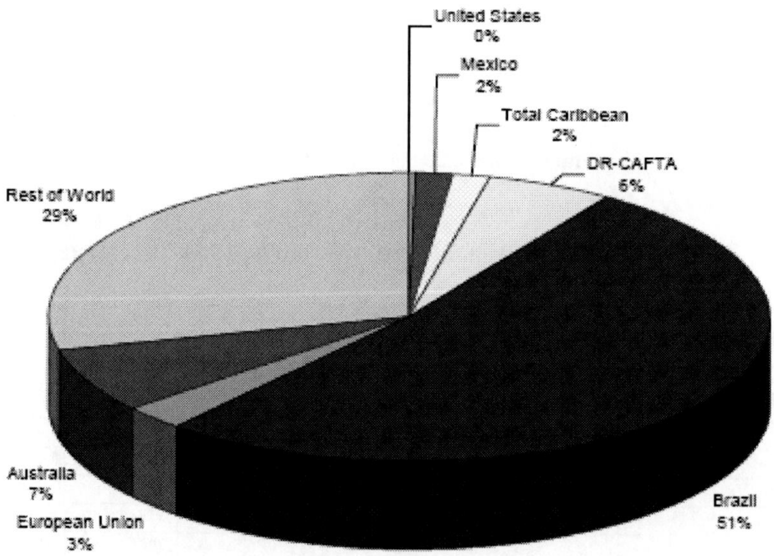

Source: U.S. Department of Agriculture, Foreign Agricultural Service.

Notes: DR-CAFTA includes Dominican Republic and Central America. The European Union (EU) data include French overseas departments of Reunion, Guadeloupe, and Martinique, but do not include intra EU trade. EU data include sugar-containing products. October-September marketing year. F = Forecast.

Figure 18. Shares of World Centrifugal Sugar Exports, 2010/2011F.

Table 18. Shares of World Centrifugal Sugar Exports, 1995/1996-2010/2011F (percent)

Country	*1995/96*	*1996/97*	*1997/98*	*1998/99*	*1999/2000*	*2000/01*	*2001/02*
United States	0.9	0.5	0.4	0.6	0.3	0.3	0.3
Mexico	1.8	2.5	2.9	1.4	0.8	0.4	1.0
Total Caribbean	12.7	11.3	8.0	9.7	9.5	9.0	8.4
DR-CAFTA[a]	5.2	5.7	6.3	5.3	5.3	6.1	5.3
Brazil	16.4	15.3	19.1	23.3	27.1	20.1	27.4
European Union[b]	13.1	13.8	16.9	14.2	14.7	17.3	11.3
Australia	12.0	12.0	12.1	10.9	9.9	8.0	8.5
Rest of World	37.8	38.9	34.4	34.7	32.6	38.8	37.8
Country	*2002/03*	*2003/04*	*2004/05*	*2005/06*	*2006/07*	*2007/08*	*2008/09*
United States	0.3	0.6	0.5	0.4	0.7	0.4	0.3
Mexico	0.1	0.0	0.3	1.7	0.3	1.3	2.8
Total Caribbean	4.8	5.2	2.5	2.5	2.3	2.4	2.4
DR-CAFTA[a]	4.9	5.1	5.5	5.3	5.3	4.8	5.9
Brazil	29.7	32.7	38.4	34.3	40.5	37.8	44.1
European Union[b]	11.9	10.5	12.8	16.7	4.7	3.2	2.7
Australia	8.7	8.9	9.5	8.4	7.5	7.2	7.2
Rest of World	39.7	36.9	30.5	30.7	38.6	42.9	34.7
Country	*2009/10E*	*2010/11F*					
United States	0.4	0.3					
Mexico	1.5	1.8					
Total Caribbean	2.2	1.7					
DR-CAFTA[a]	5.6	5.6					
Brazil	46.9	51.8					
European Union[b]	4.6	2.8					
Australia	6.9	7.2					
Rest of World	31.8	28.8					

Source: U.S. Department of Agriculture. Foreign Agricultural Service Production, Supply and Distribution Online database, http://www.fas.usda.gov/psdonline /psdHome.aspx.

Notes: P = Preliminary.

F = Forecast.

[a] DR-CAFTA includes Dominican Republic and Central America. 1995/1996-2003/2004 data are EU-15, 2004/2005-2005/2006 are EU-25, and 2006/2007 to present are EU-27.

[b] The EU Includes French overseas departments of Reunion, Guadeloupe, and Martinique. EU trade data does not Include intra trade. Beginning 2004/2005, the data reflects the EU enlargement by accession of 10 countries. EU exports include sugar-containing products.

MAJOR U.S. AGRICULTURAL IMPORTS

- High-value horticultural products (fruits, nuts, vegetables and preparations; wine and malt beverages; nursery stock and flowers, and others) are the largest category of U.S. agricultural imports, and are forecast to be $39.4 billion in FY2011.
- Other sizeable commodity imports forecast for FY2011 are grains and feeds ($8.2 billion), livestock and dairy ($8.9 billion), and oilseeds and products ($7.3 billion).
- Imports of tropical products such as coffee, cocoa, sugar, and products are forecast to be $16.7 billion in FY2011.

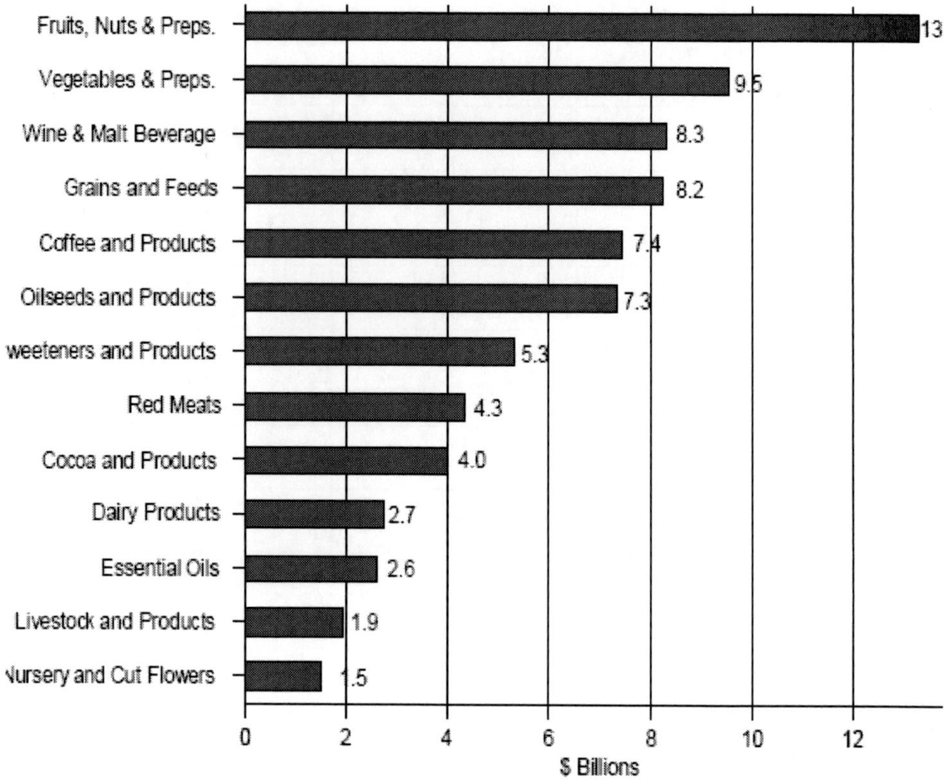

Source: U.S. Department of Agriculture. Economic Research Service.
F = Forecast.

Figure 19. Major Agricultural Imports by Commodity, FY2011F.

Table 19. Major U.S. Agricultural Imports, FY2011F ($ billions)

Commodity	FY2011F
Fruits, Nuts & Preps.	13.3
Vegetables & Preps.	9.5
Wine & Malt Beverage	8.3
Grains and Feeds	8.2
Coffee and Products	7.4
Oilseeds and Products	7.3
Sweeteners and Products	5.3
Red Meats	4.3
Cocoa and Products	4.0
Dairy Products	2.7
Essential Oils	2.6
Livestock and Products	1.9
Nursery and Cut Flowers	1.5

Source: U.S. Department of Agriculture, Economic Research Service, Outlook for U.S. Agricultural Trade, AES70, May 26, 2011, available at http:// usda.mannlib. cornell.edu/usda/ers/AES// 2010s/2011/AES-05-26-2011.pdf.

Note: F = Forecast.

U.S. Agricultural Imports by Country of Origin

- NAFTA partners Canada ($17.8 billion) and Mexico ($15.9 billion) and the EU-27 ($14.5 billion) are forecast to be the source of more than 50% of total U.S. agricultural imports ($93 billion) in FY2011.
- Agricultural imports from Brazil are expected to reach a forecast $3.4 billion in FY2011; Indonesia is expected to ship $3.7 billion of farm products to the United States in FY2011.
- Australia, with whom the United States entered into a free trade agreement (FTA) in 2005, is forecast to provide the United States with $2.2 billion worth of agricultural imports in FY2011. Colombia, a prospective FTA partner, is forecast to ship $2.6 billion of farm products to the United States in FY2011.

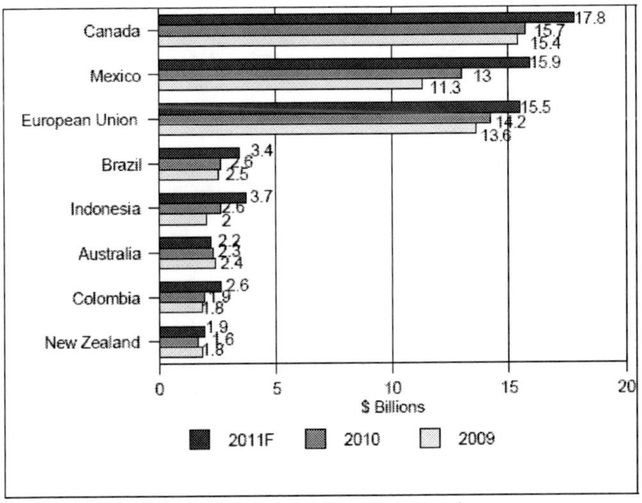

Source: U.S. Department of Agriculture. Economic Research Service.
F = Forecast.

Figure 20. U.S. Agricultural Imports by Country of Origin, FY2009-FY2011F.

Table 20. U.S. Agricultural Imports by Country of Origin, FY2009-FY2011F ($ billion)

Country	FY2009	FY2010	FY2011F
Canada	15.4	15.7	17.8
Mexico	11.3	13.0	15.9
European Union	13.6	14.2	15.5
Brazil	2.5	2.6	3.4
Indonesia	2.0	2.6	3.7
Australia	2.4	2.3	2.2
Colombia	1.8	1.9	2.6
New Zealand	1.8	1.6	1.9

Source: U.S. Department of Agriculture, Economic Research Service, Outlook for U.S. Agricultural Trade, AES-70, May 26, 2011, available at http://usda.mannlib. cornell.edu/usda/ers/AES //2010s/ 2011/AES-05-26-2011.pdf.

Notes: F = Forecast.

Regional Market Growth in U.S. Agricultural Exports

- Economic growth in Asia has contributed to relatively consistent long-term growth in U.S. agricultural exports to the region.
- Despite some year-to-year variation, the EU, the United States' fifth-largest agricultural export market, has been a relatively stable market for U.S. agricultural exports with little growth since 1992.
- Agricultural exports to countries in the former Soviet Union have declined in value since the 1992 break-up of the USSR.
- Agricultural exports to Latin America, including Mexico, and to Canada have grown rapidly since the early 1990s due in part to geographic proximity and NAFTA, among other factors.

Growth in U.S. Agricultural Exports to Asian Markets

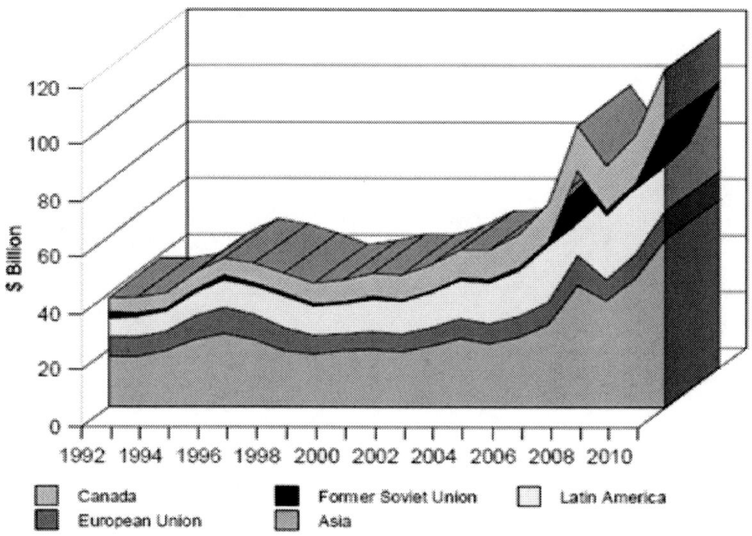

Source: U.S. Department of Agriculture. Economic Research Service.
F = Forecast.

Figure 21. Growth in U.S. Agricultural Exports, FY1992-FY2011F.

- Like the EU, Japan also has been a relatively stable and slow-growing market for U.S. agricultural exports.
- U.S. agricultural exports to China, fueled by rates of GDP growth in excess of 9%, have grown rapidly since the early 1990s (18.54%). FY2011 U.S. agricultural exports to China are forecast to be more than 10 times their value in FY2001, when China became a member of the World Trade Organization.
- Rapid income growth in Southeast Asia also has stimulated demand for U.S. agricultural exports since 1992.
- Agricultural exports to South Asia also have shown growth since 1992.

Table 21. Growth in U.S. Agricultural Exports to Selected Markets, FY1992-FY2011F ($ billion)

Year	Asia	European Union	Latin America[a]	Former Soviet Union	Canada
1992	17.8	7.2	6.5	2.2	4.8
1993	17.8	7.2	6.9	1.6	5.2
1994	19.9	6.6	7.4	1.0	5.3
1995	24.0	8.4	8.2	1.2	5.8
1996	26.0	9.2	9.9	1.6	6.0
1997	23.9	9.0	10.0	1.3	6.6
1998	19.7	8.5	11.3	1.0	7.0
1999	18.5	7.0	10.4	0.8	7.0
2000	19.7	6.4	10.6	0.7	7.5
2001	20.1	6.5	11.6	1.1	8.0
2002	19.5	6.5	11.5	0.7	8.6
2003	21.7	6.3	12.4	0.7	9.1
2004	24.3	7.0	13.6	1.1	9.6
2005	22.5	7.2	14.4	1.2	10.4
2006	24.9	7.2	16.5	1.1	11.6
2007	29.3	8.0	20.0	1.4	13.3
2008	43.2	10.7	27.5	2.3	16.2
2009	37.8	7.6	22.8	1.8	15.5
2010	45.8	8.5	23.8	1.4	16.6
2011F	59.5	10.0	29.9	1.7	18.5
Rate of Growth[b]	6.22%	1.66%	7.93%	-1.28%	6.98%

Source: U. S. Department of Agriculture, Economic Research Service, Outlook for U.S. Agricultural Trade, AES-70, May 26, 2011, available at http://usda. mannlib. cornell.edu/usda/ers/AES// 2010s/2011/AES-05-26-2011.pdf. Notes: F = Forecast. [a] Including Mexico. [b] The rate of growth is the change in U.S. exports from 1992 to 2011F. Calculations were made by CRS using a compound rate of growth calculator.

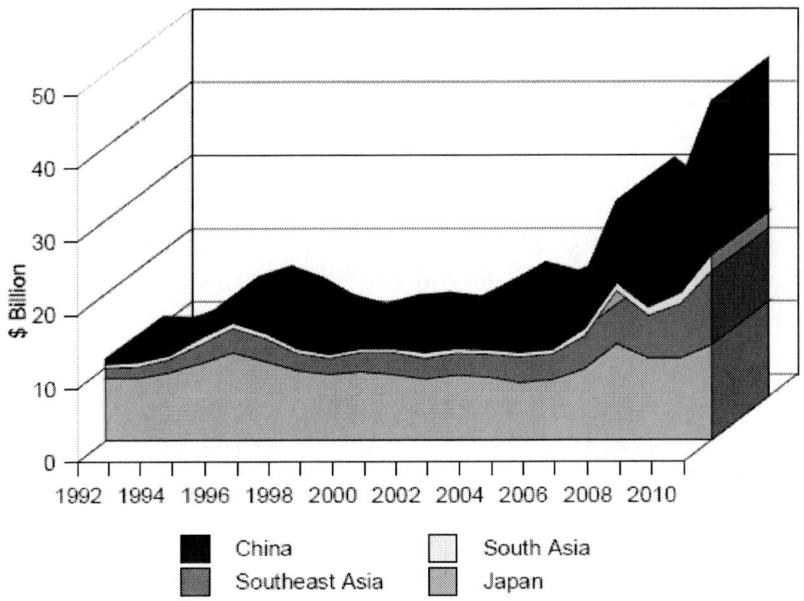

Source: U.S. Department of Agriculture. Economic Research Service.
F = Forecast.

Figure 22. Growth in Agricultural Exports to Asian Markets, FY1992-FY2011F.

Table 22. Change in USAgricultural Exports to Asian Markets, FY1992-FY2011F ($ billion)

Year	Japan	South east Asia	South Asia	China
1992	8.4	1.5	0.5	0.7
1993	8.5	1.6	0.6	0.3
1994	9.2	1.8	0.6	0.9
1995	10.5	2.6	1.0	2.4
1996	11.9	3.4	0.7	1.8
1997	10.7	3.1	0.7	1.8
1998	9.5	2.3	0.6	1.5
1999	8.9	2.2	0.5	1.0
2000	9.4	2.6	0.4	1.5
2001	8.9	2.9	0.6	1.9
2002	8.3	2.9	0.8	1.8
2003	8.8	2.9	0.6	3.5
2004	8.5	3.1	0.7	6.1
2005	7.8	3.4	0.7	5.3
2006	8.2	3.4	0.7	6.6
2007	9.7	4.4	1.0	7.1
2008	13.1	7.1	12	11.2
2009	11.2	5.7	12	11.2
2010	11.2	7.3	1.5	15.1
2011F	13.0	10.0	2.2	21.0
Rate of Growth[a]	2.21%	9.95%	7.69%	18.54%

Source: U.S. Department of Agriculture. Economic Research Service, Outlook for U.S. Agricultural Trade, AES70, May 26, 2011, available at http://usda.mannlib. cornell.edu/usda/ers/AES// 2010s/2011/AES-05-26-2011.pdf. Notes: F = Forecast.

[a] The rate of growth is the change in U.S. exports from 1992 to 2010F. Calculations were made by CRS using a compound rate of growth calculator.

Growth in Agricultural Exports to North and South America

- Growth in U.S. agricultural trade with Canada and Mexico, both NAFTA trading partners, and with Latin America has been particularly strong since 1992.
- U.S. agricultural exports to Canada are forecast to be $18.5 billion in FY2011.
- U.S. agricultural exports to Mexico are expected to be $17 billion in FY2011.
- U.S. agricultural exports to Latin America (excluding Mexico) are expected to reach $12.9 billion in FY2011, up from $9.9 billion in FY2010.

U.S. Agricultural and Trade Policies

Domestic Support

The Food, Conservation, and Energy Act of 2008 (P.L. 110-246, 2008 farm bill) was enacted into law in June 2008 and will govern most federal farm and food policies through 2012. The 2008 farm bill provides price and income support to U.S. agricultural producers through 2012. In addition, the farm bill authorizes programs for conservation, rural development, nutrition (domestic food assistance), trade, and food aid administered by USDA. Budgetary outlays for all U.S. agricultural programs were $129.5 billion in FY2010.[1]

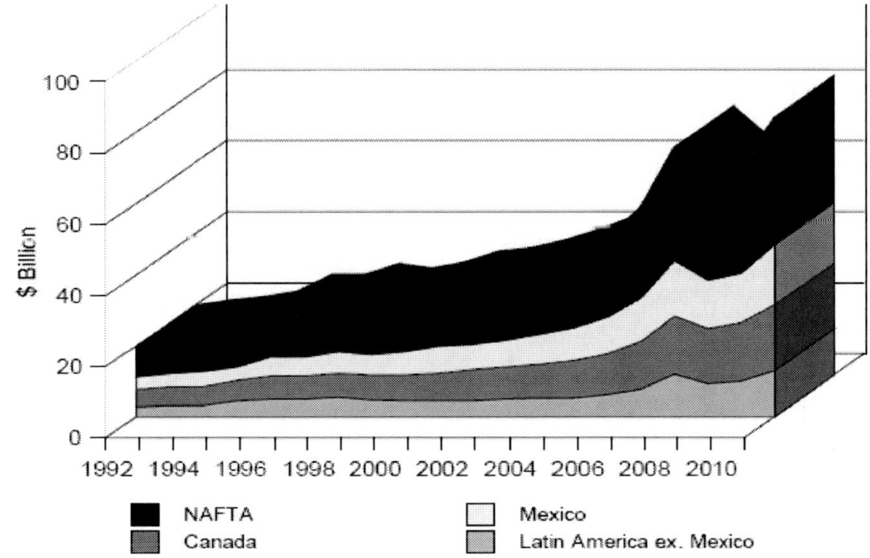

Source: U.S. Department of Agriculture. Economic Research Service; F = Forecast.
Figure 23. Change in Agricultural Exports to North and South America, FY1992-FY2011F.

Table 23. Change in Agricultural Exports to North and South America, FY1992-FY2011F ($ billion)

Year	Latin America ex. Mexico	Canada	Mexico	NAFTA
1992	2.8	4.8	3.7	8.5
1993	3.3	5.2	3.7	8.9
1994	3.2	5.3	4.1	9.4
1995	4.5	5.8	3.7	9.5
1996	4.9	6.6	5.1	11.7
1997	4.9	6.6	5.1	11.7
1998	5.3	7.0	6.0	13.0
1999	4.7	7.0	5.7	12.7
2000	4.3	7.5	6.3	13.8
2001	4.3	8.0	7.3	15.3
2002	4.5	8.6	7.1	15.7
2003	4.8	9.1	7.6	16.7
2004	5.2	9.6	8.4	18.0
2005	5.2	10.4	9.3	19.7
2006	6.1	11.6	10.4	22.0
2007	7.7	13.3	12.3	25.6
2008	12.0	16.2	15.6	31.8
2009	9.3	15.5	13.5	29.0
2010	9.9	16.6	13.9	30.5
2011F	12.9	18.5	17.0	35.5
Rate of Growth[a]	7.94%	6.98%	7.92%	7.41%

Source: U.S. Department of Agriculture, Economic Research Service, Outlook for U.S. Agricultural Trade, AES-70, May 26, 2011, available at http://usda.mannlib. cornell.edu/usda/ers/AES// 2010s/2011/AES-05-26-2011.pdf.

Notes: F = Forecast.

[a] The rate of growth is the change in U.S. exports from 1992 to 2011F. Calculations were made by CRS using a compound rate of growth calculator.

By one widely used measure, the producer support estimate (PSE) calculated by the Organization for Economic Cooperation and Development (OECD), the United States provided an estimated $30.6 billion in agricultural support to producers in 2009 (provisional estimate).[2] PSEs measure assistance to producers in terms of the value of monetary transfers generated by agricultural policy. Transfers are paid by consumers or by taxpayers in the form of market price support, direct payments, or other support. They are a broader measure of support than direct government spending alone. The percentage PSE measures support in relation to gross farm receipts. As a percent of gross farm receipts, the PSE for the United States is 10% in 2009, the third-lowest among OECD countries (*Figure 24, Table 24*). OECD attributes an increase of 2% (over 2008) in the PSE expected for the United States for 2009 to an increase in market price support for dairy. Over a longer period, the trend in producer support in the United States has been downward, dropping from a PSE of 22% in 1986-1988 to 10% in 2009.

Table 24. Producer Support Estimates (PSEs) in Selected OECD Countries (percent)

Country	1986-1988	2007-2009	2007	2008	2009P
Australia	10	4	5	4	3
EU	39	23	24	22	24
Japan	64	47	46	48	48
Korea	68	52	58	46	52
US	22	9	10	8	10

Source: Organization for Economic Co-operation and Development (OECD), Agricultural Policies in OECD Countries: At a Glance 2010.

Note: P = Provisional.

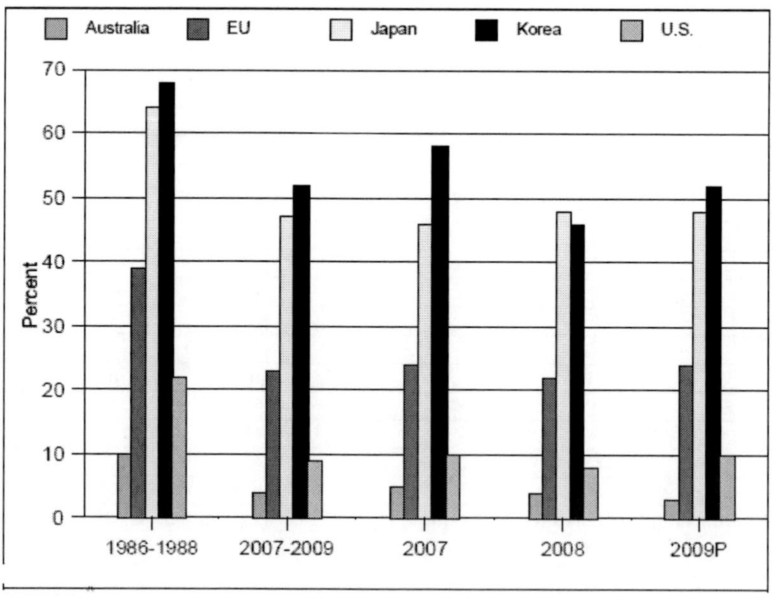

Source: OECD 2010.

P = Provisional.

Figure 24. Producer Support Estimates (PSEs) in Selected OECD Countries.

Among U.S. commodities, sugar is the most highly subsidized product in the United States, with a provisional single commodity transfer estimated at 21% of the gross value of sugar production in 2009 (*Figure 25, Table 25*).

Table 25. Producer Single Commodity Transfers (PSC) in the United States, by Commodity (percent)

Products	1986-1988 (Average)	2007-2009	2007	2008	2009P
Wheat	46.5	6.1	7.6	0.2	14.4
Corn	34.8	0.6	0.5	2.8	-0.5
Rice	50.2	0.6	0.7	0.4	1.1
Soybeans	1.7	1.8	0.6	5.6	-0.8
Sugar	55.9	27.3	34.1	26.3	20.8
Milk	34.9	13.0	24.8	0.0	14.3
Beef and Veal	1.1	0.0	0.0	0.0	0.0

Source: Organization for Economic Cooperation and Development (OECD), Agricultural Policies in OECD Countries: At a Glance 2010.

Note: P = Provisional.

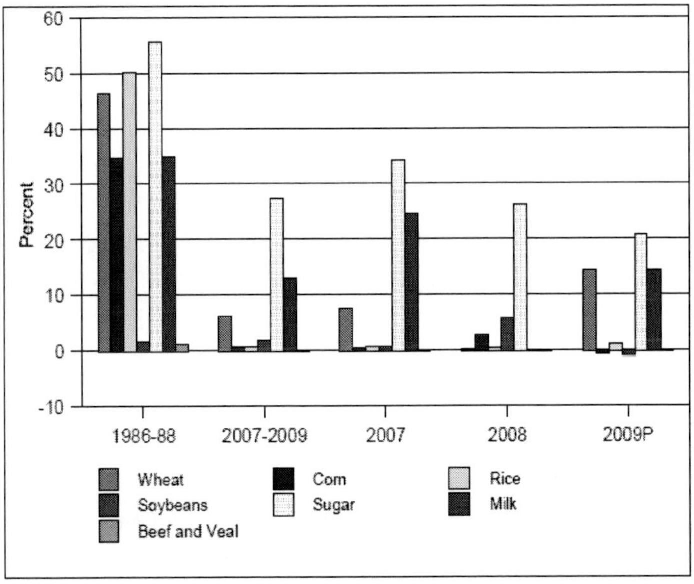

Source: OECD 2010.

P = Provisional.

Figure 25. Producer Single Commodity Transfers (PSCs): Selected Commodities in the United States.

Trade Measures

With agricultural exports totaling $137 billion in FY2011, the United States is the world's largest exporter of agricultural products. The United States applies tariffs and tariff quotas[3] to products entering the United States from abroad. According to the World Trade

Organization (WTO), the United States average applied tariff for agricultural products is 8.9%, which is slightly above the average applied U.S. tariff for non-agricultural products (4%), but relatively low compared to other WTO member countries.[4] About 170 tariff lines (a tariff line is a product as described in a schedule or list of tariffs) are subject to tariff quotas, including beef, dairy products, and sugar. The average in-quota tariff was 9.1% in 2007, while the out-of-quota was 42%.[5]

Under the WTO Agreement on Agriculture, the United States made export subsidy reduction commitments for 13 commodities.[6] The 2008 farm bill repealed authority for the Export Enhancement Program (EEP), which was used to fund subsidies for those products, with the exception of dairy products. Export subsidies, in the form of cash bonuses, can be provided to exporters of dairy products under the Dairy Export Incentive Program (DEIP), which was reauthorized in the 2008 farm bill through 2012. Prior to its repeal, no expenditures were made for EEP from FY2002. Spurred by declining prices for dairy products in 2008-2009, USDA announced in May 2009 DEIP allocations for nonfat dry milk, butter fat, and cheeses. DEIP bonuses of $19 million were awarded in FY2009. In FY2010, DEIP bonuses of $2 million were awarded.

A federally chartered public corporation operated by USDA, the Commodity Credit Corporation (CCC), makes credit guarantees available to private financial institutions who finance the purchase of U.S. agricultural exports. Under the GSM-102, the CCC guarantees repayment of credit made available to finance U.S. agricultural exports on credit terms of up to three years. Exporters tallied $3.1 billion of agricultural exports under the GSM-102 program. The CCC also operates the Facilities Guarantee Program (FGP), which guarantees credit to U.S. banks that finance export sales of U.S. goods and services that are used to improve agricultural export-related facilities in emerging markets (storage, processing, and handling facilities).

Export market development programs, the Market Access Program (MAP), and the Foreign Market Development Program (FMDP) assist producer groups, associations, and firms with promotional and other activities.

Food Aid

The United States is the world's leading supplier of food aid. It provides more than half of the global total.

The United States provides food aid mainly through P.L. 480, also known as the Food for Peace Program. Wheat and wheat flour are the main commodities provided as food aid, but rice and vegetable oils are also important in P.L. 480 programs. Higher-value products are made available in special feeding programs. Responsibility for implementing food aid programs is shared by USDA and the U.S. Agency for International Development (AID).

P.L. 480 food aid is provided on a grant basis through Title II of the Food for Peace Act of 2008, the successor legislation of the Agricultural Trade and Development Assistance Act of 1954 (P.L. 480). Two other food aid programs are conducted under Section 416(b) of the Agricultural Act of 1949 and the Food for Progress Act of 1985. The former provides surplus CCC inventories, if available, as donations; the latter provides concessional credit terms or commodity donations to support emerging democracies or countries making free market economic reforms. A recently enacted food aid program, the McGovern-Dole School Food for Education Program, finances school feeding and child nutrition projects in poor countries.

End Notes

[1] U.S. Department of Agriculture, at http://www.obpa.usda.gov/budsum/FY12budsum.pdf.

[2] OECD countries include Australia, Canada, the European Union, Iceland, Japan, Korea, New Zealand, Norway, Switzerland, Turkey, and the United States.

[3] A tariff quota is defined by WTO as a trade measure applied at the border where quantities inside a quota are charged lower import duty rates than those outside (which can be high).

[4] WTO, *Trade Policy Review: United States 20108*, p. 90, available at http://www.wto.org/ english/tratop_ e/tpr_e/ tp_rep_e.htm#bycountry.

[5] Ibid, p. 81.

[6] Wheat and wheat flour, coarse grains, rice, vegetable oils, butter and butter oil, skim milk powder, cheese, other milk products, bovine meat, pigmeat, poultry meat, live dairy cattle, and eggs.

INDEX

A

B

C

D

E

F

G

S

T

U

V

W

Y